A Guide to the Harpsichord

A Guide
to the
Harpsichord

Ann Bond

Amadeus Press
Reinhard G. Pauly, General Editor
Portland, Oregon

Copyright © 1997 by Amadeus Press (an imprint of Timber Press, Inc.)
All rights reserved.

ISBN 1-57467-027-1

Printed in Hong Kong

Amadeus Press
The Haseltine Building
133 S.W. Second Avenue, Suite 450
Portland, Oregon 97204, U.S.A.

Library of Congress Cataloging-in-Publication Data

Bond, Ann.
A guide to the harpsichord / Ann Bond.
p.   cm.
Includes bibliographical references and index.
ISBN 1-57467-027-1
1. Harpsichord. I. Title
ML651.B66   1997
786.4'19—dc20   96-41086
CIP
MN

Contents

Acknowledgments

My thanks are due to a number of people. In the first place, to my former harpsichord pupils at Croydon High School, without whom I would not have had the idea of writing this book. As the scope of the undertaking expanded, Jane Chapman, Malcolm Greenhalgh, David Sanger, Peter Bavington, Maggie Cole, Mary Cyr, and John Raymond all contributed helpful information or sparked ideas in discussion. In particular I am grateful to Bernard Harrison, of the University of Lancaster; Elizabeth Dodd, gambist and authority on historical dance; John Raymond, of the Russell Collection, Edinburgh; and Robert Deegan, harpsichord builder, who have read parts of the manuscript and made helpful suggestions, and to Bonnie Garrett who scrutinized the entire work from the viewpoint of the U.S. reader. John Edmonds, in Cumbria, and Claire Andreoli, in New York, did sterling work, far beyond the call of friendship, in helping me to check available editions.

The staff of Amadeus Press has coped heroically with the task of editing a book being written at the other side of the world, and I am grateful for their patience and help. It is my husband Peter, however, who has shared the greatest burden, making it possible for a totally non-technological person like myself to benefit from advanced computer technology and, latterly, the resources of the Internet. He created the font of ornament type, drew the diagrams, smoothed away my problems with music file writing, and gave invaluable help with formatting. Above all, he encouraged me in moments of doubt and despondency. Without him, this book would never have seen the light, and I dedicate it to him.

Acknowledgments are also due to the following:

The Russell Collection, Edinburgh University, for the jacket illustration and figures 2, 3, 5, and 6.

The Wallace Collection, London, for figure 4.
Fuzeau Editions, for figure 7.
Oxford University Press, for figures 8 and 12.
The Victoria and Albert Museum, London, for figures 9 and 10.
Performers' Facsimiles, New York, for figure 11.
The Library of the Conservatoire Royal de Musique, Brussels, for
    figure 12.
The National Portrait Gallery, London, for figure 13.
Gerrit Klop, for figure 14.

Ann Bond
Silverdale

The following reference system to pitch (Great C staff) is used in this
book:

FF - BB   C - B   c - b   c' - b'   c" - b"   c'" - g'"

1

Setting the Scene

That lovely instrument.
—PIER FRANCESCO TOSI, *Observations on the Florid Song* (1723)

I have always found the harpsichord irresistible, and I hope that before the end of this book you will catch some of my enthusiasm. I first encountered the instrument when I was a music student at Cambridge. My predominantly organ-playing background may have predisposed me, long before I had proper harpsichord lessons, to respond immediately to the most obvious aspect of the instrument's nature: its genius for musical line drawing, or counterpoint. But it was not until later, when I had an instrument of my own, that I discovered another side of the harpsichord's nature: its capacity for color, sonority, and fascinating textures, especially in the work of the French school. Later still, under the tutelage of Robert Woolley and David Roblou, I became aware of its rhetorical power and the subtleties of touch that can release this power. Although harpsichord mechanism is of primary simplicity, it can be used to reflect with extreme accuracy a wide range of musical ideas. Provided one is taught to unlock its resources, it is a highly gratifying instrument to play.

As my harpsichord upbringing was not smoothly processed through the preordained channels of the music conservatory, I hope that readers who have not had a traditional musical education will take heart.[1] Indeed, I have much to say to those who are not players at all. Many people today are fired with enthusiasm for the harpsichord playing that they hear in recitals or recordings, but need some initiation into its rewarding world. I shall start, however, by addressing the player and the would-be player.

9

Beginning players come in many guises, ranging from the early music enthusiast to the conservatory student who needs to complete a harpsichord module as part of an accompaniment course; from the retired person who has built an instrument in kit form and wants to learn to play it, to the capable pianist who would like to play Bach's music on the instrument for which it was written. Additionally, some schools are now fortunate enough to have their own instrument—in fact, the idea for this book dates from a time when I taught the harpsichord in a school and realized that the students had hardly any background knowledge of the instrument.

In order to learn the harpsichord, you need a teacher who has to some extent specialized in that instrument—not simply a keyboard teacher. In Great Britain, one way to find a suitable teacher is by contacting the National Early Music Association, which has several forums in different parts of the country and publishes an invaluable yearbook that lists players and teachers. Similar organizations exist in many other countries. In the United States, help can be sought from the regional historical keyboard societies. (Addresses of these can be found in appendix B.) Those who already have a teacher may be able to amplify what they learn from this guide, and I also commend this book to teachers in the hope that it will support their efforts. But there may be many people who cannot find a good teacher within convenient range, or whose teacher has only a limited overview of the subject: they should be able to get a practical foundation from this book, as well as acquiring plenty of background information.[2]

As well as a teacher, you will need your own instrument: practicing for an hour a week on someone else's harpsichord does not get you very far. But please read chapters 2 and 3 before making any decision on what sort of instrument to acquire. There are many types of harpsichord, and some are more suited to specific purposes, others to general use. Harpsichords can be acquired from a variety of sources today: there are numerous builders and also a few reputable second-hand agencies. Again, details are given in appendix B.

Chapters 5, 6, and 8 explore the basis of harpsichord touch, explaining its mechanisms in relation to the musical effects you want to produce. These chapters are supported by a detailed study in chapter 7 of four pieces in commonly encountered musical styles. Chapter 11 contains guidance about buying music, reference to graded anthologies, and advice about facsimile editions. Throughout the book, many important and enjoyable individual works are singled out for comment. Suggestions for available editions are given in the relevant chapters.

Fingering makes up the whole of chapter 9, which is addressed both to those who want to use historical fingering, or at least understand its principles, and to those who want to stay mainly with traditional methods. Fingering is one aspect of the engrossing topic of historical performance—sometimes referred to as "period style" or, more controversially, as "authenticity." Historical performance style is of such crucial interest to player and listener alike that it forms a kind of ostinato throughout the book, and has a vital chapter of its own.

Many topics interest both player and listener. Chapter 2, which deals with the construction of the harpsichord, will enable you to recognize its components and understand how they function. I then pass naturally in chapter 3 to the diversification of the instrument during the two centuries of its heyday, examining the forms it took in different countries. (It is gratifying to be able to distinguish a French harpsichord from an Italian, or a muselaar from a bentside spinet, whether you are buying an instrument, attending a concert, or looking at something in a museum.) This in turn lays the foundations for studying the repertory of the chief national schools of harpsichord composition, to which six chapters are devoted. Particular attention is paid to the French and Italian styles of the seventeenth and eighteenth centuries, since these styles have an important bearing on the way much early keyboard music should be played.

The emphasis may seem to be on the player again in the chapters on ornamentation—a vital component of harpsichord style—and continuo playing, chapters 18 and 19 respectively. But continuo playing is an especially universal function of the harpsichordist, and listeners would do well to read about it in order to get an idea of the fascinating processes that occupy the player. Far from merely playing some notes propped up on the music desk, continuo playing often involves highly skilled forms of creative activity.

Finally, I explore the fascinating subject of how the instrument is tuned and the historic tunings that were used. This is fundamentally a mathematical topic, but there is a great need for an account of it that is sufficiently simple to be understood by the ordinary reader. I first wrote such an account as an appendix to the second edition of *Making Music on the Organ* by the distinguished recitalist Peter Hurford, and the present book expands my earlier writings. How the harpsichord is tuned—not in the equal temperament of the piano, but in systems based on historic practice—is intimately linked to the way the music was written and how it should sound, and much attention is now given to this matter by those in charge of concerts and recordings. A brief survey of temperament should be important background reading for everyone. In addition, if you have your own instrument, you will need this information to tune it. Tuning is one aspect of looking after your instrument. The book concludes with advice on how to care for what I hope will become a valued companion.

Many of the chapters are designed to be read singly, as essays on various topics. For this reason, you may find that some points are referred to more than once during the course of the book. All technical terms dealing with the harpsichord are explained: those wishing to look up further musical points will find either *The New Grove Dictionary of Music and Musicians* (London, 1980) or *The New Harvard Dictionary of Music* (Cambridge, MA, 1986) an invaluable aid. I have deliberately kept scholarly references to a minimum, as this book is meant for a wide range of music lovers. My aim is to steer those who are new to early music toward an understanding of its basic issues without foundering in complex argument. Modern musicology is impressively thorough, but it can prove somewhat daunting to the beginner. This book is meant as a guide, and I do not want the wood to be obscured by the trees.

The statements I make are based on a consensus of many of the standard sources from the period. Where these are contradictory or controversial, I have taken what seems to me a commonsense view. While I realize that this may strike the scholar as facile, I am keenly aware that the beginner's need is for reasonably clear guidance without constant qualification. But I am also aware that interpretation has many hazards—and this is nowhere more true than in the case of articulation, where ideas rightly remain fluid, and where few people are consequently willing to commit themselves to the permanence of print. It has nevertheless proved a fascinating exercise to determine what can usefully be written on the topic, and I hope you will enjoy the result.

The Early Music Scene

If you are to understand the history of the harpsichord and its place in today's musical world, it helps to know what the phrase *early music* signifies. As you begin to investigate the harpsichord's double life—its two incarnations—you will discover how attitudes toward the music of previous periods have shifted and undergone interesting transformations.

For some readers, the concept of early music will probably be bounded by the world of amateur viol or recorder consorts, sixteenth-century vocal music, or even plainchant—a common enough definition. The topic of early music, however, has in recent years become enmeshed within the broader issue of historical performing style, with which it has a great deal in common; and professional practitioners take this into account when they speak of early music. Their definition might read something like this: *early music includes any music that involves the use of specialist skills of transcribing or editing to recover the original text, or that relies for its true effect on the use of historic instruments*[3] *(or modern copies of them), linked with an understanding of how they were originally played.* Under this definition, a performance of Schubert using the instruments and style of about 1820 could be regarded as early music, and Schubert songs accompanied on the fortepiano have indeed figured in the York Early Music Festival. Generally, however, the mental end line for early music might be drawn a little before 1800. The harpsichord and its music certainly fall within this time limit, and within the main area of the definition given above.

Beneath the present impressive blossoming of early music there lies an extensive root system. To play music of the past, one needs to draw on the support of a number of other activities. For instance, there is research into the history of instrument building, which finds further expression in the work of the large numbers of builders now engaged in creating copies of old instruments; research into manuscript and printed musical texts, and the publishing thereof (sometimes in facsimile editions); and research into performance—conducted both by musicologists who investigate sources and by musicians who experiment with the playing techniques of original instruments—which aims to discover more about how the music was originally played. Musicological scholarship has long been important in universities, and Chairs of Historical Performance Studies are becoming common in both universities and conservatories.

This book is concerned with keyboard music from approximately 1580 to 1780. It embraces the majesty of Frescobaldi; the passionate rhetoric of d'Anglebert; the vigor, expressiveness, and color of Rameau. And, of course, the lofty and universal intelligence of Bach: but I left Bach out of that list for the reason that his keyboard music—unlike that of the other composers just mentioned—remained accessible to the musical public, even during the nineteenth century. By then it had been transferred from the harpsichord, which had come to be considered obsolete, to the piano. (The sonatas of Scarlatti, and a few unrepresentative pieces by Couperin and Daquin, also enjoyed this dubious form of preservation.) But the harpsichord itself, whose nature and tone color had called forth the music in the first place, had disappeared below the musical horizon just before 1800, having been eclipsed by the piano and by the growth of new composition styles. With it disappeared familiarity with d'Anglebert and his fellows, whose music was exclusively linked to the harpsichord.

The processes that led to the revival of the harpsichord—over one hundred years later—are discussed in chapter 4, but here I am concerned with the fact that, by the time the instrument reappeared, people's musical attitudes had understandably changed. New styles and new enthusiasms had taken root, and musical taste had acquired different orientations. It is particularly relevant to my argument that by the end of the nineteenth century the public had come to absorb a kind of musical version of the Darwinian theory—a view that can be observed in Victorian histories of music. This resulted in the belief that the piano was musically superior to the harpsichord, and piano music to harpsichord music, reflecting the natural process of an evolutionary survival of the fittest. This attitude was an obstacle, to say the least, to the revival of the vast forgotten areas of the older repertory. Another obstacle was the tone of the new harpsichords that were beginning to be built in the 1920s as a result of pressure from isolated enthusiasts. Some of these instruments were in truth not very impressive (probably meriting some of the witticisms directed at them by the more waspish critics) and their thin sonority did not really help the cause of harpsichord revival.

In addition, the repertory available to the few specialists who were brave enough to commit themselves to these instruments (for few historic harpsichords were still in playing order) was not extensive, because good editions of harpsichord music were scarcely available in the early decades of the present century. Of the enormous repertory available today—still growing, as other music comes to light—only a fraction had been reprinted by the 1930s. The herculean labors of the great pioneer musicologist Charles van den Borren in Brussels and of the great English scholar and harpsichordist Thurston Dart in Cambridge were necessary to set the editorial revival of harpsichord music in motion.

England and the Netherlands are still the European centers of early music, although other countries now strongly challenge this position. The United States also supports a vigorous early music movement, with Boston playing a leading role. The revival of true historical harpsichord making, which characterized the 1970s and is crucial to my story, took place more or less simultaneously in England, Holland, the United States, and Germany. By that time, many other period instruments—the cornett and sackbut, the lute and theorbo, the whole range of renaissance wind instruments—had also emerged from their eclipse, and the string family was beginning to experience a reincarnation in copies of eighteenth-century instruments. These were strung at a lower tension and used a lighter, more versatile bow. The clear timbres of all these instruments have proved a revelation. I hope that if you have not yet heard them you will try to do so, since period instruments will open your ears to the sounds typical of the renaissance and baroque periods, and will add depth and perspective to your mental picture of the harpsichord.

But can we hear these instruments in the same way people did in, let us say, 1670? We differ so greatly from our forebears. In particular, the enormous changes that have taken place in music since 1800, and the equally far-reaching ones in the world around us, have all conspired to coarsen our ears. The development of heavy industry and modern transport has led to noise levels in daily life that would have been inconceivable in Handel's day. The orchestration of Wagner and of Brahms, the heavy stringing of the modern concert grand piano, and the voice production of the modern opera singer are all in their different ways proportional to these levels. The total string tension on a full-size concert grand may amount to over eight tons; the tension on even a large harpsichord would not exceed one ton. Inevitably there were problems and misconceptions when period instruments began to resurface; their subtler, gentler methods of sound production proved a shock to the modern ear. The harpsichord may genuinely have sounded tinkly to people in the 1930s; at any rate, it is a fair guess that the impact of its sound was quite different from what the seventeenth-century listener experienced.

In fact, our attitude to harpsichord sound was obliged to undergo a two-fold adjustment in the middle years of the present century. On the one hand, builders had to rediscover the full sonority of the genuine historic harpsichord, and, on the other, our ears had to rediscover the pleasures of gentler, unforced sound production. Happily, these two processes have by now converged. Concerts and recordings have familiarized us with fine reproduction instruments and many superb players, and the false "Dresden china" image of the harpsichord has been laid to rest. We are now in a much better position to experience the original impression made by a good harpsichord: its sheer presence, and its potential for strength and brilliance as well as pathos and tenderness. Likewise, the riches of its repertory have been opened up by historical awareness and improved editorial methods, and much pleasure awaits you as you investigate them.

Those new to early music and the harpsichord may take a little while to find their bearings among a lot of unfamiliar names, of both composers and performers, but names do not matter at first: the main thing is to enjoy the music. You may find that concerts of early music have a more informal and relaxed atmosphere than the high-powered, personality-centered world of traditional concerts. Early music concertgoing is not dressy or socially ostentatious, and there is generally not much promotional pressure. However, the commercial aspect is certainly not absent; the recording industry has embraced early music enthusiastically, to the extent that almost half of all recordings currently issued are period-instrument performances, often of previously unrecorded works.

Festivals of early music are now well established. They often take place in venues that are more appropriate in size for the music than the modern concert hall—in stately homes, churches, and historic buildings. Since music for the harpsichord was meant for fairly intimate surroundings, concert promoters are learning to present baroque music in the acoustics and the settings where it will sound best. Another welcome development is the growth of summer schools of early music, which also often take place in delightful surroundings. Here one can receive superb coaching and tuition and spend many hours of the day—and night—playing music with like-minded enthusiasts. This is a particularly valuable opportunity for the harpsichordist, because by getting involved in ensemble music you strike at the root of the keyboard player's besetting problem—isolation. (Bear in mind that the main use of the harpsichord was originally as an ensemble, rather than as a solo, instrument.) The chance for the amateur to mix freely, both socially and musically, with professionals of several instruments, and to absorb some of the attitudes and atmosphere of their work, brings obvious benefits.

Certainly both amateurs and professionals can now accept that early music has a secure and important place in musical life. Young performers entering careers in early music today may hardly even be aware that players of period instruments were once castigated as failures in the regular branch of the profession. Likewise, those of my readers under the age of, say, thirty may well be surprised by the notion that period instruments were once regarded patronizingly or even with contempt. You most likely have not had to make any of the adjustments I have described; the attitudes of our heritage- and conservation-conscious age will in fact predispose you to accept quite naturally the proposition that music sounds best on the instruments for which it was originally written. It probably seems an insultingly obvious idea.

Yet accepting this idea calls for humility—for a readiness to acknowledge that builders and composers of the past were no mere primi-tive forerunners of modern musical excellence, but indeed knew what they were doing and could create instruments and music that were valid in their own right and inseparably wed. Perhaps it is appropriate for me therefore to end this introduction to early music by saying that this new attitude has had to be worked for, and even fought for; and I pay tribute to the great pioneer figures who have done so. David Munrow, the Kuijken family, Frank Hubbard—to name only a few—did not find their opportunities ready-made. Nor did the older generation of outstanding harpsichordists who are still active. Yet names like Kenneth Gilbert, Gustav Leonhardt, and Ton Koopman are now universally familiar, and they and the many excellent players following in their path continue to enlarge our musical world and give us tremendous pleasure.

Notes

1. A Cambridge music degree course is a wonderful experience, but does not include actual instrumental tuition except in the case of organists and singers.

2. I am often asked if I can recommend a modern harpsichord instruction book for those unable to find good lessons. There is no simple answer, but Rosen-hart, *The Amsterdam Harpsichord Tutor* (Amsterdam: Groen, 1977) has much in its favor, as it builds up technique from historic examples of music. There is however no commentary on either fingering or the mechanics of touch and articulation, vital topics which I discuss in chapter 6, 8, and 9. See also endnote about Boxall (chapter 9:1).

3. Throughout the book, I make a distinction between two usages: a *historic* harpsichord means an antique instrument, whereas a *historical* harpsichord means one that is built using antique instruments as a model in some or all of its aspects. *Historic* and *historical* are also similarly distinguished in other contexts.

2

The Mechanics of the Harpsichord

To understand the production of tone in the harpsichord, we must first investigate how the instrument is constructed. Comparisons with a later instrument, the piano, may seem an odd and anachronistic way of going about the task; but since most people are familiar with piano characteristics, I find that they nearly always approach the structure of the harpsichord from the piano point of reference. (A harp would be a better but less familiar alternative.) The basic difference between harpsichord and piano is that in the harpsichord a lightly stretched string is plucked by a tiny quill called a plectrum, whereas in the piano a strongly tensioned string is struck by a hammer. There are several other significant differences that appear on inspection.

The piano has a heavy iron frame; thick strings (some wrapped with wire); pedals (one to control the dampers, the other to reduce the tone); and one keyboard, usually of seven octaves. The harpsichord, however, has a light wooden frame; thinner strings; and no sustaining pedal, although there may be other pedals. There may be one, two, or (extremely rarely) three keyboards—called **manuals**. These are shorter than the piano's; depending on type, the compass varies from a little over four octaves to five octaves (FF–f''') or even more. The normal black-and-white key color may be reversed, although this is not significant; the keys may be of various woods, or inlaid. Middle C lies somewhat to the right of center. The length of the keys from back to front can vary, but in most pre-1700 instruments (and their modern copies) it is short. In particular, you will probably notice the shortness of the part of

18

the keys in front of the raised sharps. Only in English and German instruments of the eighteenth century does the length of key remotely resemble that of a modern piano. The width of the keys may also be marginally less.

When you come to play the instrument, several other differences will emerge. The most obvious is that you cannot readily vary the amount of tone by depressing the key gently or strongly, as you can on the piano, since the volume of tone obtainable is set when each individual harpsichord is voiced. To make one note sound louder than another demands a different approach, involving accurate control of the moment of pluck and of the duration of hold for every note. All real music making (as opposed to mere playing) on the harpsichord depends on the cultivation of this control; the technique is discussed in chapters 5, 6, and 8.

When you depress a harpsichord key, the back of the pivoted key (which extends some distance inside the case and cannot be seen) rises as the front goes down. Supported vertically on top of the back end of each key is a narrow wooden strip called a **jack**. Protruding from the side of this jack, near the top, is the little **plectrum**—made originally from bird quill but often today from a synthetic such as delrin (see figure 1a). As the jack is pushed upward by the back of the key, the plectrum presses up against the string until it cannot help plucking it. The beginning of the note—the moment of plucking—is crisp and extremely definite, unlike the relatively cushioned attack of the piano. The string is set in motion, and its vibrations are carried through the **bridge** to the **soundboard** (the flat surface below the strings), which amplifies the vibrations into a note, using the resonance of the air inside the cavity below. The soundboard is not of uniform thickness, but varies subtly from area to area. The skill with which the thinning is done and the quality of the timber used (usually spruce or, in Italy, cypress) are the most important factors determining the sound quality of a harpsichord.

As long as your finger depresses the key, the jack stays up, and the **damper**—a small piece of felt at the top of the jack—is held above and away from the string, so that the vibration can continue. Contrary to general belief, harpsichord tone can last as long as piano tone while the damper is off the string. However, the rate at which the sound dies away is initially faster. This means that to some extent harpsichord tone is naturally articulated, especially in slow passages.

When you release the key, the back of the key falls, and the jack drops back with it. The plectrum does not of course pluck the string again on the way down; it is enabled by an ingenious hinged **tongue** to

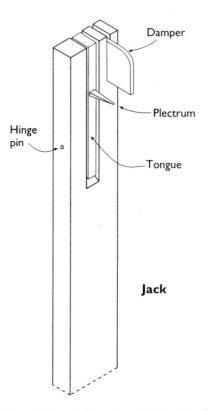

Damper

Plectrum

Hinge
pin

Tongue

Jack

Figure 1a. Diagram of a typical jack (shortened). *Peter Bond.*

slide past the string without plucking it. As the key comes to rest, the damper drops onto the string, stopping the sound.

To see all this happen, the **jack rail** must be removed. First prop up the lid securely with its stick, then remove the music desk. You are now able to lift out the jack rail—a wooden bar that runs right across the instrument, behind the tuning pins. It may have a catch at one end, which must be undone; or it may be held in place by friction. (In this case, notice which end is which before you put it down, because it must go back the same way around or it will not function properly.) You can now see the rows of jacks—one, two, or three rows. A spinet or virginal (to be discussed later) has one row, a harpsichord usually two or three. Looking at the jacks from above, you will notice that all the plectra of any particular row project from the same side. On a two-row instrument, the rows of jacks face in opposite directions, one set plucking the strings on the left of the jack, the other plucking the strings on the right.

Each row of jacks controls a complete set of strings (sometimes called a **choir**), with one string for each note. So a two-row harpsichord has two sets of strings, and a three-row has three sets; here it differs from the piano (whose strings are mostly in threes), however, because each set can be used either singly or in combination with the others, to provide different tone colors. This is done as follows:

- Each row of jacks stands in a slotted strip, running from side to side of the instrument, which is called a **register**.
- Each register can be moved very slightly to right or to left, perhaps by about 2 millimeters, and when moved it pulls the jacks with it. (The bottom of each jack is restrained by another slotted strip from moving out of its place above the back of the key.)
- When the register is positioned so that the tip of each plectrum is under its string, that row of jacks is ready for action (see figure 1b).
- When the register is positioned so that the jacks lean slightly out of the vertical, the tip of each plectrum misses the string as the jack rises. That row of jacks is now out of action, even if the keys are played.

This simple system allows one to select the **registration** one wishes. Different harpsichords have different mechanisms to move their registers. Some have levers or knobs on the board above the keys; some have pedals; in the past, some had knee levers. Some—the simplest of all—require the player to lean forward and pull or push the end of the register that sticks out of the case on the right-hand side. When you meet a new instrument, a little experimentation and observation is needed to find which mechanism moves which register, unless these have been labeled.

The asymmetrical shape of the harpsichord arises naturally from the varying length of its strings. There is a long, straight **spine**, a curving **bentside**, and a short straight **cheek** to the right of the player. The main strings cover practically the whole area of the instrument, from the **hitchpins** just inside the case to which they are anchored, over the curved bridge, past the jacks, over the **nut**, and so to the **tuning pins** or wrestpins, which are set in a heavy oaken **wrest plank** near the front of the instrument. These full-length strings are known as **eight-foot strings** (a term borrowed from organ building, meaning that the strings sound at unison pitch). Some harpsichords also have a shorter set of strings, lying under the eight-foot strings, and starting at hitchpins halfway along the soundboard. These shorter, **four-foot strings** have their own nut and sound an octave higher than normal. All these details are shown in figure 1c.

21

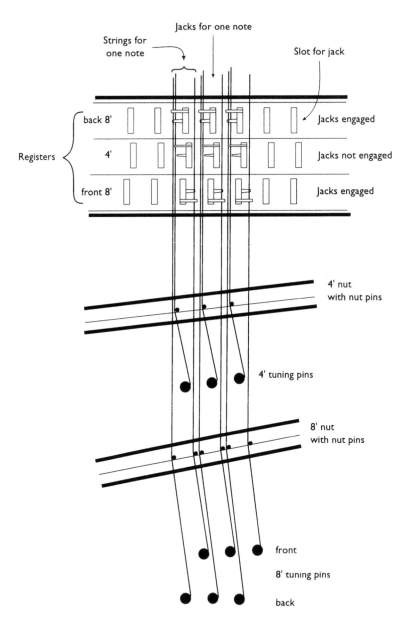

Figure 1b. Close-up view of three notes on a three-register harpsichord. When a register is engaged, the plectra project marginally beyond their strings. *Peter Bond.*

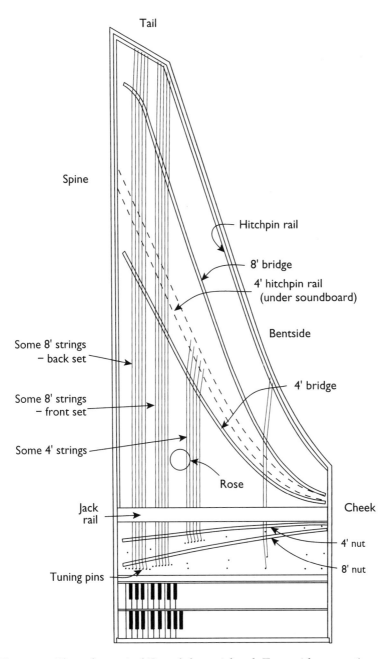

Figure 1c. Plan of a typical French harpsichord. To avoid congestion, only a small group of each set of strings is shown. *Peter Bond.*

23

Notice that the bass strings are made of brass or copper. In an instrument of the Italian type, the upper strings will also be brass: otherwise, they will be iron or steel. The gauge of the wire is subtly graded from bass to treble, becoming progressively more fine. (The way in which this is done must be respected when a string has to be replaced.) There is a complex relationship between the gauge or weight of the wire, the tension at which it is stretched, and its actual length; this relationship is known as **scaling**. If all the strings were of the same gauge and tension relative to their pitch, an impossibly long instrument would result, and the scaling of any particular harpsichord shows the necessary compromises that have been made. Different schools of builders favored different patterns of scaling: Italian harpsichords, for example, have short scaling in the treble, which accounts for the distinctive sharp curve of their bentside.

A one-manual harpsichord (a **single**) usually has two eight-foot registers. These registers differ slightly in tone because one plucks proportionally a little nearer the end of the string than the other throughout, as is apparent when the jack rail is removed. The register that plucks nearest to the keyboard (the **front 8**) has a more nasal, rich sound than the mellower sound of the register that plucks nearer the middle of the string (the **back 8**), because the different point of pluck favors different harmonics, or overtones, of the sound. Once you have replaced the jack rail, you can explore this difference by playing chords on each eight-foot in turn; then savor the timbre of using both at once.

A two-manual harpsichord (known as a **double**) has the front 8 on the upper manual and the back 8 on the lower manual. To use both 8s together, you must **couple** the manuals. This is done by lever, pedal, or knob, or by a shove coupler. The latter is a mechanism that you engage by pushing the whole of the top manual away from you. It is rather like shutting a drawer: one needs to keep the manual straight by pushing at both ends, or it may stick. Having coupled the manuals, play on the lower one, and the upper set of keys will be mechanically drawn down as well. The touch will be slightly heavier, and you will need to play positively, although the timing of the action is finely set so that the two strings do not pluck absolutely instantaneously but are staggered. To uncouple, use the knob or lever again, or pull the upper manual back toward you.

The manuals of historic French instruments were coupled by pulling the lower manual toward the player, so if you are playing a copy of such an instrument, follow this procedure, which is the reverse of the one just described. English eighteenth-century instruments had no coupling mechanism.

Both singles and doubles may have a four-foot register; on a double, it will be played from the lower manual. The function of a four-foot is to add brilliance to one or both eight-foot registers. (On a double, it is worth exploring the effect—not immediately obvious—that can be obtained by using the four-foot with the *front* 8; to do this, you will need to disengage the back 8, add the four-foot to the lower manual, and then couple the manuals.) The four-foot is not normally used on its own, although players occasionally exploit it for special effects in French music.

The best echo effects in baroque music come from contrasting the coupled manuals, played from the lower keyboard, with the top manual on its own. (J. S. Bach's famous Italian Concerto, which he carefully marked *f* and *p* throughout, responds well to this treatment.) Another possibility is to use the eight-foot and four-foot of the lower manual, uncoupled, for the *forte* and the top manual for the *piano* passages.

There are other musical uses for two manuals, besides the obvious one of getting contrasts of volume or timbre. We shall note in chapter 14 how French composers explored interesting textures in the *pièce croisée*. Also, in two-part writing it may occasionally be a good idea to play with one hand on each manual, especially if the right-hand part is prominently melodic. This expedient can solve problems of balance on difficult instruments, and the juxtaposition of the two timbres may also be attractive in its own right, although one should not regard this manner of playing as the norm.

Many harpsichords have a **buff**. This consists of a set of small felt or leather pads that can be moved into place by a batten situated just behind the nut, so that they press against the ends of one set of eight-foot strings (note carefully which set). This damps the tone of that register and gives an attractive lutelike effect. Although it is useful for melody-and-accompaniment textures and special effects, one should use it sparingly. One-manual harpsichords and spinets sometimes had a divided buff affecting treble or bass halves of the instrument, so that accompaniment figures in the lower half of the keyboard could be subordinated to a right-hand melody.

Possibly you may have access to a harpsichord with a sixteen-foot (suboctave) register. As we shall see later, this register is of dubious authenticity, although it was popular on post-war revival harpsichords where it helped to shore up the often weak tone of the eight-foot registers. But the addition of sixteen-foot tone tends to congest the contrapuntal texture and, although superficially impressive, soon becomes wearisome to the ear. No reputable historical copies include this register, and it should not be used in performances of baroque music.

Spinet and Virginal

The plucking mechanism of the spinet and virginal (or virginals) is the same as that of the harpsichord, but their geometry, size, and construction are different. Notably, their strings do not run straight ahead in front of the player, as in the harpsichord, but are set at a different angle to the keyboard. Both spinets and virginals have only one eight-foot register. Their compass may also be fairly short, which enables the size to be modest—these are purely domestic instruments. In appearance, historic specimens range from undecorated or even quite roughly built to exquisitely ornate. Generally, they are richly resonant in relation to their size, having more strength in the fundamental pitch and less in the higher harmonics than the harpsichord.

Differentiating historically between the spinet and virginal is not always easy. For example, a definition may be masked by language: to a seventeenth-century French person, *épinette* (little thorn) referred to anything that was played with a quill—spinet, virginal, or even harpsichord. Most valid distinctions are technical, depending on such factors as whether both nut and bridge, or only the latter, were on the soundboard. The point of pluck (i.e., how far along the string) is another important distinguishing feature.

Nevertheless, in about 1600, many people would have agreed that a spinet was polygonal, but a virginal was rectangular. The Flemish, however, made a different and rather confusing distinction: to them, a **spinett** (sic) was any instrument—rectangular or polygonal—whose keyboard was offset to the left of the long side, while a rectangular instrument whose keyboard lay to the right was known as a **muselaar**. Both types of instrument can be seen in many paintings of the Dutch school. The muselaar was a distinct subspecies of the virginal family that, because the geometry of its keys caused it to be plucked relatively near the middle of the string, had a powerful, rather "plummy" sound throughout its range. Its unusual resonance makes it capable of sustained tone, and it excels in slower moving music. Another distinctive feature of the muselaar is the **arpichordium** stop; when engaged, this adds a buzzing sound to the tenor and bass registers—a tone color that evokes the renaissance sound-world of crumhorns and curtals.

The Ruckers family of Antwerp showed a great deal of ingenuity in the construction of smaller keyboard instruments. One specialty was the building of virginals in different sizes and pitches, varying from four to six feet long. There was also a delightful "mother and child" model, in which an octave virginal could be placed on top of a larger one so that

26

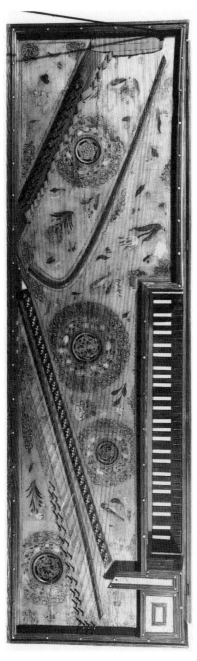

Figure 2. Virginal by Stephen Keene (1668). A late example of the English virginal, richly decorated, with four roses. The tuning pins and curved bridge lie to the right; the nut is on the left, just outside the angled jack rail. The compass is long—FF-d‴, but with no FF-sharp. This bird's-eye view of the soundboard enables one to appreciate that the instrument is almost harp-shaped within its rectangular case. *Photograph reproduced by kind permission of the Director of the Russell Collection of Early Keyboard Instruments, University of Edinburgh, St. Cecilia's Hall, Edinburgh.*

Figure 3. English bentside spinet by John Harrison (1757). Note the shape of the instrument. The keys are longer than those of the virginal; the key-well is outside the case. No music stand is provided, as was not uncommon at the time: the player might lay the music flat over jack rail and nameboard. *Photograph reproduced by kind permission of the Director of the Russell Collection of Early Keyboard Instruments, University of Edinburgh, St. Cecilia's Hall, Edinburgh.*

the jacks coupled together. When not in use, the octave virginal could be stowed away inside a cavity of the main virginal; hence the name.

Italian virginals were also of various types, but the most characteristic came from Venice. These had notably good resonance, since they were built with both bridge and nut resting free on the soundboard. The virginal kept its popularity as a domestic instrument in Italy for a surprisingly long time, and did not succumb to the advance of the piano until the early nineteenth century.

Elsewhere, however, use of the virginal was declining by about 1650. In view of the preeminence of the early seventeenth-century English virginalist school, it is sad that no actual English instruments from the time of Bull or Gibbons survive. The virginal by Stephen Keene, whose soundboard is shown in figure 2, is a late English specimen of 1668. It has the coffered lid characteristic of all English virginals, which directs the sound strongly toward the player; its sound is refined and satisfying.

All the instruments considered in this section, however named, have had their strings running parallel to the keyboard. This has an important practical consequence: the back portion of the key (behind the pivot) has to increase in length as one ascends the keyboard, in order to reach the shorter strings at the back of the instrument. This, in turn, means that the touch of the instrument cannot be uniform through its compass: as the pivot points are all the same distance from the front of the key, the principles of leverage cause the touch to be deepest in the bass. Bass notes can also be slower to speak.

This disadvantage might have been one reason for the development of a new initiative—to put the strings at an angle of about thirty degrees to the keyboard. The idea seems to have come from Italy, but it was the English who took it up in the 1670s and developed the characteristic **bentside spinet**, which soon replaced the virginal and established itself as a highly successful domestic instrument. A bentside spinet is basically a small harpsichord whose layout is rearranged for economy of space: the player sits beside the strings rather than at the end of them. It is fundamentally harpsichord-like in tone, having a higher proportion of energy in the upper harmonics than the virginal. Eighteenth-century bentside spinets were particularly elegant pieces of craftsmanship, sharing the beautiful woodwork of the English harpsichord (figure 3).

There is no specific repertory associated with the bentside spinet. It can cope with any harpsichord music within its keyboard range, although it is essentially a domestic instrument and does not aspire to the grand style. The virginal, on the other hand, has its own special literature, represented most notably by the great English *Fitzwilliam Virginal Book*. Virginal music can certainly be played on harpsichord or spinet, but without the typically forthright virginal tone an intriguing quality is lost.

Buying Your Own Instrument

Acquiring your own instrument is a big step to take and should not be done without the advice of your teacher or another experienced person. If you are a beginner, you do not need a large and sophisticated instrument: most people, after all, do not learn to drive on a Maserati. A beautiful copy of a French double may seem tempting, if finance permits, but in fact it is not much use for Italian music, or for accompanying; and until your technique has reached a certain level of refinement, its splendors will be wasted on you. Also, you may spend a lot of time trying to keep the four-foot in tune. A good single with two eight-foots, on the other hand, confronts the student immediately with the essentials of harpsichord playing—the relationship between finger end and plectrum—without the distraction of a lot of varied registration. There are various national types of one-manual harpsichord to consider, as you will see in the next chapter. Roughly speaking, Italian-type harpsichords are best for continuo playing, while Flemish or German singles are a good general purpose investment.

For many people, however, the best way of getting acquainted with the harpsichord world is to buy a bentside spinet. Its single eight-foot register, which operates exactly like a harpsichord, focuses your mind even more clearly on touch and phrasing. Its compact size enables it to fit into small houses, and its lower price may mean that you can afford a better quality instrument. Musically, its scope is perfectly adequate for much of the repertory—spinets are now often made with a full five-octave compass. A spinet can be used (and easily transported) for continuo playing in small groups. It is simple in tuning and upkeep, and it will not lead you into any habits that need to be unlearned when you move on to a harpsichord.

Whether you decide to buy a spinet or a harpsichord, do try as many instruments as possible, looking for one whose action seems reliable, responsive and comfortable and whose tone you really enjoy. Also listen to the instrument from a distance, if possible, while someone else plays; the person at the keyboard is not necessarily in the best position to form a balanced picture of the tone, because many instruments seem to develop power and richness as the sound travels.

Don't order a new instrument from a builder unless you already have experience of his work or know another satisfied buyer. It is sometimes easier, and it is certainly cheaper, to buy a good secondhand instrument from a reputable agency, which will have thoroughly overhauled it. Addresses of such agencies are given in appendix B. Instruments privately advertised in periodicals should be avoided, unless you can have them inspected by a knowledgeable person; all too often, they suffer from undisclosed problems. Kit-built instruments should not be dismissed—they can at their best be highly satisfactory—but they also need expert assessment. Anything described as "suitable for beginner" should, however, be shunned like the plague; it is a common but disastrous fallacy to imagine that an inferior instrument will suffice when you begin. In practice, it will prove discouraging, because a lot of expertise is needed to produce a tolerable sound from a third-rate instrument; and the more sensitive you are, the more likely you will be to acquire undesirable habits as you seek to cover its defects. Finally, a poor instrument will be hard to sell. For the last reason alone, a good spinet is greatly preferable to an inferior harpsichord.

3

Harpsichord Building in the Past

I mentioned in the last chapter that since about 1970 builders have generally concentrated on building harpsichords based on certain historic instruments, or at least on national types. We should therefore now consider the national types that existed during the two hundred years of the harpsichord's heyday. Copies of several historical types are now widely available, and you may well have access to one; you may hear recordings made on such instruments, or on genuine historic instruments (although old instruments in good working order are not too common). A detailed history of the harpsichord is not appropriate to a book of this nature, but you can find it in a good standard reference work, such as the classic by Frank Hubbard, *Three Centuries of Harpsichord Making.*[1] I propose instead to focus on the salient characteristics of the various national types.

The harpsichord as we now define it seems to have come about by applying a keyboard mechanism to the psaltery, an instrument whose origins lay in Biblical antiquity but which was still in use in the Middle Ages. The psaltery has the same basic characteristics as the harpsichord—its strings are also stretched across a sound box and plucked by plectra. The addition of a keyboard may have taken place sometime around 1400, and harpsichords were certainly known to exist in the fifteenth century. There was a continued evolution in Italy and in the Netherlands during the sixteenth century, and a few harpsichords of outstanding quality survive from this period. An initial peak was reached in Flanders in the early part of the seventeenth century; later in the century the center of interest shifted to France, and in the eighteenth century England and Germany also became important. Each national school of harpsichord building had its own traditions and characteristics. Like many historic crafts, harpsichord building tended to run in family businesses, such as that of the Ruckers family in Antwerp.

The Netherlands

Flemish builders usually decorated their harpsichords around the key-well with beautiful printed papers patterned with sea horses or classical motifs. (These papers can also be found on modern copies of Flemish instruments, since they are available in excellent reprints using the original blocks.) Patterned paper was used also around the inside of the case above the strings and on the borders of the lid. The soundboard was painted, mostly with stylized flowers and birds and patterned arabesques. Latin mottoes were painted on the ash-grain paper that covered the inside of both sections of the lid, and these were surrounded by more arabesques and red and black lines. In addition, the outside was generally painted with a marbled finish. The stand was sometimes tall by modern standards. Some of these characteristics can be seen in the numerous Dutch paintings of the period that depict harpsichords (figure 4).

The general effect of a Flemish harpsichord was vivid and colorful. The visual image was striking, and the same could be said for the rich, resonant sound, with an almost drumlike bass, which was the Ruckers' special distinction, whether the instrument was large or small. The Ruckers family—Johannes (1578–1643), his brother Andreas I (born 1579), and Andreas II (born 1607)—were the most famous members of the Flemish harpsichord school. Their illustrious work was carried on by the Couchet family. Hans Moerman (in the sixteenth century) and Anton Dulcken (in the eighteenth) were also outstanding builders.

Flemish harpsichords were highly prized and, as old Italian violins are today, eagerly sought after. Unfortunately, however, in previous centuries people did not have the sense of responsibility to the past that is now considered essential, and instruments were often altered to meet the demands of changing taste. French musicians of the eighteenth century had a particular regard for the tone qualities of Flemish harpsichords, but by that time music being written for the instrument demanded more notes than the original Flemish keyboard possessed, so French builders often subjected Flemish harpsichords to a process called **ravalement**. Ravalement means that an extra section of soundboard is

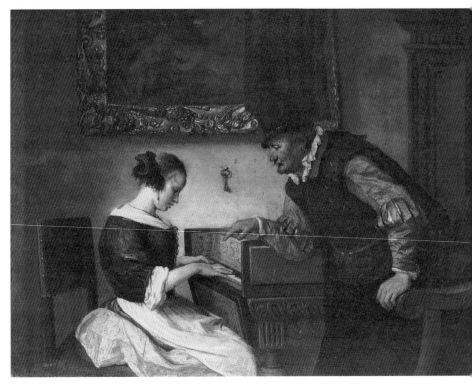

Figure 4. *The Harpsichord Lesson* by Jan Steen (1626–1679). This rather amusing picture shows us a well-to-do young lady being taught by her music-master: instruction is clearly by rote. The instrument has typical Flemish decoration— marbled painted case, sea-horse papers in the key-well, and probably a Latin inscription on the fall-board. The lid appears to be shut. Note the position of the player, turned to the right, as advocated by many contemporary writers. *Reproduced by permission of the Trustees of the Wallace Collection, London.*

inserted at the cheek end or along the spine, and the case is enlarged accordingly. This creates enough width to accommodate extra jacks and strings for extra notes at both ends of the keyboard. Contrary to what one might think, this drastic-sounding process does not spoil the instrument, but as it inevitably alters the scaling, the character of the instrument changes slightly. The frequency with which ravalement was done is one reason that a Flemish harpsichord in its original state is comparatively rare.

Just as Flemish virginals were noted for being built in a variety of pitches, Flemish harpsichords were available in different versions—for example, singles at a pitch a fifth above normal, resulting in a smaller instrument. This idea is in keeping with the building of viols at different pitches, and should not surprise us unduly. But a disconcerting feature of historic Flemish instruments to the modern player is that, in the case of a double, the two keyboards were not always aligned immediately below each other. This offset type of harpsichord, called a **transposing double**, in effect combined two instruments in one (figure 5). The two sets of strings, an eight-foot and a four-foot, could serve either keyboard; the two strings that served, say, the middle-C key on the upper manual would serve the key for the F above that on the lower manual. Obviously the manuals were never coupled. The chief advantage of this rather odd arrangement was the housing in one case of a high-pitched and low-pitched instrument that could accompany voices or instruments of different pitch (say tenor/bass) without rewriting the music in another key. Whatever the reason for the layout, it was usually eliminated in later rebuilding of the instrument; which is another reason why it is rare to find a Flemish harpsichord in an unaltered state.

Italy

Cembalo (occasionally **gravicembalo**) is the Italian term for harpsichord. In general, Italian harpsichords were less complex than Flemish. They were almost invariably single-manual, with two eight-foot registers; and these two were normally played together, being separated only for tuning. Cypress wood was often used for the soundboard and case. The tone of an Italian harpsichord is dry and incisive, making it a particularly suitable instrument for continuo playing (i.e., accompanying an ensemble). In fact, there was no particularly extensive literature for the solo instrument.

An Italian harpsichord is easily recognizable by its shape; it is sharply curved behind the cheek because of its short scaling, and it has a long thin tail. It is usually strung throughout in brass. In addition, historic Italian instruments are unusual in having an outer and an inner case; the outer case is complete with legs and lid, and the inner case—the instrument itself, with keyboard and strings—slides into this. All decoration is on the outer case, the inner being quite plain. Italian harpsichords, especially those owned by wealthy families, could be sumptuously decorated with marquetry, inlaid mother-of-pearl, embossed leather with brass studs, or paintings. Opera house instruments, however, would be quite plain to cope with the heavy wear and tear of their environment.

The most notable Italian builders were Baffo, Trasuntino, and Vin-

Figure 5. Flemish harpsichord by Jan Ruckers (1638). A unique surviving example of an unaltered transposing double. Many Flemish instruments of the period were built to this pattern, which enabled players to accompany at alternative pitches. As the manuals also have the short octave layout in the bass, some complex mechanical arrangements of the keys are called for. There were at one time two strings each, and split keys, for E flat/D-sharp and A-flat/G-sharp, to mitigate the "wolf" effect of meantone tuning. *Photograph reproduced by kind permission of the Director of the Russell Collection of Early Keyboard Instruments, University of Edinburgh, St. Cecilia's Hall, Edinburgh.*

centius, although many other builders are known, often on the evidence of only one instrument. A typical Italian harpsichord made in 1574 by Baffo is now in the Victoria and Albert Museum in London (see figure 9 in chapter 13).

Like other seventeenth-century keyboard instruments, Italian harpsichords often had a peculiarity in their key arrangement known as a **short octave**. Because the music of the period made little use of the chromatic notes in the lowest octave—C-sharp, E-flat, etc.—these notes were omitted. Their keys were allocated to other diatonic notes, and the strings tuned accordingly. What looks like a low B may consequently sound the G below that, and the A and B may be played from the lowest C-sharp and E-flat keys.

Apparent key : B   C   C♯ D   E♭ E   F . . .
Key sounds   : G   C   A   D   B   E   F . . . (chromatic thereafter)

Another arrangement has a keyboard that apparently starts at E, but this key sounds the low C; D and E are played from the F-sharp and G-sharp keys respectively.

Apparent key : E   F   F♯ G   G♯ A . . .
Key sounds   : C   F   D   G   E   A . . . (chromatic thereafter)

These mutations sound alarming, but you will soon adjust to them when playing music contemporary with the instrument (which is really the only music suited to this particular type of keyboard). You simply need to make a careful study of which sound comes from which key. Seventeenth-century music often contains tenths in the left hand, and these large intervals are easily reached with short-octave layouts.

You may also come across instruments in which one or more of the lower black keys are divided into a front and back half. This is another space-saving device called a **broken octave**, or **split-sharp short octave**. Here one half (usually the front half) of the key plays the expected note, while the back half plays the note that has been substituted in the manner described above. Such devices were obviously an impediment to rapid scale work in the lowest bass register, but this does not matter greatly as Italian seventeenth-century music generally avoids writing of this kind. Incidentally, both these features (broken and short octave) may be reproduced in modern copies of the historic instruments that possessed them.

The history of the Italian harpsichord was not an eventful one. Eighteenth-century instruments looked and sounded much like seventeenth-century ones, although the compass tended to increase—possibly to five octaves (GG–g'''). Among later Italian builders, one might mention Grimaldi, whose instruments were unusual in that the grain of the wood ran across, rather than along, the soundboard. This was combined with an unorthodox internal construction to produce an unusually bright sound.

Spain and Portugal

Only a few old Spanish and Portuguese harpsichords survive, but those that do tend to follow the Italian model. Scarlatti's patron Maria Barbara of Spain had eight harpsichords at the time of her death, most of them Italian in style. Some of these must have had the full five-octave compass that was common in Italy by that time, to judge from the range of Scarlatti's sonatas. German harpsichords were also exported to Spain, and there was a little reciprocal influence of style.

A notable Portuguese harpsichord has recently been restored and can be seen and heard in the famous Burnett collection of old keyboard instruments at Finchcocks in Kent. Built in 1785 by Antunes, it is basically Italian in shape and specification (2 × 8, i.e., two eight-foots), but has certain French and even English characteristics. (Several English harpsichords were exported to Portugal during the 1770s.) Its tone combines Italian incisiveness and French resonance.

France

The French term for harpsichord is **clavecin**—although in the sixteenth and seventeenth centuries the term *épinette* was also used for both spinet and harpsichord. Technically, French builders developed from the Flemish tradition, and their instruments exhibit great sophistication and elegance, worthy of the splendid music of the great French *clavecinistes*. Visually, however, eighteenth-century French harpsichords are more refined than the exuberant Flemish instruments, displaying the same shapes and motifs as French furniture of the Louis XV period—cabriole legs, gilt or lacquer decoration, or possibly chinoiserie on the outside (see figure 10 in chapter 14). The inside of the lid might be decorated with classical pastoral paintings, often by well-known painters, and the soundboard was painted with floral motifs.

Tonally, the mature eighteenth-century instrument was equally sophisticated. It was lightly quilled and possessed a great smoothness

38

and sweetness of tone; its action was also refined and particularly well suited to the highly ornamented French style. Whereas some seventeenth-century French instruments had both eight-foot registers on the lower manual (the "grand clavier") and the four-foot alone on the upper, the classic arrangement of one eight-foot on each manual plus the four-foot on the lower became normal by the eighteenth century. An extra eight-foot register, the **peau de bouffle**, was also frequently found; this seems to have evolved originally as a way of filling up the empty register that was left after a Flemish transposing double had undergone ravalement. The jacks of this register had plectra of buffalo leather that produced a gentle, rather muted sound.

The system of coupling the manuals by moving a keyboard appears to have been a French invention. Coupling would have made possible the full range of permutations of these different registers. Here, however, it may be appropriate to point out that it is not always easy to be certain about the original disposition of any historic instrument; internal evidence about the arrangement of the registers, the stringing and so on, can be doubtful, and written references are often problematic to interpret.

The most famous of the many French builders were Nicholas Blanchet, (1660–1731), his son François (1695–1761), the great Pascal Taskin (1723–1783), Jean-Antoine Vaudry, and Henri Hemsch. Their work stood somewhat aside from the rest of the European tradition, but had a remarkable homogeneity. It is never possible to be certain whether instrument makers influence composition or vice versa, but it is beyond doubt that the mature French clavecin composers required from their builders an instrument that could encompass a wide range of qualities: elegance, formality, strength, tenderness, and passion. The uniqueness of French culture made for a homogenous school of composition, whose idiom retained its integrity almost until the time of the Revolution of 1789, and held its own with some success against the invasion of the preclassical style from Vienna and Italy and the novelty of the Érard piano. Eventually, however, harpsichord composition succumbed, and many an instrument ended its days as firewood. Its identification with the aristocracy and the old régime cannot have helped its fate.

Germany

German has no specific word for harpsichord; the generic *Klavier* (keyboard) sufficed in the majority of cases. The Italian term *cembalo* was also used.

39

Harpsichord building was never preeminent in Germany, and because of the devastating effects of the seventeenth-century wars few instruments from before 1700 survive. Eighteenth-century German harpsichords exhibit, like the music of Bach, a blend of national characteristics, with French influence uppermost. The most famous builders were the Hass family, Christian Zell, and Gottfried Silbermann—the latter more familiar as a great organ builder. In fact, some of the methodology of organ building seeps through into German harpsichord design during this period.

Both J. A. Hass and Silbermann seem to have experimented with sixteen-foot (suboctave) tone, and an isolated instrument by Hass is definitely known to have had three manuals—possibly following a Spanish pattern—with a third manual devoted to a sixteen-foot and a two-foot register. Both these extreme features impose severe constraints on the design of an instrument. The short strings of a two-foot register are obviously unstable in tuning, and in addition the strings cannot be continued above treble c″ because the string length becomes so short that there is no room to accommodate all the necessary rows of jacks along it; so the experiment was not followed up. Sixteen-foot strings have to be thicker and under lower tension than eight-foot, and need a separate section of soundboard in order not to interfere with the tone of the eight-foot strings. In fact, sixteen-foot registers hardly got beyond the experimental stage; but unfortunately even this was enough to provide a bad precedent for harpsichords of the revival period, as we shall see in the next chapter.

Another experimental instrument made in Germany—the **lautencymbel**—was strung with gut eight-foot strings but had a four-foot choir in brass throughout. The eight-foot was said to produce a tone very similar to the lute's, although gut strings present many practical problems. Two specimens of the lautencymbel feature in Bach's inventory, however, so the instrument was obviously taken seriously.

Historic German harpsichord cases are often sumptuous but tend to be heavy in appearance. Their stands may also be ornate, with elaborate stretchers connecting the legs (usually six in number).

England

The famous music historian Charles Burney wrote in 1775 "the Germans work much better out of their country than they do in it"[2]; it is certainly true that at least two of the best eighteenth-century English builders were of German or Swiss descent. These were Jacob Kirckman

40

and Burkat Shudi (or Tschudi). The Shudi dynasty formed a partnership with John Broadwood, which eventually became the foundation of the famous English piano firm of Broadwood. Together with the Englishman Thomas Hitchcock, these builders were relatively late arrivals in the field: indeed, composition for the instrument had already entered the Indian summer that heralded its eventual demise.

Earlier English traditions of keyboard instrument making had tended to concentrate first on the virginal, then on the bentside spinet, and few native harpsichords from the seventeenth century survive. The majority seem to have been imported. As latecomers to the scene, however, English builders had a particular advantage in that they were able to observe and build on the best of other European styles of building. An unusually large number of eighteenth-century English instruments survive, and many people consider these English harpsichords to be unequaled. Certainly their tone is rich and singing. The Germanic influence led to a propensity for sheer power and scope: Shudi experimented with scalings and different plucking-points, and extended the downward compass of several instruments to CC, in order to achieve an even more impressive sonority.

The exterior of the instruments, however, was relatively plain, in keeping with the restrained character of English classical architecture. The legs were square and the trestle functional, much plainer than any continental type. But the keys were usually of ivory, and the casework was veneered in beautiful wood, often with marquetry. Kirckman produced some particularly striking instruments with maple-gold marquetry around the key-well. Paint was never used, on either the exterior or the soundboard.

The typical English talent for invention found a ready outlet in the development of various technical devices. One was a way of cutting the jacks in a special dog-leg shape so that one of the eight-foot registers could be played from either manual (an idea that probably originated in the Netherlands). Another involved a modification of the instrument's layout to accommodate an extra row of jacks that plucked one of the existing eight-foots very near the nut, giving a nasal, edgy sound. This type of eight-foot is called a **lute**—not to be confused with the kind of lute effect obtained by using felt dampers on a buff batten.

With these extra tone colors, the need became apparent for devices that enabled one to switch easily from one group of registers to another: the **machine** pedal or stop was the result. This mechanical device, which centers on a shallow box mounted on the outside of the spine, instantaneously changes more registers than one could possibly manipulate in

Figure 6. English harpsichord with swell by John Broadwood (1793). The last known harpsichord by Broadwood, of later pianoforte fame. Although there is only one manual, there are three sets of strings (8, 8, 4), and a further tonal option is given by a fourth set of jacks, which plucks very near the eight-foot nut for a lute effect. The left pedal works on the principle of preselected gears, making possible quick changes of register. The right pedal opens or closes the Venetian swell. Apart from this last feature, the appearance of the whole instrument is entirely typical of harpsichords of the English school. *Photograph reproduced by kind permission of the Director of the Russell Collection of Early Keyboard Instruments, University of Edinburgh, St. Cecilia's Hall, Edinburgh.*

a single movement of the hand. (Taskin, in France, had experimented with knee levers to procure the same effect.)

In retrospect, it can be seen that the later years of the English harpsichord were not entirely free of decadence. This is epitomized by Shudi's invention in 1769 of a harpsichord with an inner lid covering the strings, which had louvers like a Venetian blind (see figure 6). These louvers could be opened or closed with a pedal to give small crescendos and diminuendos. The louvers, however, alter the natural tone of the instrument radically when closed, masking much of the sharpness of the pluck. Add to this the occasional use of leather plectra, and we are faced with an instrument whose tone was not so very far removed from that of the fortepiano, and which could make good sense of classical compositions such as Haydn's sonatas.

Crescendos and diminuendos are nevertheless artistically foreign to the harpsichord's nature; and in the end, the integrity of the instrument was pushed beyond its limits by attempting to cope with changes in composition styles. Although English harpsichord building continued vigorously until almost 1800, with the wisdom of hindsight we can see that the final two decades of the century were a period of decline, whose compromises helped consign the instrument to temporary oblivion.

Notes

1. Hubbard 1965–67. A comprehensive study by a writer who was also an eminent builder of harpsichords in the United States. As well as historical accounts of the major schools, it also contains valuable appendixes and pictorial illustrations from contemporary sources.

2. Burney 1775, 2: 145.

4

The Eclipse and Rebirth
of the Instrument

The gradual replacement of the harpsichord by the piano that occurred during the last decades of the eighteenth century was inescapably linked to fundamental changes in musical style. It is true that much music of the 1780s and 1790s, such as Beethoven's "Pathétique" Sonata, was inscribed "for harpsichord or pianoforte"; but this was due mainly to practical and commercial prudence. Publishers wanted to ensure that people who had not yet acquired the new instruments were not discouraged from buying the latest works. Music of the Viennese classical period, however, is conceived in a decorated harmonic style, and its dynamics are governed by essentially dramatic procedures: its textures and its ethos are basically foreign to the level tonal scheme of the harpsichord. As a result, by 1800 the instrument entered a period of eclipse that was to last for well over a hundred years.

Music is ideally inseparable from the instruments for which it is written, although it is sometimes hard to say whether composers or instrument builders provided the stimulus for new developments. The nineteenth century was the great era of the piano; names such as Chopin, Schumann and Liszt, Rachmaninov and Debussy epitomize the triumphant progress of piano composition, while those of Érard, Broadwood, and Bechstein represent the enormous development in its construction. In general, the Romantic period was no more conspicuous than any previous century for its interest in older keyboard music. There were certain notable exceptions—Guilmant, for instance, investigated early French organ music, and Mendelssohn did much to popularize the keyboard music of Bach, which (especially *The Well-tempered Clavier*) had never fallen completely below the horizon. But during the nineteenth century, harpsichord music from the baroque period, if it was known at all, was played on the piano, which was automatically assumed to be superior to the harpsichord. A kind of musical Darwinism had resulted in a belief that the fittest instrument had survived, and vestiges of this attitude still persist. You probably played your first Bach keyboard music on the piano; and people often express surprise when I explain that the harpsichord, which they regard as old-fashioned and obsolete, is widely made and used today.

An isolated initiative to revival occurred as early as 1889, when at the Paris Exhibition two rival French piano firms, Pleyel and Érard, showed harpsichords copied from eighteenth-century instruments by Taskin.[1] But the first real renaissance of the harpsichord is indelibly linked with the name of Wanda Landowska. It was for her that Pleyel constructed in 1912 the instrument on which her virtuosity became legendary. Pleyel's was, however, quite unlike any historic harpsichord; it had an iron frame in a heavy case, in an attempt to eliminate the need for frequent tuning. The iron frame in turn led to the adoption of high-tension stringing and a precision action with metal components, and some of the registers had leather plectra instead of quill for smoothness of tone. There were also pedals to facilitate—or perhaps I should say orchestrate—frequent changes between the numerous registers (which included a sixteen-foot). Such features resulted in a formidable instrument, but one which was scarcely a harpsichord any longer: it subsequently acquired the unkind but apt nickname of "pianochord."

Landowska's enthusiasm and deep musicality were nevertheless responsible for a growth of interest in the historic repertory. Although her musicological standards would not withstand scrutiny nowadays, she should be given great credit for a real attempt to revive the keyboard music of the past. The work of Arnold Dolmetsch was another powerful stimulus to the revival of the harpsichord. He made an instrument for the London Arts and Crafts Exhibition in 1896 that was used in a performance of *Don Giovanni* at Covent Garden the following year. (Oddly enough, the harpsichord was revived for the purpose of accompanying operatic recitative long before there was any serious interest in other continuo playing. In a few opera houses, indeed, its use had never been interrupted.)

Germany was also an early protagonist of the harpsichord renaissance, but there the revival fell victim almost immediately to an unfortunate circumstance. An instrument in a Berlin collection, which had been rebuilt some time during the nineteenth century with a sixteen-foot and eight-foot on the lower manual, and an eight-foot and a four-foot on the *upper* manual, was mistakenly believed by scholars to have a direct historical connection with J. S. Bach. A copy of this instrument was made as early as 1899, and eventually there was a widespread copying of the so-called Bach harpsichord under factory conditions. By the 1930s the false model had become the norm in German universities and concert halls, and it was widely exported. The ensuing confusion resembled the confusion which prevailed in Germany and elsewhere during the same decade over the nature of the so-called Bach organ. Neither error was fully cleared up until the 1960s.

With few exceptions, builders in the 1930s continued to embrace the philosophy that modern technological development could correct the apparent shortcomings of the historic instrument. Some even clung to the idea of an iron frame and heavy case, with the intention of producing a harpsichord that was as stable in tuning as a piano—although this kind of construction inhibits the sonority of the instrument. Builders seemed unwilling to believe that an instrument built on simple historical principles could have a free, resonant, and singing tone; they preferred the paths of technological intervention. These "revival" harpsichords of the 1930s were nevertheless built in considerable numbers. As well as being used for Bach's music and for continuo playing, they fitted the vogue for neobaroque composition that flourished in Germany as a result of Hindemith's work and became widespread throughout Europe.

This vogue produced various harpsichord works such as the *Concert Champêtre* for harpsichord and chamber orchestra by Francis Poulenc, the *Concertino* by Walter Leigh, and the Sonata for Violin and Harpsichord by Walter Piston: the idea of ensemble writing seemingly attracted composers at this stage. Unfortunately these attractive works labored under the disadvantage that no harpsichord, let alone one of the kind built in the 1930s, can satisfactorily hold its own against high-tensioned modern orchestral strings. The stratagems adopted by composers to ensure sufficient prominence for the harpsichord part often led to a preponderance of writing in the highest part of the keyboard. As this texture does not particularly suit harpsichords that are historical copies, these works tend to be neglected today.

The problems of volume and balance took a new turn in the 1950s. With the technology then becoming available, amplification of the harpsichord seemed to be the solution. Baroque music was becoming increasingly popular, but one now looks back with incredulity at the conditions in which it was played. Sometimes it formed a single item in a concert otherwise devoted to symphonic works, and conductors were then particularly keen to have the harpsichord amplified. With microphones suspended in unlikely places, harpsichords often battled heroically, in concert halls intended for large-scale symphonic music, against modern orchestral strings that were both too numerous and too loud— a travesty which lasted for well over a decade.

Reliability of action was another matter that exercised the minds of revival harpsichord builders; here again builders preferred to invent modern devices to regulate the action of their jacks, rather than to understand the methods used in historic instruments. For instance, the firm of Neupert was extolling the merits of its patent adjustable metal jacks as late as 1960—although a well-made traditional wooden jack never needs any adjusting. In retrospect, it is hard to sympathize with such misplaced ingenuity.[2]

Mid-century builders also tended to retain the rather questionable features that had been introduced by Pleyel—such as sixteen-foot registers, rows of pedals to facilitate instant changes of register, and pedals with a half-hitch position to provide full or half volume on each register. This kind of instrument encouraged a style of playing that relied heavily on changes of color during a movement, although this aesthetic is inherently opposed to baroque style. The way back to a true understanding of historical performance style has been as long and hard as the return to historical methods of harpsichord building.

It is only relatively recently that players have begun to study systematically the instruction books and other writings of the sixteenth, seventeenth, and eighteenth centuries to discover how composers expected their music to be performed. It is invidious to mention performers of the 1950s and 1960s, many of whom, although holding ideas about performing early music we might not now agree with, were wonderfully accomplished players and did much to popularize the repertory. One might however regard George Malcolm and Rafael Puyana as the last exponents of the colorist style. The truly great musicologist and harpsichordist Thurston Dart did more than any other single person to explore and open up the world of early music in the same two decades, and to his example we owe many fundamental procedures of editing and research. Yet in spite of his visionary understanding, his harpsichord performances were conditioned by the instruments available in his time, and even his superb playing can occasionally sound slightly old-fashioned, so vastly has the knowledge of early performance style and harpsichord building expanded since his untimely death in 1971.

The impetus to true historical harpsichord building seemed to come more or less simultaneously from the United States, Great Britain, and Germany. In the late 1950s Hugh Gough in London, Frank Hubbard and William Dowd in Boston, and Martin Skowroneck in Bremen (who had all been trained in revival-style building) independently began to explore the special techniques of historical building. Hubbard's work in particular was enthusiastically endorsed by the eminent harpsichordist Ralph Kirkpatrick, whose study of the complete works of Scarlatti had made a considerable impression on the musicological world. There was also a parallel within the organ-building scene, where builders were increasingly exploring concepts of authenticity as applied to organ building. Insistence on a light wooden frame was fundamental to the new harpsichord thinking, just as the appreciation of the importance of a shallow, well-designed case was crucial for the organ.

As the movement toward a lightly built, authentically strung harpsichord gathered momentum in the 1960s, keyboard collections such as the Vleeshuis Museum in Antwerp, the Russell Collection in Edinburgh, or the Skinner Collection at Yale University began to be besieged by builders anxious to measure and examine the historic harpsichords they housed. There was a reaction against factory production in favor of small individual workshops, and by the 1970s an ever-increasing number of builders, some of them highly talented, were producing copies of Italian, French, and Flemish models. German copies have also gained ground lately. (Few makers, however, offer copies of English instruments, because the fine cabinetmaking involved in these copies outweighs the actual musical work and is reflected in the price.) Copies of historic instruments proved so popular that many long-established firms such as Goble, who had hitherto relied on supplying compromise instruments, joined the historical movement and began to produce excellent work.

A further important factor was the development of harpsichord-building kits, especially by the American firm of Zuckermann. Kit building brought the construction of some kind of harpsichord within the reach of amateur builders; and although the results are inevitably of uneven quality, depending on the capabilities and patience of the builder, the caliber and sophistication of the kits themselves have increased considerably. In fact, the availability of mass-produced parts, many of which emanate from the United States, has also brought about great changes in the work of professional builders, some of whom produce excellent and individual instruments constructed mainly from such preproduced components. Other developments include metallurgical research, which has led to the manufacture of iron music wire according to historic formulae, giving a better tone,[3] and a revival of old decorative styles, including the original types of paints and materials used.

Present-day professional players are scrupulous about using the right instrument for the music they perform. A harpsichordist recording, for example, the French Suites of Bach would not dream of using an Italian-style harpsichord, nor would he play music by Sweelinck on a French-style instrument. For a concert of music by composers of various nationalities, he would possibly use a Flemish or German type, as these are the most universally adaptable in tone.

Students cannot usually be so fussy; they may have to work on whatever instrument is available—probably an instrument of the wrong national type, or even a hybrid of no particular style. Such compromises do not matter much to the beginner, except when there are problems with the length of the keyboard. (Italian and Flemish instruments have a shorter compass and cannot accommodate, for instance, all of Scarlatti's sonatas.) As you progress, however, you should aim to cultivate an increasing discrimination and appreciation of the inherent properties and potential of each type.

Of course, one can still play Bach's harpsichord music on the piano, and certain artists continue to do so, some with great integrity and sensitivity. One can even play Bach on saxophone or synthesizer and retain some of its quality, such is the greatness of his musical thought. But playing music on an instrument for which it was not written must always involve an element of compromise. It is rather like reading poetry in translation—the sense is there, but the nuances and the essential sound are not. In the case of sixteenth- and seventeenth-century harpsichord composers, the textures that they favored simply refuse to translate successfully into piano sound. Their spacing of chords, their use of ornamentation, and their contrapuntal thinking are all rooted in the nature of the harpsichord, but run counter to the grain of the piano. For a composer like Couperin, there is simply no substitute for the clavecin.

Merely using the right kind of instrument for the performance of early music, however, will not itself guarantee a satisfactory performance. The player has still a great deal to learn about the actual method and style of playing appropriate to the music. These matters come under the terms **historical performance practice** or **historically oriented performance** (*Aufführungspraxis* in German)—a fascinating, though inevitably controversial, study, which is discussed in chapter 10. But for the moment it is sufficient to say that playing on the right instrument is a vital step in the right direction. The very act of playing a harpsichord can in time give you real insights into how the music should go, if you approach the instrument sympathetically.

Notes

1. The Taskin copied by Érard was the famous instrument of 1769 now housed in the Russell Collection, Edinburgh University.

2. Feldberg, the English offshoot of Neupert, turned to building historical copies soon after 1960.

3. See *A Handbook of Historical Stringing Practice for Keyboard Instruments*, compiled and edited by Malcolm Rose and David Law. Available from The Workshop, English Passage, Lewes BN7 2AP, United Kingdom.

__ 5 __

Starting to Play the Harpsichord

The next four chapters explore the principles of harpsichord playing and touch, showing how your hands should cooperate with the action of the instrument and how you can obtain various effects. These chapters may supplement or clarify what your teacher tells you, and they will serve as a compendium of the language and scope of the harpsichord, which can be applied to any music you study.

Obviously, prior familiarity with the keyboard is useful. It is not indispensable—in the past, keyboard players naturally started directly on the harpsichord, instead of coming to it via the piano or organ; and increasingly this may be possible today. In writing this book, however, I have decided to concentrate on those who have some keyboard experience. Organists usually find the transition to harpsichord quite easy, especially if they have been taught the organ well, since the principles of articulation and key release on that instrument are not fundamentally different. Pianists need more help. Until they are shown how to unlock the musical potential of the harpsichord, they may find that it feels unresponsive and frustrating. On the other hand, if any clavichord players should be reading this, they will find they have a head start.

Whatever your previous experience, if you want to play the harpsichord properly it is essential to have access to a reasonable instrument for regular practice. Aim to play for at least a short time every day: this is far more productive than long, infrequent sessions, since it is the frequency of coming fresh to your practice material that counts. Even on a day when you think that you have no time to spare, try to fit in a couple of ten-minute sessions devoted to one specific problem—you will be amazed how much benefit this will bring.

It cannot be overemphasized that you will derive most benefit from studying music that is within your capacity to play with attention to detail. By all means explore other music, and aim gradually to widen your technical scope; but never make a habit of stumbling through music that is too difficult for you.

Posture and Playing Action

The harpsichord is best played with the lid open; with the lid closed, the tone is stifled. Some players like to have the lid opened right out—that is, with the flap extended to the front of the instrument, instead of folded back as on a grand piano. This gives the maximum reflecting surface, enabling both player and audience to hear the full tonal range, although a tall player will be slightly short of space.

First, make yourself comfortable at the keyboard; middle C (which is a bit to the right of center) should be in front of you. Make sure that your seat is at the right height: you may well need a slightly higher seat for an instrument with two manuals, in order to be able to reach the top keyboard without any strain on your neck or shoulder muscles. Put your feet flat on the floor in front of you, and get used to playing with them in this position, which is the only one that looks nice to the viewer. Check, periodically, where your feet are (you may be surprised); check, too, that your shoulder muscles have not become tense and dragged your shoulders up toward your ears—a common reflex action when you are feeling anxious or uncertain.

Harpsichord playing is essentially a finger and knuckle, rather than a wrist and arm, activity, although the arms must also remain free and relaxed. The relative shortness of harpsichord keys is a natural guide to the proper position of your hand—the fingers should be gently curved, so that (at rest) the fingertips lie just beyond the end of your thumb. Many writers, from the sixteenth-century Tomás de Santa Maria down to J. S. Bach and Rameau,[1] refer to this position. In fact, if your hands are large no other position is really possible. You will also realize that your nails need to be kept short.

The curve of the fingers means that as you play a note your finger moves slightly toward the front of the key as well as downward. The release of the note is not simply a lift of the finger, but may also be a continuation of the curve. Experiment with this movement now, away from the keyboard. Although a difficult technical point, such as an awkward trill, can sometimes be solved by flattening the fingers slightly, curved fingers should be the norm. This will ensure clarity in your playing, and by automatically bringing your fingers near the front of the keys it will give brilliance and definition to quick passages.

Relaxation is vital. Your wrist and fingers must be firm at the moment of depressing the key, especially when you are playing chords, but as soon as the plectrum has plucked you should aim to soften the position. A soft hand conveys a singing, resonant sound, whereas a rigid hand produces a pinched, hard tone. I realize that complete relaxation comes only when you are absolutely familiar with what you are doing, but try to give it some thought from the outset. Breathing *out* at difficult moments will often help release tension.

Because the harpsichord key mechanism is of primary simplicity, it reflects your attitude immediately. A tense approach may achieve exactness, but will not be conducive to expressive playing. Be firm, active, and precise, but be prepared to be gentle and flexible too. Tomás de Santa Maria put it well when he wrote "although the hands strike the keys gently, they nevertheless have to strike them with a little impetuosity."[2] If you achieve this balance of gentleness and decisiveness, the instrument will in return respond readily to your wishes.

A harpsichord key attacked from a height gives a brittle, unpleasant sound, so keep your movements reasonably compact. Bach's hand movement in playing was said to be almost imperceptible, and Rameau says "no great movement should be made where a lesser one will suffice."[3] You should certainly never pound the keys so hard that you hit the key bed, causing a thud and shaking the jack rail. On the other hand, don't be afraid of the instrument—it is by no means fragile. Harpsichord music occasionally calls for quite a lot of grip and attack, and a dramatic passage may elicit some energetic hand movement. Generally, though, you should aim at a quiet manner at the keyboard, reflecting an inner certainty and tranquillity.

Students often ask whether they should look at the keyboard when they play. There is no single answer to this. It depends whether you are sight-reading, playing from memory, or something in between. Obviously, one needs to look at the keys at certain times—when executing a big leap, or changing manuals, for instance. What matters, however, is that you should be keenly aware of **focus**. Getting accurately to the key you intend depends on your having a precise picture of the keyboard. This may be achieved either by actually looking at the keys, or by calling up your mental map of the keyboard (which, with the passage of time, becomes increasingly familiar and sharply defined). This mental picture comes from a blend of visual memory and tactile memory, and it is perfectly possible to *play on it*, especially if your eyes are occupied with reading the notes. It does not matter much which focus you use, but you need to take care when changing from one to the other.

If you are having trouble with split notes (i.e., depressing the neighboring key as well as the one you intend) or general wobbles in performance, focusing carefully on either the keyboard or the mental map will nearly always solve the problem.

Key Action

In the rest of this chapter, we explore the basic principles of how to use the instrument's key action. These simple experiments in touch are very important. For them, engage one of the eight-foot registers.

- Using the second finger of the right hand, on any convenient note in the treble, depress the key very slowly until the plectrum plucks. Feel the pluck: then let the key travel to the bottom, without pressing unduly hard, and hold it here until the sound has completely died away. Notice how long the sound continues to resonate—probably six seconds or more after the pluck (a bass note will resonate even longer). Then let the key return. Repeat this several times, listening and observing carefully.
- Now depress the same key—normally this time, not slowly—and after about two seconds release it quite quickly and let it return to the rest position. Notice the sudden stopping of the sound as the damper falls on the string.

In more advanced harpsichord playing, you will need to develop control over the precise moment of damping every note—sometimes instantly, sometimes after a delay—as an important part of your expressive technique: so be conscious of this damping from the outset. The release of the note is as crucial as its attack and must be precise and positive. (Clean release will also help to avoid a problem that can occur on a poorly regulated instrument, where the plectrum hangs above the string and makes repetition impossible.)

Next, begin to combine the basic elements of plucking and damping in different ways, experimenting as follows:

- Using the second and third fingers of your right hand, play two adjacent notes several times in slow alternation, with a very small break between the damping of one and the plucking of the next.

54

(Don't let your hand move; this is just a finger movement.) Listen for the silence, which is called a *silence d'articulation*.

• Next, play the same thing, slowly, but synchronize the damping of one note with the pluck of the next, so that there is no gap in the sound.

• Now play the same thing but don't damp the first note until after the second has plucked, and so on. Listen carefully for the over-lap: two notes at once for a brief instant.

The pluck of the plectrum is obviously the loudest and most conspicuous part of the note. It could be compared to the explosive consonant at the beginning of a word. As in good elocution, you must learn to manage it to good effect.

If you want to make any note distinct or prominent, this initial pluck needs to be *exposed*—i.e., not obscured by the preceding sound. For example, a single note in a basically continuous phrase can be made prominent by allowing the previous note to damp slightly early, so as to leave a *silence d'articulation*. The length of the silence can be varied to regulate the amount of stress you want, but it is in no way as long as the break succeeding a staccato note—just a tiny discontinuity. The overall rhythmic flow is not disrupted, and your hand should not rise from the keyboard. A useful way to indi-cate the *silence d'articulation* in your copy, when necessary, is to put a short vertical mark above the staff between the two notes con-cerned.

If you want a note to sound really weak—as in the second note of a strongly phrased pair—its pluck must be *concealed* as much as possible. Overlap the preceding note by holding it down until the second note has been plucked. The continuing resonance of the undamped first note will to some extent mask the second pluck and weaken it. The effectiveness of this depends on the fine adjustment of the instrument, and to some extent on the acoustics of the playing space: but cultivate it as a valuable part of your technique. It could be marked in your copy as a horizontal line above the two notes. Rameau included this effect in one of his tables of ornaments as an illustration of an appoggiatura from below, and shows very clearly how the accented first note is sustained beneath the lighter second note (example 5-1). (Rameau notates a long overlap to make his point, but the length may be varied according to context: your ear should guide you.)

Example 5-1. *Port de voix* (appoggiatura), from the ornament table of Rameau's *Pièces de Clavecin* (1724).

In between these two extremes of separation and overlap lie many gradations. At the center of the spectrum is the clean, basic *mouvement ordinaire* of the eighteenth-century writers—Rameau, Saint-Lambert, Mattheson, Marpurg—in which the damping of one note and the pluck of the next coincide. *Mouvement ordinaire* is not like the legato of the modern pianist, which is often slightly overlapped: it has greater clarity.

Gradually, you will come to understand how to apply this basic knowledge. What counts is how you manage the transition from one note to the next. This determines whether the *second* note is prominent and strong, or weak and tucked away, or neutrally in-between. A detached transition makes the next note more distinct; a precise end-to-end (ordinary touch) one makes it equally important; an overlapped transition makes it weaker. From this simple formula spring all the musical effects of harpsichord playing.

If you are a pianist, this will probably seem strange. You have been used to differentiating the musical weight of a note by the energy of the finger—i.e., by something done *at the time of striking the note.* On the harpsichord, however, most of this differentiation comes *from the treatment of the previous note*—i.e., it is an effect with roots in the past. You therefore have to learn to think ahead continually as you play.

Harpsichord touch focuses your attention on new aspects of continuity and shaping, and this may challenge you at first. The exercises given above, however, will teach you the underlying rationale; it is important to review them every time you practice. Before long, control of your transitions will start to become instinctive, and then your playing will develop real life.

When teaching children, I have them take the three notes, E, D, C, of the old nursery rhyme and then vary the transitions so that they play first: THREE blind MICE; and then: three BLIND mice. This tiny exercise, which I strongly recommend to adults as well, seems to summarize nearly everything there is to learn about articulation on the harpsichord, and it contains the answer to those tiresome people who say that the harpsichord cannot produce accents.

In conclusion, it is not too early to note that this idea of using words can be developed into a useful tool to help your practice. Students who have difficulty in accenting phrases suitably will usually respond readily if I find words that fit the rhythm of that phrase, and then suggest that they "play the words." Indeed, the relevance of words and the voice to instrumental playing should never be ignored: not for nothing did so many historic writers insist on the primal importance of vocal music.

Notes

1. Rameau's remarks in *De la Méchanique des Doigts sur le Clavecin*—the Preface to his *Pièces de Clavecin*, 1724—are typical:
   "The first and fifth fingers, being at the [front] edge of the keys, cause the other fingers to curve, so that they can position themselves likewise . . . one should neither straighten nor bend them further. . . . The movement of the fingers comes from their root [i.e., where they join the hand]."
   Erwin Jacobi, ed., *J. P. Rameau: Pièces de Clavecin* (Zürich: Bärenreiter, 1972), 17.

2. Santa Maria 1565 (Rodgers 1971, 223). This much-quoted source from Santa Maria is aimed at players of the keyboard in general: it includes organ and clavichord as well as harpsichord, which inevitably makes it more prone to generalization. The fingering is not printed with the music, but separately in the text, and the matter of fitting the two together has exercised editors considerably. Rodgers' solutions seem acceptable.

3. Erwin Jacobi, ed., *J. P. Rameau: Pièces de Clavecin* (Zürich: Bärenreiter, 1972).

6

Articulation in Harpsichord Music

You will constantly come across the word **articulation** in connection with harpsichord playing. Literally, it means "breaking up into jointed lengths"—we speak, for instance, of an articulated vehicle. By extension, it also means the art of expressing something clearly in speech by making all the parts of a sentence distinct and relating them to and balancing them with each other so that their meaning is obvious. An articulate person is one who can convey an argument clearly. Applied to harpsichord playing, the word refers to the variety of ways in which notes are joined to, or separated from, each other (i.e., the transitions), in order to display the musical argument clearly. Articulation is part of the music, not an extraneous element: it should not draw much attention to itself, but make its effect through the shaping of the music.

The word articulation has unfortunately tended to be linked too much with the separation aspect—the *silence d'articulation* between two separated notes. This limited use of the word is misleading, because it tends to focus on the discontinuity element, when in fact continuity is vital (the vehicle is after all one unit, although it is in jointed sections). Rather, you should think of articulation in the sense of microphrasing: something that governs the handling of detail and the small units from which the music is constructed. It is inseparable from the subject of **touch**.

How is Articulation Indicated?

The slur is practically the only marking used for indicating articulation. A few composers used staccato marks (either our modern dot, or the wedge-shaped mark we now associate with *marcato*), but this was infrequent. Articulation markings of any kind are scarce in keyboard music before about 1660; even after this date, the growth of articulation marking was hesitant and lagged far behind actual practice. Many eighteenth-century composers were still cavalier about their markings: you should not look for many indications in, for example, the works of Scarlatti.

As in many other matters, the French baroque school was the most highly organized in respect of articulation. By about 1710 it had evolved markings that were detailed, significant, and commendably consistent. But in other music, consistency is something of a nightmare. If, for instance, a composer has a slur over a little figure the first time it appears, does this mean that the same figure should always be slurred thereafter? The answer is not always simple. Bach, whom one might assume to be a model of Germanic thoroughness, can pose great problems in this respect, even when his manuscript is clearly legible.[1]

This may not sound comforting to the beginner, especially as many people are used to editions that are thoroughly marked in the modern manner. In fact, to satisfy such desires, twentieth-century editions that appeared before the development of historical performance practice (and even a few since then) tended to subject music of the baroque period to a heavy peppering of markings. These of course did not carry any authority, or even bear much relationship to baroque musical style. The phrasing was aimed at pianists, and when it is applied to harpsichord music a mincingly artificial style usually results.

Modern musicology has reversed this trend, to the extent that any reputable edition today will bear only the composer's own markings. But as I have said, these were often sparse, and we need to know what principles to apply to unmarked music. Absence of markings by no means implies absence of varied articulation.

How Can One Decide About the Articulation?

There are three lines of approach to deciding about the articulation. We can

- apply our own musical sense,
- listen carefully to what the instrument itself can tell us,
- inquire about the general practice of the time of composition.

Many treatises and instruction books of the seventeenth and eighteenth centuries are now available in reprints. These writings occasionally contain information about articulation, and musicologists now study them closely and write about their conclusions. The relationship between articulation and the type of fingering used is a favorite, if rather controversial, topic for scholarly discussion. I have, however, left original (historical) fingering until a separate chapter, because the beginner should not have to cope with too many issues at once.

Delving in historic treatises can be fascinating, but it must be admitted that they are sometimes obscure, random, or even inconsistent, and they often lack a pedagogic sense. I cherish the memory of one viol book that progresses, in three musical examples, from the most elementary fingering to a passage of hideous difficulty. These books are equally apt to be vague or unsubtle in keyboard matters. The instruction "raise the finger from A and depress B" could cover quite a variety of transition types (whose effect could depend on many variables—for instance, on how far the key dips before it plucks); it might have a basic meaning to a beginner, but a more complex one to an expert. To whom was it addressed? This example highlights two truths: first, that articulation is not easy to write about; and second, that although historic sources should certainly be consulted, their inferences need careful sifting by the expert performer, and do not offer sufficient advice for a beginner.

Further help is therefore needed, and the practical experience of professional performers can be one way of supplying it. Historical performance studies are now well developed, and there are many players who have read the sources and experimented with various historical techniques. From their study of sources and the music itself, they have evolved convincing articulation styles. Their playing can offer us models, and listening to and studying with experienced players is one of the best ways to develop your ideas on articulation.

You might think it a good thing if informed players could commit the results of their researches to printed editions, but there are three objections:

- It is best to provide the player with a clean page (i.e., without editorial intervention), since any articulation markings are too readily taken as infallible by the inexperienced.
- No articulation should ever be regarded as unchangeable or unique. Even within a framework of historical reference, a player would be unlikely to produce exactly the same articulation in two consecutive performances. Certainly, over the years, that player's

ideas would develop. In addition, what is right for one player, occasion, or room is not necessarily right for another. While there are some obviously undesirable articulations, there is never just one correct or supposedly approved version which excludes all others. Even the well-marked music of Couperin still leaves a lot of room for individual choice.

• Copious articulation-marking tends to defeat its own ends, and can result in a stilted style (like a centipede unsure which leg to use next). It is pretty impossible to indicate the subtler nuances of articulation in any case.

Some readers may wonder if all this agonizing is necessary. "Won't it do," you may ask, "if I just play it *musically*?" Of course that will take you a long way, and you certainly should never suppress your own natural musical impulses. What you deduce and sense from the music itself is extremely valuable. Other ideas, such as analogies with string bowing, may be helpful too. But always remember the risk that your twentieth-century attitudes may blind you to attractive but unimagined possibilities in earlier music. You will enjoy the music more and penetrate it further if you augment your own musical ideas by taking note of what can be learned from the past.

It is now time to summarize some of these findings and to make a few suggestions based on experience and experiment. In doing so, I want to focus on six main topics. These are good guidelines for you to use when dealing with any music written before about 1750.

• the use of imitation in contrapuntal writing
• the presence of dissonance
• rhythm and meter
• patterns derived from the instrument itself
• figures and motifs used in composition
• expressive elements

The Sixteenth and Early Seventeenth Centuries

One might compare the articulation of sixteenth and early seventeenth centuries to a painting executed with plenty of primary color. Many sources, such as Tomás de Santa Maria's *Arte de tañer fantasia* (1565), tend to suggest that the articulation style at this time was basically crisp, even detached, since it is often stated that the finger should be raised from one key before the next is depressed. There are many factors, too complex to discuss here, that color the interpretation of these sources. But it is best for the beginner to treat such references as an invitation to play with crisp clarity and clean release, rather than as an instruction to insert *silences d'articulation* between every note. The result should never sound spindly, fussy, or lacking in continuity.

In fact, the desired clarity arises naturally from the fingering style of the period, which made little use of the thumb except for larger chordal stretches and the beginning of scales. (The second and third, or third and fourth, fingers were often alternated in pairs in scale passages: see chapter 9.) Even if you decide not to use historical fingering, sixteenth- and seventeenth-century music always benefits from an active finger movement, with plenty of detached transitions.

In playing music composed before about 1650, the six principles listed above might be applied as follows:

- Alert your ears to the detail of the music. In contrapuntal pieces, it is important that the subject, or any imitative material, is clearly spelled out. Many fantasias start with long individual notes that benefit by being separated somewhat (indeed, long notes in general are rarely sustained for their entire length). Apart from such initial notes, aim to phrase the subject distinctly (and distinctively) and to allow enough daylight into the surrounding voices, so that detail can be heard. You should not, however, lose a sense of the direction of each voice, and how its notes relate to each other.
- Music of this period was governed by a sensitivity to dissonance, which was reckoned in terms of the intervals above the bass note. Fourths, sevenths, and ninths (or seconds) above the bass could only occur on main beats in certain carefully regulated contexts: they were sustained, repeated, or tied over from the preceding note, and then resolved. This disciplined handling of dissonance was an important part of a composer's expressive technique. If you play contrapuntal music with an intelligent use of detached touch, these suspended dissonances will be naturally highlighted, as the sustained notes will be more prominent.
- In playing pieces in a more chordal style, it is natural to make the most prominent *silences d'articulation* before the most important chords, so that there is an alternation of musical weight between the stronger and weaker beats. The seventeenth-century musician distinguished clearly between "good" notes on strong beats and "bad" notes on weaker. Dance music, in particular, needs its phrase ends clearly marked, and its rhythmic structure alertly presented: in other words, you should here be linking the articulation to the

meter. Example 6-1, the first half of a corrente by Frescobaldi, does not have phrases of regular length, but your articulation should convey its captivating rhythmic sway. Experiment with these measures (playing only the right-hand part if necessary) until you capture the shape and emphasis you want.

Example 6-1. Girolamo Frescobaldi, *Corrente Quarta*, from *Toccate e partite, libro primo* (1637), mm. 1–15.

• The technique of any instrument imposes its own articulation patterns to some extent, which means that fingering patterns and musical patterns often coincide. Example 6-2 presents an excerpt of music by John Bull, coming home in fine style at the end of a pavan: it is almost inevitable that the left-hand figures should be slurred as shown. (The passage is easier than it looks, and creates a splendid turbulent swish in the lower strings.)
• A viable rule of thumb for articulating almost all music before 1700 (and even some later music) could be: within each main division of the measure, join adjacent (conjunct) notes more closely than those proceeding by leaps (disjunct), which should be detached. There will naturally be exceptions, however: for instance (as in example 6-3), paired notes are normally slurred, even when they are disjunct.

This example leads us to another factor to be considered—the figuration of the piece. Seventeenth-century writers devoted considerable space to theorizing about the **figures** *(figurae)*—rhythmic or melodic motifs and patterns from which the music was constructed, which they in turn linked to the study of rhetoric.[2] Note patterns and manner of

Example 6-2. Dr. (John) Bull, end of *Pavana*, from the *Fitzwilliam Virginal Book* No. 136 (CXXXVI), with author's fingering and slurs.

Example 6-3. Jan Pieterzoon Sweelinck, Toccata, from the *Fitzwilliam Virginal Book* No. 96 (XCVI), mm. 49–50 (entitled *Toccata 9mi. Toni* in the Lubbenau MS).

movement mattered greatly to baroque composers, and their music needs intelligent and consistent articulation, so as to highlight the motifs from which it is built and the way such motifs are imitated between the parts. When this is done habitually and well, your playing will acquire interest and luster, like silver chased by a silversmith.

You will also come to enjoy the tensions that can arise between articulating by meter (as mentioned above) and by figure. For instance, the little figure in the left hand of Farnaby's *Hanskin* (example 6-4) can be highlighted by a slur that crosses the beat and imparts a lively rhythmic sparkle. Similarly, in this figure from a march by Henry Purcell (example 6-5), one possible articulation involves slurring the figure onto the following *weak* beat, as shown in the first measure. I have shown here a different possibility in each measure: naturally, once you have chosen your preference, you should apply it consistently throughout the sequence. Slurs call for a joined touch, possibly with a slight overlapping of the first note.

Example 6-4. Richard Farnaby, *Hanskin*, from the *Fitzwilliam Virginal Book* No. 297 (CCXCVII), mm. 39–42 (author's slurs).

Example 6-5. Henry Purcell, March, mm. 16–21. A transcription by the composer from incidental music to the play *The Married Beau*, from *A Choice Collection of Lessons* (1696) (author's slurs and staccato dots).

What you should *not* do, however, is slur over the half measure (e.g., from the F to the G in the first measure shown) or over the barline. Slurring from weak beat to strong disturbs the natural stress and should be done only for special effect. Even then, it is usually advisable to redress the metrical balance by an articulation in the other hand (i.e., the left, if the slurred figure is in the right). Cross slurring, in short, is something you should never do unintentionally. Alas, it is a common fault of the beginner, so please guard against it.

Music of this period is often eloquent, yet to strive self-consciously for expressiveness is unnecessary. The music will make its own impact in a variety of ways, and these are more likely to be effective if its formal aspects are given plenty of scope.

The Late Seventeenth Century

At this point we begin to be aware of subtler shades in articulation styles. More overtly expressive methods of articulation were evolving in the later part of the seventeenth century, as one can see from the great finesse of writing and the increasing use of appoggiaturas in the work of composers such as d'Anglebert, whose *Pièces de Clavecin* were published in 1689. This tendency was also evident in the techniques of other instruments: more sophisticated bow strokes and new methods in the tonguing of wind instruments were developing.

The French, ever innovative in matters of texture and timbre, opened up a new awareness of tone color and instrumental effect. Many of their keyboard terms and effects depended on sophisticated methods of touch and articulation—particularly the delayed release or overlapping of the key. In his famous unmeasured preludes, written before 1660, Louis Couperin had already explored evanescent textures where one chord melts into the next—an effect made possible by deliberately delaying the release of certain notes. This technique proved epoch making. The closely related *style brisé* also became popular, and in the eighteenth century it was often used for character pieces. (Both these effects are discussed in chapter 14.)

The Eighteenth Century

We are, however, chiefly indebted to Louis Couperin's nephew, François "le Grand," for his outstanding resourcefulness in devising new keyboard textures, often for picturesque purposes. His close attention to subtleties of touch led him to indicate the slurring that he wanted in great detail. François Couperin's music was beautifully and precisely engraved, using elegant square brackets rather than the customary rounded slurs. Straight lines between two disjunct notes are another of Couperin's ways of indicating legato, or even a slight degree of overlap—in this case, between notes that would not normally be joined. He often slurs across the beat for special effects: always look carefully at his markings.

Eighteenth-century articulation was certainly influenced by the refined aesthetic of playing that developed in France and spread through Europe. Expressiveness, even sensuousness, was by now deliberately sought after: the French in particular loved indications such as *languissament* or *tendre*. But structure remained important, and the six points outlined above should still be kept in mind. A good performance of any eighteenth-century work will always display the actual musical material clearly. In particular, the ends of phrases should be clear (a point often overlooked by the beginner); and sequences, imitated motifs, prominent melodic intervals, and other *figurae* should be tactfully highlighted.

Paired notes still call for special attention in eighteenth-century music. Their effect can be freely emphasized. Some paired notes are obvious from the figuration (example 6-6, m. 2); these need to be elegantly slurred. In addition, an awareness of consonance and dissonance—either through your ear, or your brain—will reveal to you other pairs of notes that benefit from slurring. For instance, I like to slur measure 4 of this example lightly as shown, to display that the whole measure is really built on an F major chord, with dissonant leaning notes on the second and third beats. Similarly, measure 8 is built on a D minor chord. On the analogy of string playing, and on musical grounds, I feel that a melody note that is dissonant with its bass should be slurred to the next melody note, using adjacent fingers (although sources with original fingering do not always allow this phrasing).

Example 6-6. J. S. Bach, opening of *Menuet II*, from French Suite No. 1 in D Minor, BWV 812 (author's slurs).

By about 1715, both Couperin and Bach were stressing the importance of legato playing.[3] But legato in this context probably means simply a somewhat smoother approach than the crisp, almost articulated *mouvement ordinaire* which was still common. It does not imply anything like the grandiose Romantic legato, which on the piano often involves marginal overlapping. The nineteenth-century concepts of long sweeping phrases, imperceptible bow changes, and sostenuto singing were the product of a later musical aesthetic and are fundamentally foreign to harpsichord style. It is evident, however, that both Bach and Couperin were deeply interested in the relationship of note, phrase, and instrumental sonority.

Paradoxical as it may initially seem, the more legato the norm of playing, the more you need to employ a subtle variety of touch to bring the notes to life. Experienced players include within their basic legato separations or overlappings so small as to be barely perceptible, but which nevertheless transform the shape of the phrase. As you progress, your sense of touch will hone itself gradually, until you begin to revel in minute, intimate secrets between yourself and the keys. Bach's delightful two-part Inventions are the ideal place to develop a sensitively varied legato touch and what Bach significantly described in his Preface as a "singing *(cantabile)* manner of playing."

Notice that Bach indicated some slurs in the Third and Ninth Inventions. A glance, however, at the Berlin autograph manuscript (easily accessible in Dover facsimile) will suffice to show how ambiguously they are written. For instance, it is much more likely that many of the slurs in the Third Invention cover the whole measure, rather than starting on the second note (as interpreted in some Urtext, i.e., original text, editions). Separating—and thus weakening—the first note of a group of sixteenth notes, and slurring the remainder, tends to sound stilted on the harpsichord. The effect produced is quite different from the identically notated bowing effect, where the potentially weak first note can be compensated by a strong down-bow.

You are entitled to be skeptical when editors make guesses about how to locate Bach's unclear markings. But if you keep before you the ideal of displaying the structure of the music to the listener, you will not go far wrong. For instance, you will naturally want to differentiate between the trumpetlike eighth-note figures and the running sixteenth-note figures in Bach's Eighth Invention (in F major), and to show how they invert—that is, change places between the hands. In the Sixth Invention (in E major), which also uses inversion constantly, you will be able to project the syncopated part against the unsyncopated by playing the former legato, but articulating the latter clearly in groups of three eighth notes. Incidentally, the notes immediately after the double bar, where the two parts collide on middle B, offers a hint that this Invention is best played on a two-manual harpsichord.[4]

Practical Considerations

Articulation is an endlessly engrossing topic, but there is always a risk of being too dogmatic, and trying to describe it analytically runs the risk of killing the subject—you really need to study it as it runs around the field, not as it lies on the dissecting table. For this reason, I offer four pieces as demonstration models in the next chapter, with some suggestions about articulation.

Remember that, although there may be a few palpably ugly articulations, several good ones exist for any given phrase. If you find you cannot decide between two possible articulations, do not worry unduly about being dogmatically consistent: let the two coexist—pull against, counterbalance, and complement each other. Your playing will be enriched merely by feeling the presence of these opposing elements. Be guided by your teacher, or by what you observe and like in the playing of experienced performers. As your discrimination develops, you will be able to bring life and contrast to the music you play by making it seem more three-dimensional.[5]

Here is a useful exercise in basic technique to develop your awareness and control of accent and articulation. Practice it with both hands.

- Play the standard five-finger exercise up and down, quite slowly, concentrating on getting the notes evenly spaced.
- Keeping the rhythm absolutely steady and even, group the notes as shown in example 6-7.

  When this is going nicely, you will hear an effect like the bite of a violin bow at the beginning of each group. Remember, it is the break between the groups that causes the accent.
- As you play the next examples (examples 6-7a, b, and c), listen to the gradual shift in accent. Your hand may relax down into the keys during the slurred group and rise up a little at the end of it, but do not take your hand right away from the keys as you articulate each group—there is no time for this. Keep all the notes even: the tiny break in the sound must create no gap in the time. If the rhythm begins to waver, go back to the beginning until it is steady again.

Example 6-7.

As you become familiar with this exercise (which, like the ones in chapter 5, should be part of your daily routine) you can practice varying the size of the articulation to increase your awareness and control. With practice, you will be able to make it smaller and smaller.

Whether you are playing a simple minuet melody in quarter notes, or displaying the grouping of sixteenth notes, you need this control to bring life and shape to the music. Later on, articulation control will also stand you in good stead in performance, steadying your rhythm (and your nerves) in busy passages, and increasing your incisiveness in ensemble playing.

A tape recorder is a useful adjunct to all your technical practice, but an honest and attentive ear is less expensive and much more valuable in the long run. Listen to yourself—to what you are *really* doing, not to what you *think* you are doing, or would *like* to be doing. Check particularly that the stresses are in the right place and of the right size. They should sound elegant rather than blatant.

Some people are apt to stop listening if they don't like the result. They may even substitute a record of a famous player in their head while they practice. Clearly, they will not progress. Be brave: instead of anaesthetizing yourself to your problems, try to analyze what is unsatisfactory in what you hear. Honest listening is the most crucial part of music making (at any level), although probably the hardest to learn. Once you can listen constructively, however, you have a priceless asset.

Notes

1. Bach's articulation marks in his manuscript are not always precisely placed. The article *In Search of Bach the Organist* by Peter le Huray and John Butt, in *Bach, Handel, Scarlatti: Tercentenary Essays*, ed. Williams, 191 ff., makes an intelligent attempt to address this problem, but it must remain an open-ended question.

2. The fascinating topic of rhetoric and its influence on the thought of German composers in particular is fully discussed by Buelow, in *The New Grove Dictionary of Music and Musicians*, vol. 15, 793–803, and in Williams 1984, vol. 3, 81 ff.

3. "It is necessary to preserve a perfect legato in what one plays" (Couperin 1716/1974, 70). The French reads: "Il faut conserver une liaison parfaite dans ce qu'on y exécute." Halford's translation may be a little misleading, in that it suggests that legato should be used constantly, whereas Couperin has just been dealing with "arpeggios which lie under the hand, pieces in lute style, and syncopations," to which legato is particularly appropriate. His little word "y" may refer to these. (The term "syncopations" is here used in its sense of notes that are tied over.)

4. Other two-part Inventions that suggest the use of two manuals, because of colliding or overlapping parts: No. 2 (see m. 18); No. 12 (m. 15); No. 14 (m.16); No. 15 (m.13).

5. Suggestions for further reading on articulation in general: Rodgers 1971; Lindley article, "Keyboard Technique and Articulation" in Williams 1985; Faulkner 1984; Neumann 1982, Williams 1984, vol. 3.

7

A Musical Interlude

In this chapter, I examine four pieces of music in detail to show some ways of using the techniques outlined in the two previous chapters. In doing so, I am acutely aware that writing about how to play is a poor substitute for actually observing the player, since everyone's approach and problems will be different. Select from this chapter what seems useful to you, though don't omit the first piece. This familiar Bach minuet is considered from the standpoint of someone who has previously played only the piano, and the touch is discussed in detail. The other pieces are meant for those who have a little more experience on the harpsichord. They offer an introduction to three seminal keyboard styles. The texts are printed in full, in case your edition is encumbered by editorial phrasing, etc. Note, however, that the fingering is not the composer's, but my own recommendation.

Never forget that, however small the piece you are playing, it has a phrase structure, which needs to be revealed to the listener. It is a common fault of the beginner to press on regardless. Think of yourself to some extent as speaking or singing the music, giving it the maximum clarity of structure and significance by intelligent use of breathing spaces. Small elasticities in the rhythm will help, especially at cadences. But I do not mean obvious ritenutos; and in the case of the final cadence, a heavy ritardando is considered to be foreign to early music styles unless it is indicated. Baroque composers generally use some notational device—a change of time-signature, or a tempo indication such as Adagio—to show a final broadening.

Minuet in G, No. 2, J. S. Bach, Clavierbüchlein für Anna Magdalena Bach (BWV Anh. 114)

You may have learned Bach's Minuet in G on the piano, but it will feel better on the harpsichord once you have overcome the unfamiliarity, because the texture of the music—mostly a single line of notes for each hand, which can sound very thin on the piano—will be enriched by the generous harmonic overtones of the harpsichord.

The tempo of the minuet should be poised, so that you can almost feel one slow, elegant beat to a measure; avoid feeling three strong beats, which will produce a dogged effect.

Your first task is to consider the large phrase units. You might decide to group the measures thus: 2 + 2 + 4; 2 + 2 + 4; 4 + 4 + 4 + 4.

Next, decide the more detailed articulation: which notes should be joined to their neighbors, and which need to be separated? Consider both hands at the same time when making your decisions: a *silence d'articulation* in both hands at once gives a choppy, broken effect, and should be reserved for phrase endings or moments of greater emphasis. Generally speaking, a *silence d'articulation* in one hand is best supported or complemented by legato in the other.

A common failing of the beginner is to obliterate or confuse the basic metric structure. For instance, a pianist would probably slur the four eighth notes of measure 5 into the first note of the next measure and accent this note by extra weight on the key. But any extra weight on the first note of measure 6 will of course produce no effect on the harpsichord, where accents have to be achieved by other means.

To show how to achieve a satisfactory pattern of accents, I have marked the music with small *vertical* lines indicating where the basic legato should be broken. This should be done gently and without fuss: try to think more about the groups than the gaps. Ignoring the *horizontal* dashes for the moment, practice the piece in this way, listening carefully to the result.

I stress that this fairly minimal scheme is only one of several possibilities, but it will work well as a starting-point. Notice

- that gaps in articulation happen in both hands at once only at the more important phrase ends, or where a more emphatic accent needs to follow. For example, in measures 25–26 I have emphasized the little sighing units, and the warmer effect of the divided left-hand texture, by separating out these measures.
- that an articulation in the left hand can help suggest a smaller

Menuet

J.S. Bach: BWV anh. 114

See text for meanings of markings

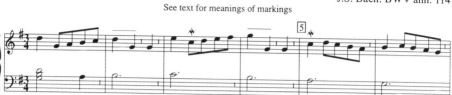

73

accent in the right hand even if the latter is not articulated—as at the beginning of measure 2.

The appoggiatura in measure 8 is best played as an eighth note. The lower-note shakes in measures 5 and 13 start on the beat. Other ornaments can if you wish be left out at this stage; they are not vital. Spread the final chord gracefully, playing the B in the right hand on the beat with the left-hand G, and holding each note down as you play it.

This initial version might be developed somewhat when you feel ready to explore further. Don't do anything, however, that makes your playing sound fussy. You may need to save the following effects for a later stage, when you have learned to make your articulation-gaps calm and unobtrusive:

- The rising scales in measures 21 and 29 can either be played legato (turning the thumb under normally on the fourth note), or in a more sophisticated paired phrasing which could be obtained by the use of some historical fingering. (This is discussed in chapter 9.) As an experiment, finger the passage 343434. Keep the hand in its normal position, with the fingers curved: odd contortions are unnecessary. Simply withdraw the fourth finger after you have used it while your hand moves gently sideways to place the third finger. Once you get the knack (and most people manage nicely after one or two tries) you will find that this fingering naturally creates a strong-weak pattern of accents, by making you articulate after every other eighth note. The first, third, and fifth notes will sound more conspicuous than the others.
- It is also possible to apply more detailed articulation to other groups of eighth notes: for example, in measures 17–18 they can be grouped either in pairs, or as three-plus-one (i.e., with a small articulation *both before and after* the fourth note: think about this, as it is an important point to grasp). The eighth notes in measures 5–6 and 13–15 could also be articulated in pairs, on the grounds that the first note of each pair is an appoggiatura (dissonant with the bass) and the second resolves onto a consonance.

Oddly, it is hardest to decide about the measures containing only quarter notes in both hands, perhaps because of their very plainness. I have shown one possible pattern in measures 23 and 31 (right hand, legato; left, slightly articulated) that sounds good; but it would be possible to apply the same articulations to the right hand as well, to make a more emphatic approach to the cadence. They would need to be discreet, however—a sharp, pecking staccato is unpleasant and rather counterproductive on the harpsichord, since it hardly allows the string to sound.

When you are familiar with the whole piece, consider it further. If you feel that the results are still a bit inexpressive and wooden, try holding down the notes marked with a tenuto sign (a horizontal bar over the note) a little longer, so that they overlap slightly with the next note— a technique discussed in chapter 8. This will give them a little more warmth: though you must be careful, in the early stages, only to use this delayed release intentionally—not out of laziness.

Some measures benefit from a feeling of tapering or shading away from the main beat—for example, measures 20, 25, and 26. Try playing the beginning of these measures well down in the keys (holding the first note until fractionally after you have played the second), but letting your hand rise out of the keys toward the end of the measure (so that you merely touch the last note briefly on the way up). This will confer elegance on the phrase and keep your hands flexible.

The suggestions here made are obviously not the only way of playing this piece: treat them as a sampler that displays some of the basic effects offered by articulation. If you observe carefully what is happening as you practice, you will learn how to use the choice that governs your progress from note to note, until you have made it a musical resource.

In the following pieces, write in the places where you need to articulate, or overlap a note with the next one, using the system of vertical and horizontal dashes suggested above.

Giles Farnaby's Dreame, Giles Farnaby, Fitzwilliam Virginal Book No. 194 (CXCIV)

Giles Farnaby's Dreame can serve as an excellent introduction to the virginalist repertory. Written in basically chordal style, this is a miniature pavan with the customary three strains. Contrary to normal practice, the composer did not write out varied repeats in this short piece, but this gives an opportunity to devise your own, and some simple suggestions are made for doing this. Further suggestions for decorating this type of piece can be found in Howard M. Brown, *Embellishing Sixteenth-Century Music* (1976).

The general articulation style of this piece should be of primary sim-

Some suggestions for simple divisions in the right hand

plicity; try to feel a basic alternation of stronger and weaker beats, without striving too hard for a legato. I have suggested some historical fingering: if you use this, hold your hands easily just above the keyboard, with the middle three fingers particularly available. Keep your hands very supple and make sure that you release notes promptly and cleanly.

> **m. 1.**   You might soften one of the left-hand chords with a slight spread: possibly the one which coincides with the expressive top D of the melody. The spread begins on rather than before the beat, but don't be too wooden about this. (For the use of spread, see chapter 18. Note that I avoid the term "arpeggiation," which suggests to most people a regularly spaced spreading of the chord, and thereby blinds them to the immense variety of possible spacings.) Chords tend to sound more pleasant when given at least a slight amount of spread; a completely unspread chord makes a hard sound, although this effect can have a distinct musical purpose.
> **m. 2.**   The given right-hand fingering will enhance the syncopation.
> **m. 5, m. 8.**   There is a choice of ornaments (see chapter 18) but the best ornament in this context is a lower-note mordent, played with the first note on the beat.
> **mm. 6–7.**   This fingering of the old type will phrase the descending scale naturally in pairs and point out the canon between the voices.
> **m. 9.**   The third finger will pass easily over the fourth to emphasize the C-sharp on the third beat.

The final whole-note chord should be quickly spread. If on your instrument the left-hand chord sounds very congested, release the two middle notes once you have played them.

The courtesy chord at the very end (in square breves) is intended for the end of the dance. If you play this chord, try to think of it as a final flourish in a piece of calligraphy. It could be arpeggiated up, down, and up again, holding each note as you pass it. You can experiment with various ways of pacing the arpeggio: one good way is to dwell deliberately on the first low note, accelerate as you go up and down, then flick the final stroke quickly upward, with litheness and grace.

Prelude in C, Matthew Locke, Melothesia (1673)

In 1651, Froberger visited London, and it is likely that Locke would have come to know his partitas. Froberger's allemandes—such as the famous *Lamento* for Ferdinand IV which depicts his final ascent to heaven on a scale of C major—were often written in a fragmented texture, which has connections with both the Italian toccata and the unmeasured rhetorical prelude of the French lutenists. This prelude by Locke (the prelude to a collection of pieces in C, although the composer does not call it a suite) is written in a similar texture, and can serve as a brief introduction to the performance of both these seminal styles. It needs more sophistication and variety of touch than the preceding piece by Farnaby.

This rather unpromising looking piece of notation can blossom into inviting music if you in turn accept the composer's implied invitation to improvise with some given ingredients. You may tackle it as suggested below: you may also discover other ways. It needs gracious elasticity of movement, although the basic beat should never be entirely lost. In such an impressionistic and sparse score, every note is interesting and needs to be played significantly.

m. 1. The slur over the right-hand arpeggio is Locke's own, and it means that all the notes should be held down after playing. Imagine that the entire opening chord, as far as the low left-hand C, resembles the illuminated initial in a manuscript; its function is to state the tonality. Then take a breath and move on to the little dotted motif, articulating and enjoying the imitation.

m. 2.   Treat the two right-hand sixteenth notes as a heavily sighing appoggiatura and resolution—overlap them, i.e., don't release the D until the E is established.

m. 3.   Similarly, feel the F-sharp as an appoggiatura to an expressive G. Then feel the breadth of the chord-change to a beautifully spaced F major chord.

m. 4.   The breathless appoggiaturas and the chromatic bass need due emphasis here. Slightly overlap the two pairs, E–F and F-sharp–G in the right hand, then the two pairs B–C and E–F in the left hand. Respond to the tensions in the part writing by sometimes pressing forward, sometimes yielding. It would be impossible to offer a formula for this complex measure, as it answers to several patterns of treatment. Try to feel that you are improvising the passage, and are aiming toward measure 5.

m. 5.   Multiple appoggiaturas crowd together at the beginning of the measure with striking effect before gradually relaxing into a C major chord. The spacious low E (which should be deliberately placed) and the high C mark the midpoint of the piece and its turning-point. Deliver the high right-hand phrase broadly.

m. 6.   Again, the phrase marks are Locke's, and they indicate that the notes should be held to form a chord.

m. 7.   The pause mark could mean that the right-hand chord should be arpeggiated: it is effective if the bass note is played first, alone, and then the chord is spread down, up, and held. The rest of the measure could be played with a certain impetuosity, treating the sixteenth-note D as an appoggiatura to C and slightly spreading the left-hand octave Gs. Repeating the fourth finger in the right hand, as shown, will draw attention to the 6/4 chord.

m. 8.   "Chirrup" the two double (upper-note) shakes by shortening the final note, and play the written-out trill rather flamboyantly, slurring the 32nd-notes in pairs, and accelerating slightly at first. At the end of the measure, hold back a little, and show that the last D leads to the E in the final chord This could be done by adding the ornament (example 7-1) known to Locke as a *beat*:

Example 7-1.

Courante in D Major, Jacques Champion de Chambonnières

The courante discussed here is from a suite in D from Chambonnières's *Pièces de Clavessin*, engraved and published in Paris in 1670.

Only two ornaments are involved: the *pincé*, or lower-note mordent, and the *tremblement*, or upper-note shake. Both begin on the beat (see chapter 18). The upper-note shake is always a four-note ornament, starting on the note above the written note, even in contexts where this involves repeating a previous melody note. This first note can be elongated at will, especially on a long or expressive note, or before a cadence.

Chambonnières also indicates some spread chords: these are all spread from the lowest note up, fairly quickly but fluidly: avoid convulsive, hard spreads. The original notation (given in figure 7) involves only the right hand, but there is no reason why the whole chord should not sometimes be spread: I have indicated this for the first chord of measure 2.

The rhythmic subtlety of this piece is typical of the French courante and involves a constant ambiguity of meter. Look out for the varied groupings of the quarter notes; the difference between 6/4 and 3/2 should be made apparent and enjoyed. Courantes are suave, buoyant and gracious but not jaunty.

The touch should be sometimes joined, sometimes detached: the chords should be weighted as for the appropriate meter. More expressive measures (e.g., those containing A minor chords) should be warmer and more lazily legato, with a very relaxed hand.

m. 1.   6/4. It is effective to join the right-hand F-sharp to the G bearing the *pincé*, the ornament then releasing the slur.

m. 2.   Strongly accented 3/2.

mm. 3–4.   Suavely 6/4, leading into the minor mode.

m. 5.   3/2, smooth, with long upper-note C-natural in the shake.

m. 6.   6/4, and more matter of fact.

m. 7.   The ornaments establish the meter here as 3/2, so the right hand should be strongly phrased to emphasize this.

mm. 9–10.   Both 6/4. Notice how the top part of measure 9 is imitated in the tenor part of measure 10. It would not be out of order to imitate the ornament on the C-sharp too.

m 11.   3/2. The ornament on the first note in the right hand needs C-natural, because of what is to come. The second ornament in this measure is best played with a long first note to introduce the cadence.

81

m. 12.   6/4. The composer's notation could imply that the four left-hand notes beamed together should be played as a group, followed by a group of two.

m. 13.   Delightfully ambiguous. The right hand is in 6/4, with bustling ornaments: the left hand falls naturally into 3/2—you need not strive to emphasize it.

m. 14.   3/2. This ornament is more relaxed, and needs a pathetic C-natural to follow up the preceding harmony.

m. 15.   The left hand should be distinctly grouped in 6/4; the ornament on the fifth quarter note will make the point that the right hand is in 3/2.

m. 16.   Place the final D (left-hand thumb) deliberately when you repeat. Add a *pincé* if you like.

Figure 7. Courante in D Major by Chambonnières. Engraved and published in Paris in 1670. The right hand part is in the soprano clef and the left in the baritone clef, the first notes being D in both cases. The hook-shaped signs below the right-hand chords in m. 2 and elsewhere are a direction to spread the chord from the lowest note upward (for a downward spread, Chambonnières positioned the sign slightly above the notes). A pragmatic view of notation prevails—for instance, just before the double bar, where the left hand has a full six beats but the right hand only five, the sixth appearing as upbeat to the second section on the following page. The first note of m. 6 is sustained beneath the second. Note the repetition of accidentals within a measure, standard at the time; e.g., the C-flats (flats were used to lower a note, i.e., C-natural here) in m. 5. In full chords, such as at the beginning, the little hook represents the tail of the middle note, and not an ornament. This piece appears in modern notation on page 81. *Reproduced by permission of Facsimilés J. M. FUZEAU, BP 6 - 79440 Courlay, France.*

8

Techniques for the More Experienced Player

Some of the techniques in this chapter will be adopted only gradually by the beginner, but it is never too soon to understand the full range of the instrument's resources, so that when you hear experienced players you may know and appreciate what they are doing.

I begin by repeating that relaxation is vital to effective performance. A tense hand—symptom of a tense mind—produces hard, unforgiving playing that, not surprisingly, is intense rather than expressive. You have by this stage realized that you cannot accent a note by merely playing it more strongly, but remember to make sure that you are not imagining the accents you want, instead of working actively to project them to the listener. Also check that you are not trying to simulate an accent by a physical movement, such as pushing down from the shoulders.

The more sophisticated harpsichord touch that is particularly appropriate to music composed after about 1680 deals in relative values, relying on subtle distinctions of transition from note to note within the phrase. As your playing develops, you will be able to differentiate the apparent weight of the notes in a phrase; featureless uniform legato will become a thing of the past, and tapered effects and even small simulated crescendos will become possible.

Drawing Attention to a Note

There are at least four ways of making a particular note prominent or expressive:

- You can precede the note by a *silence d'articulation*, to highlight its initial pluck, as already explained.
- Another important technique is to depress the key in a rather clinging manner, delaying the release until after the next note has been struck. Look at the seventh piece (BWV Anh. 119) in the book for Anna Magdalena—another Minuet in G. Here the first note of the second measure, the high G, will respond well to this treatment; so will the first notes of measures 13 and 14, the melody notes E and D. This technique focuses your attention on the note and will help your listeners to do likewise.
- A chord or note can be elongated, easing the meter slightly. This is an eloquent technique, but must be used with great discretion if your natural rhythmic sense is not strong. The time is adjusted later in the measure or phrase. For a discussion of rubato, see chapter 10.
- Delaying or "placing" a particular note or chord is a common resource in music making, comparable to the actor's timing of words. Allow yourself time to listen to a prominent note; this usually ensures that your audience attends to it too. In this closing passage from the somber *Les ombres errantes* (Couperin, *Ordre* 25, example 8-1), the eloquent low F at the beginning of the penultimate measure has a special musical point—it outbids the previous G—and needs placing appropriately.

Example 8-1. François Couperin, *Les ombres errantes* (*Ordre* 25), mm. 26–28.

The extra dimension of metric flexibility shown in these last two categories is a valuable means of compensating for the harpsichord's rather uniform dynamics.

Making a Note Insignificant

A note can be made inconspicuous by two main devices:

- overlapping the release of the previous note, so as to conceal the pluck of the note in question; or
- using a glancing touch, usually in a rebound movement after a prominent note.

By mixing these techniques, or playing them off against one another, you can achieve a great deal of light and shade. As your playing develops, you will begin to think in terms of various kinds of stroke: brusque, or caressing; exclamatory, or pensive; relaxed, or instinct with energy.

Suspension and Spread Chords

Pianists often use a technique where the left-hand part is played in time but the right-hand note is delayed. This has become a particular hallmark of Chopin performance, but it is in no way a peculiarly pianistic or romantic device. Couperin and Rameau were already familiar with the effect and used a special symbol, the suspension (discussed in chapter 18), to indicate this expressive device—the musical equivalent of a catch in the breath. Couperin's explanation clearly shows how the left-hand note is played *on* the beat, and the right hand *after* it. His useful symbol ⋊ could well be revived for marking your own copies.

Playing the right hand later than the left could of course be regarded as a form of spread chord; and a thoughtfully spread fuller chord is a powerful expressive device, used in many sarabandes. Slight arpeggiation warms and softens a chord, and produces a better sound than a *secco* (dry) attack. Dwelling briefly on the lowest note (played on the beat) can further enhance the expression, especially in slow movements.

The fact that arpeggiation is indicated in certain places by no means rules it out elsewhere; observe and analyze what good players do, and in what musical contexts.

Resonance

In the left-hand part of the same Bach minuet, measures 5 and 6 will benefit if the first notes, the low C and B (the true basses), are held down until after the G has been played. This kind of overlapping is often notated, especially from Purcell onward, and its purpose is to increase the natural resonance of the instrument.

There is not much harpsichord music that thrives on a bleakly clinical approach, and I believe that the principle of resonance can be applied in many more contexts than were actually notated. By sustaining selected notes within the harmony, one achieves an effect of warmth. This technique has some analogy with the use of the sostenuto pedal on the piano, but with the added advantage of holding only those dampers you choose off the strings. As with piano pedalling, though, you need to listen critically for unwanted smudges.

In the work of some composers, a slur placed over a chordal figure can be a way of indicating resonance—each note being held down as it is played, until the end of the slur. This meaning is given by Saint-Lambert: "All the notes that the slur encloses are played, and . . . held after being played, even if their value has expired."[1] It is also found in the ornament table to Rameau's *Pièces de Clavecin* (1724). The effect can with discretion be applied elsewhere.

Sometimes it makes good musical sense to treat a slur over a *scale* as an indication of sostenuto. In this case, however, only the first note is sustained:[2] be guided by your ear and reject anything that sounds confused.

Arrange your fingering to take account of any resonance to be used.

Differentiation of Repeated Notes

Returning to the beginning of the Bach minuet, we have seen in measure 2 how the first two right-hand notes can be played strong-weak by a discreet squeeze of pressure on the top G, which causes a delayed damping of that note. You would think it was logically impossible to apply this overlapped technique to a repeated note, such as in measure 5: but the effect can be simulated. Experiment with the following phrase (example 8-2) until you can make the second note of each pair sound minimal. It is more easily done than described: press the key gently but firmly down almost to the key bed and keep it there as long as you dare. Then, just before the second note is due, release the key, keeping your finger in contact, and ask it to repeat with a little light pressure before it has quite returned to its place. Releasing the second note fairly quickly completes the effect.

Example 8-2. "*Ah, vous dirai-je, Maman?*" (trad.)

In playing strong-weak pairs of notes, play as near to the front edge of the key as possible, which gives you the greatest control, and keep in relaxed contact with the key. Your left hand should also be able to play strong-weak pairs: this is particularly necessary if your continuo playing is to sound elegant and not stilted. (Bach sometimes asks for this left-hand effect by putting a slur over repeated bass notes.)

Now try the phrasing of a Bach fugue subject with repeated notes. In the D Major Fugue in Book II of *The Well-tempered Clavier* (example 8-3) it is desirable to stress the second D to show where the beat lies, but to make the third one weak. (Three identical pecked Ds are not attractive.)

Example 8-3. J. S. Bach, subject of Fugue in D Major from *The Well-tempered Clavier*, Book II, BWV 874/ii.

Another interesting example is the subject of the G-sharp Minor Fugue in Book I (which I have here transposed down into G minor for simplicity). Here, the beginner's temptation is to separate the repeated notes and join the others, because this is the easiest thing to do (example 8-4). But slurring across the beats produces accents in the wrong place in the second measure. A better approach is shown in the second version, where the repeated notes are played strong-weak. This may be a little harder to control at first, but is far more musical and expressive, in keeping with the spirit of this elegiac fugue.

Example 8-4. J. S. Bach, subject of Fugue in G-sharp Minor from *The Well-tempered Clavier*, Book I, BWV 863/ii (transposed by the author).

I feel that one has a certain duty to the listener, who is without a score, to make quite clear where the beat falls—especially in an unaccompanied melodic phrase such as a fugue subject. The F Minor Fugue subject in Book II offers an interesting challenge in this respect (example

8-5). Experiment until you can make the first of the three F's the most prominent, and the second F the least strong. Then consider other possibilities if you like; but do reject the awful lurching effect of a slur over the bar-line from the C to the F, which is commonly heard. It will start the poor listener on the wrong foot.

Example 8-5. J. S. Bach, subject of Fugue in F Minor from *The Well-tempered Clavier*, Book II, BWV 881/ii.

The repeated accompaniment figures of Scarlatti's sonatas offer striking possibilities. With the sound of flamenco in mind, experiment with this passage from K. 490 (example 8-6) until you can conjure images of pride, even of menace, from its hypnotic rhythm. You will also discover the mechanism of up and down strokes in the process. If

Example 8-6. Domenico Scarlatti, Sonata in D Major, K. 490, mm. 49–61.

you want to convey a menacing impression, play the left-hand chords with hardly any spread. In measure 58, however, you might soften the sternness by using a slight amount of spread on the first beat, and generally relaxing the hands (and the tempo), until in measure 59 the desperation returns with the flattened Bs. This chord might well be played absolutely unspread in both hands, like a sudden cry of pain. The full chords in measure 60 can then be spread slightly again. Experiment with these details of phrasing and try alternatives.

Sophisticated harpsichord playing runs the entire gamut between the two extremes of sensuous warmth and brittle brilliance. It is not just a question of using one manner or another for a certain piece: you may well juxtapose these extremes in the course of two phrases. In general, the more you get down into the keys, the warmer the sonority, because it takes you marginally longer to quit the key and drop the damper. You can even simulate a slight crescendo by relaxing further into the keys as a phrase progresses. When using a lazy release, however, never forget the ideals of clarity and transparency of texture. If you sacrifice them, it must be for a definite artistic purpose.

When you begin to master these techniques, you will realize that the harpsichord has an expressive potential far greater than might be expected from a mechanism of this primary simplicity. Ultimately, the instrument can convey whatever your own musicality allows.

Notes

1. Saint-Lambert 1702/1984 in Harris-Warrick translation, 1984, 29.

2. And also the last, according to Saint-Lambert 1702/1984, 30.

90

9

Fingering

This chapter is not an easy one to write. In the first place, all my readers will have different standards of keyboard dexterity—ranging from those with a mastery of the full range of scales and arpeggios and a sophisticated technical foundation, to those who have difficulty getting the right notes at all. But there is the further problem that beginners usually come to the harpsichord with a background of *piano* fingering: and identical fingerings will not always produce the same musical effects on both piano and harpsichord. In addition, there is the major consideration that, historically, the harpsichord was fingered on a slightly different principle.

In the case of other period instruments, the approach to this **historical fingering** is straightforward. For instance, the exquisitely detailed fingering given by Marin Marais in his gamba music springs from a complete integration of instrument and music: and the viola da gamba's fingerboard is so distinct from the cello's that it is inconceivable that a player would try to apply cello fingering. Harpsichord players, however, are not quite so fortunate, for historical harpsichord fingering feels unnatural at first to those who are pianists, although the shapes of the keyboards are the same.

Need one bother about this original fingering at all? Surely one can simply finger the harpsichord like the modern piano? Of course, one can, and many people will prefer to do this, especially if their hands are conveniently small. It is not easy for older people with a long experience of playing the piano or organ to adapt to the mechanics of early harpsichord fingering. On the other hand, young professional students usually find little problem in learning new and old systems in tandem, and if they are serious about their harpsichord future they should certainly become proficient in historical fingering. A full account of the subject is beyond the scope of this study, but there are several helpful publications.[1]

The present book would, however, be incomplete without some discussion of early fingering, and even if you doubt your ability to master such fingering, I hope you will not skip this section, because historical fingering radically affects the way the music is articulated and therefore the way it sounds. You should inquire into the subject, if only so that you can reproduce, by means of more familiar fingering methods, the articulation effect that was originally intended. This information will supplement what is written about normal modern fingering later in the chapter.

Fingering is discussed in instruction books from the mid-sixteenth century onward, and is also occasionally found in actual pieces of music. The information contained in the instruction books and treatises is admittedly not always clear or consistent; and there is an annoying tendency to concentrate purely on examples of scales—and even then, to ignore the presence (or absence) of raised ("sharp") keys. Music that contains fingering is more specifically informative, but there is not a great deal of it. Neither will I claim that all the extant fingerings are easy to understand or comfortable to play.

Nevertheless, there is overwhelming evidence that—until at least the early eighteenth century and sometimes longer—passages consisting of a single, conjunct line in each hand used **paired fingering**, such as 3434 (RH, ascending), 3232 (RH, descending), or 2121 (LH, ascending. All these fingerings are given in modern terms; original virginalist fingering, however, numbered off the fingers from left to right in both hands, so that, for example, the left thumb was 5). This type of paired fingering arises naturally from the circumstance that on early keyboards there is little depth between the front of the raised keys and the front of the keyboard (it may also be linked with the fact that sometimes players performed in a standing position). It tends to promote a highly articulated delivery—an alternation of light and shade, of strong and weak.

Many writers referred to notes as "good" or "bad" according to whether they occurred on the beat, or off it; and the aim was to allocate "good" fingers to good notes. There was, however, disagreement about how this was done: the English regarded the third finger and thumb of the right hand as good, but most other writers preferred the second and fourth. Ornaments in the right hand were usually fingered with the third finger on the main note, and their presence can be a key factor in deciding fingering patterns. (There is no doubt that for any delicate work the middle fingers—2, 3, and 4—give the greatest control.)

The inferiority of the left hand was deeply rooted in our culture until quite recently, and this must have led naturally to the assumption that one should if possible use its stronger fingers, i.e., those nearest the thumb. The left thumb is certainly indicated more often than the right: 43212121 was a common indication for an ascending left-hand scale, and left-hand ornaments were often played with the thumb and forefinger. Where chords with big stretches occurred, however, the thumb of either hand was obviously invoked. In addition, there is evidence that even before 1600 both English and Spanish musicians were using more modern, consecutive type fingerings for rapid passages: the sixteenth-century Spanish theorist Venegas actually lists 4321321 (LH, ascending) and 54321321 (RH, descending), and he specifically mentions that the fingers pass over the thumb. In spite of all this, there is hardly any doubt that before at least 1700 the middle fingers of the right hand, and those nearest the thumb of the left hand, were considered dominant. At that time music was commonly written in keys involving relatively few accidentals. The later expansion and systemization of fingering was directly linked to the use of more ambitious keys: the more accidentals there are in a key, the more inevitably the thumb turns under the other fingers.

Example 9-1. Girolamo Diruta, right-hand scale fingering from *Il Transilvano.*

To get the feeling of paired fingering, try an ascending scale of C in the right hand, as Diruta gives it in *Il Transilvano* (example 9-1). Think of the first note as an up beat. Keep the hand level, and the fingers well curved: resist the notion that you are crossing fingers over each other, or performing any kind of contortion. You are simply doing something similar in principle to the string player who shifts position on the fingerboard. As you use the fourth finger on the way up, bend it well and draw it toward your palm; at the same time, shift your hand without fuss to the right, and let your third finger move to the next note. If you relish the idea that you are exploring a historical technique, it will help you get over the feeling of awkwardness and unfamiliarity. Make sure that you keep your hand supple and relaxed.

I mentioned above that historical fingering can suggest to us how the composer expected the music to sound. *Le moucheron* (*Ordre* 6) by Couperin, written in 1716, offers a useful example (example 9-2). This is not an easy passage, and I would not expect a beginner to attempt it; but we can observe two interesting points.

Example 9-2. François Couperin, *Le moucheron* (*Ordre* 6), mm. 14–16.

- The two places where the consecutive use of the same finger is indicated. These show that a definite articulation was intended at these points, perhaps to highlight the cadence at the beginning of measure 15. Note the use of the same finger on consecutive notes when the *second* note needs to be made prominent. This is a particularly useful aspect of historical fingering: it can even save fingers in places where they seem to be in short supply. Watch for places where you can apply this technique—it has Couperin's full approval in *L'art de toucher le clavecin* and other sources.
- The fingering 343 in the third beat of measure 14 causes the first two eighth notes to be joined, but the third to be detached. This kind of extension of the hand was common. From the viewpoint of modern technique, such fingering might appear to make the hand rigid—but this happens only if you try to connect the second and third notes instead of articulating and carrying the hand a little to the left after the D. Notice, incidentally, that the fingering over a shake always refers to the finger on the *main* note—so both this and the next shake start on the fourth finger.

This passage gives the strong impression that keyboard articulation could be intricately patterned, although one should perhaps beware of reading too much into it.

Alongside such finely etched effects, a more cantabile style of playing had begun to evolve in the last years of the seventeenth century. This style called for, and gradually obtained, rather less constrained patterns of fingering. Couperin himself played a part in this evolution; although he mostly stood by the old fingering techniques, he was also an impressive innovator in matters of keyboard texture, and many of the points made in *L'art de toucher le clavecin* show new ideas that he developed to meet the demands of these textures.

One notable example of these developments was the technique of **finger substitution**—i.e., changing fingers on a held key—which enables a good sostenuto to be obtained in passages of *style brisé*, as shown in example 9-3. This technique, with its carefully contrived legato bass, is obviously designed to make the most of the rich resonance of the typical French instrument.

Example 9-3. François Couperin, *Premier Prélude*, from *L'art de toucher le clavecin*, mm. 1–4.

Finger substitution can also facilitate clear part playing. In example 9-4, the right-hand pattern of finger substitution makes it obvious that there are two parts, not one part in continuous eighth notes. (It is perhaps surprising that no indications of finger substitution are found in the few extant fingered passages of Bach's music, since this type of pattern occurs constantly in contrapuntal music.)

Example 9-4. François Couperin, *Première Courante* (*Ordre* 5), mm. 19–20. Quoted in *L'art de toucher le clavecin*.

The gradual movement toward the equality of the fingers and the modern method of turning the thumb is interesting to trace, but it was not fully systematized until the work of Marpurg and C. P. E. Bach in the mid-eighteenth century. Nevertheless, a glance at the fingering in Bach's *Clavierbüchlein für Wilhelm Friedemann* reveals that Bach was already using patterns that we would unhesitatingly recognize today. The pieces in that collection, however, are elementary: Bach's major keyboard works require fingering that stretched the capability of the hands to a level unprecedented in his day, and still remains challenging.

Those interested in Bach's style of fingering might also study the prelude for organ manuals, BWV 870a, with the fingering that was probably inserted by Vogler, a pupil of Bach; this is printed in several publications.[2] Organ and harpsichord fingering have certain features in common, and in this extract (example 9-5) the repetition of the fifth finger in the right hand after the bar-line (although the fourth would have been equally possible) shows that it was felt important to secure a clear projection of the melodic F—especially as notes in the lower voices are fairly static.

Example 9-5. J. S. Bach: Prelude in C for Organ, BWV 870a, mm. 7–8. (fingering probably by J. C. Vogler).

One last example from Couperin (*Les charmes* from *Ordre* 9) serves to emphasize that, by using a modern, technological fingering, you might overlook salient musical points built into the original fingering (example 9-6). The repetitions of the second finger show very clearly that he intended articulations at these points. This helps to taper the resolution of the suspension in the lower right-hand part, to reveal clearly the small figures from which the longer phrase is built, and to make it clear that there are two right-hand parts. Without such "precautions," as Couperin here describes his fingering, the intricately woven texture of the right hand would easily unravel into a dull and undifferentiated string of single eighth notes, and the division of the phrases into sighing units of three beats would be lost.

Example 9-6. François Couperin, *Les charmes* (*Ordre* 9), mm. 20–24.

All this underlines the difference of attitude that distinguishes historical harpsichord fingering from the modern piano methods stemming ultimately from the work of Czerny. Piano pedagogy has progressively devised techniques that make fingering easy and natural, offering to both player and composer the possibility of ever more impressive digital feats. Many players have scientifically studied the use of the hand and worked to improve the ergonomic equality of the fingers. These modern techniques, however, are almost always based on a legato norm, and they tend to reduce music to an undifferentiated stream of notes, on which accent and phrasing can be superimposed at will. The consequence is that phrasing, accent, and fingering are not so inseparably linked on the piano as on the harpsichord.

I am certainly not maintaining that early fingering is better merely because it calls for greater effort. But I strongly suggest that its overall effect is to emphasise the uniqueness of individual notes and, by linking fingering and phrasing, to draw attention to the place of these notes within the musical structure.

If you feel unsure of your ability to come to terms with historical fingering, try the first movement *(Fugue)* of *La Forqueray* from Rameau's fifth *Pièce de Clavecin en Concert*, which trips so easily and naturally down the scales in the right hand that your confidence immediately soars. (Use the fingering 515 for the octave leaps, then 4 32 32 32 1 for each scale.) The last couplet of Couperin's *Les ondes* *(Ordre* 5) also contains very manageable and interesting fingering.

Even if you decide you cannot aim for fully authentic techniques, there are many contexts where it is physically helpful to use bits of old fingering. Notes are easily phrased in pairs using 3434 or 2323. In appropriate ascending scale passages, passing the third finger of the right hand over the fourth, instead of turning the thumb under, can soon become a natural and useful extension to one's fingering pattern. Passing the third or fourth finger over the fifth (when travelling away from the center) or the fifth under the fourth (travelling toward the center) can also be very useful, provided that articulation is desirable at that point (example 9-7).

Example 9-7. J. S. Bach, Invention 10 in G Major, BWV 781, mm. 27–28 (author's fingering).

Admittedly, few players would be happy adopting the posture advocated by Couperin: turning one's body slightly toward the right side of the keyboard, i.e., toward the audience (and the king or nobility, if present). This position must have imposed a strain on the back over long periods, and hampered the left hand and elbow. Couperin's recommendation sprung from social conditions that are outmoded today. Yet when we try to understand its intention—as body language that implied respect for, and projection toward, the audience—we discover a point that is still extremely relevant.

The rest of the chapter takes a more pragmatic view of fingering. I shall simply assume that you have a moderate present-day keyboard capability, knowing the fingering for major and minor scales in keys up to three sharps or flats (fourteen keys out of a possible twenty-four), as well as understanding certain basics, such as that you do not put the thumb on black notes except in unavoidable situations. Now, how do you go about fingering a piece of typical eighteenth-century music—perhaps by Handel, Bach, or Scarlatti?

If there is editorial fingering in your copy, this may provide a good deal of help. But remember it may be the work of a pianist, and is neither immutable or authoritative. Although much piano fingering works satisfactorily on the harpsichord, some can produce quite undesirable effects—wrong phrasing and emphasis in particular—and some is uncomfortable, because harpsichord keys are shorter from back to front. Generally, Urtext editions have no fingering written in, and this is an advantage since it enables you to take an unbiased view. If there is any fingering that is stated to be the composer's own, however, you must give it careful attention.

Good harpsichord fingering is obviously *fingering that enables you to move comfortably and fluently around the keyboard*. It is based on patterns of hand positions, and you should of course begin by finding out which groups of notes fall naturally in the same hand position and where you need to change position, much as one would on any keyboard instrument. But even more crucially, it is *fingering that will produce or assist good articulation and phrasing*, so you need to devote some time to thinking about musical matters before you play. Try to hear the music in your head, and consider its tempo, phrasing, and expression: then look for fingerings that will promote those musical intentions. This priority is important; otherwise you run the risk of letting convenient fingering dictate the phrasing. I repeat that fingering determines phrasing and articulation on the harpsichord much more inevitably than on the piano.

Fingering

In particular, you need to look for fingerings that will

- avoid unwanted bumps and unintentional gaps that produce accents in the wrong places
- produce desired articulations in the right places

If you need to change hand position by lifting your hands from the keys, this *must* coincide with a place where you want a gap—i.e., either between phrases or before accents—because it will create one anyhow. This is particularly important in chordal passages (example 9-8).

Example 9-8. Martin Peerson, *The Fall of the Leafe,* from the *Fitzwilliam Virginal Book* No. 272 (CCLXXII), mm. 13–14 (author's fingering).

On the piano, you can use the pedal to cover changes of hand position: on the harpsichord, you must use your wits. But the answer need not be complicated. The kind of simplistic fingering that might be frowned on by a piano teacher can often serve very well. In the following passage (example 9-9), you can simply replace the hand and tuck

Example 9-9. J. S. Bach, Invention 10 in G Major, BWV 781, mm. 19–22 (author's fingering).

the fifth finger of the left hand neatly in on the first note of each measure. This is both comfortable and musical. It guarantees articulation at the bar-line; and it enables you to use the same fingering for each measure, and to warm the tone slightly if you wish by overlapping the first note briefly.

Using this as an example, encourage yourself to be flexible and adventurous: harpsichord fingering, far from limiting you, can actually be more liberating than orthodox piano fingering.

Where the music ranges widely over the keyboard, you will need to economize on fingers, taking every opportunity to work your fingers forward so that you have enough to continue in the required direction. Conversely, you sometimes have to contract your hand and use non-consecutive fingers on adjacent notes in order to cope with a change of direction, especially in contrapuntal music. But generally, you can rely a lot on simple 1–5 hand positions, which are evident in example 9-9. The occasional repeated finger on consecutive notes is also possible. At all times, though, make absolutely sure that any shifts that take your hands away from the keys occur *before* a note where an accent is acceptable.

As you work out your fingerings, write them in: not on every note, or you will merely stupefy your brain, but on every salient note, thumb turn, extension or contraction of the hand, and every place where you repeat a finger. Be prepared to modify them as you work on the piece, but as soon as possible arrive at a definite fingering and use it invariably. Only those gifted people with a natural keyboard facility can afford to live dangerously: for everybody else, fingering involves habit and repetition.

Of course, this involves self-discipline, and many students would prefer to muddle through. But imagine giving a computer a different command every time you tried to perform the same operation: the result would be chaos. The difference in the progress of students who accept the discipline of consistency and those who don't is remarkable, especially among older pupils. Consistent fingering is the only way to build up security and accuracy, and the only way to achieve reliability when you play in public. The habit of writing in and observing your fingering saves a lot of time in the long run. You will automatically build up a store of good fingering patterns. Also, when you come back to a piece after not playing it for a long period, you will not need to work the fingering out again.

Methodical habits of practice are also a great time saver. Try to plan your work for the most effective use of time. For instance, even an odd five minutes can be put to use—perhaps for the calm sorting-out of one fingering problem. In a longer session, always do a little work on touch—playing the exercises in chapters 5 and 6—before you begin to work on pieces.

Students vary, however, and everyone needs to work out practice methods that suit them personally. Some, for instance, may find it vital to practice the hands separately, others may not. But always practice music in small sections at first, progressing gradually to larger units. Never go back to the beginning every time you make a mistake: instead, isolate the measure and look at it carefully, repeating it slowly and often.

If you continue to have problems with a passage, even after you believe you have a good fingering, consider the following points:

- Is there a similar, or nearly similar, passage somewhere else in the piece, which you are fingering differently and so confusing your subconscious? If so, rationalize the two passages, or at least be aware of their differences (often, the awareness will suffice). Scarlatti sonatas are full of pitfalls of this kind.
- Conversely, are there two identical passages that you have assumed can be fingered identically but which need to be fingered differently in one or more places, because they lead differently into the next passage? (Scarlatti can be tiresome here too.)
- Look at your problem passage very carefully in slow motion, observing in turn what each finger has to do. You may find, for example, that you are asking your third finger to get from one place to another in an extremely short time, or by an awkward route. Perhaps you can amend the fingering. But if not, merely being aware of what you want a particular finger to do and visualizing the trajectory of that finger as you play may solve the problem.
- Are you preparing the approach to the problem passage properly, or are you rushing at it blindly? Be calm; your mind should move a little in advance of your fingers and focus on the note you need to reach—both seeing and feeling it *in your imagination* before you play it. Focusing your concentration on your fingertips is a great aid to accuracy, and an invaluable technique to players of every level of ability. (If things start to go adrift in performance and you are preoccupied with looking at your copy, summon your mental map of the keyboard and play on that.)
- Think about both hands. If you have problems in your right hand, it may well be that your left hand has been ignored, is uncertain or inconsistent about what it is doing, and is therefore dividing and undermining your attention.

In contrapuntal music, where you have to be fairly ingenious to distribute your fingers between the various parts, it is tempting to indulge in finger substitution. But although there are places where it is unavoidable, try to avoid doing it routinely, as it easily becomes a lazy habit (also prevalent among bad organists). There is almost always an alternative. Remember too that the hands can help each other by taking occasional notes from the other's staff.

Fugues are not intended to be played in a seamless legato, but in a manner that reveals most clearly how the parts are set against one another. Look around for places where articulation gaps are acceptable and even desirable, and use these places to lift and reposition the hand. Or you may be able, when short of fingers, to use the same finger twice in succession—provided, of course, that you want the second of these notes to bear more stress (refer back to example 9-5). Some fingering for Bach's fugal *Canzona* (BWV 588), inserted in the eighteenth century by J. G. Preller, is given in Faulkner (1984) and is well worth studying.

The strong fingers are of course those nearest the front of the hand—2 and 3—and these have always been regarded as the best to use for playing ornaments. In more complex music, however, it is quite often necessary to play ornaments with 3 and 4, or 4 and 5. The exercise at the end of chapter 18 (example 18-9) will help you to strengthen the weaker fingers. Practice it with both hands. As well as helping with ornamentation, this exercise will encourage the weaker fingers to contribute effectively to fugal playing, which involves all the fingers equally.

Finally, here are sundry pieces of useful information:

- If you are dealing with historical fingering for ornaments, remember that the figure always applies to the *written* (main) note of an ornament, which is not always the first one.
- Some eighteenth-century fingering uses a cross (+) for thumb, and 1, 2, 3, and 4 for the other fingers. You may find this in facsimile editions. There were various other methods of referring to the fingers in earlier times, some quite bizarre, but you are unlikely to come across these.
- Playing near the front edges of the keys gives the greatest control, and ensures clarity in brilliant passages.
- Remember to keep your fingers bent and your hands level and relaxed.

Notes

1. le Huray, ed., 1981. Music by Byrd, Bull, and Gibbons with original fingerings. See also le Huray, "English Keyboard Fingering in the 16th and Early 17th Centuries" in Bent 1981.

Rodgers 1971. A comparison of sixteenth-century fingerings.

Boxall 1977. This is an instruction book starting from a basic level and containing numerous usefully graded musical items, with historical style fingering. Some of its views about articulation are open to question, and it is not always reliable in detail.

Couperin 1716/1974. Margery Halford's commentary in her 1974 translation is helpful and comprehensive.

See also Lindley article, "Keyboard Technique and Articulation," in Williams 1985. This has many passages of music by Handel, Bach, and Scarlatti, with a discussion of appropriate methods.

2. le Huray 1990; Faulkner 1984.

10

Issues of Historical Performance Practice

Discussion of historical fingering leads us naturally on to more general ideas about performing old music. A vast amount has been written about **authenticity**, a subject that arouses heated debate; although the debate sometimes proves merely that its participants are lacking in real knowledge and experience. My aim is to stimulate your ideas on the subject rather than provide infallible answers. Suggestions for further reading are given at the end of this chapter.

Authenticity is actually a word that most experts avoid, for it conceals a minefield of dangerous assumptions. Safer, and more sharply focused, are phrases such as "historically oriented performance practice" or "a historically informed approach." Whatever words they use, all professional players of early music now take for granted the vital importance of a historically based outlook. Unfortunately this lies outside the range of the average musician, whose experience tends to be bounded by the Viennese classics, the Romantic composers, and a larger or smaller amount of twentieth-century music. This limitation is a natural consequence of the traditional conservatory training that they, or their teachers, have received; traditional conservatory training does not generally rely on a historical point of view. It is true that a few pianists may still boast of a direct chain of teachers linking them back to Liszt, or singers to Marchesi: but generally speaking, conservatory teaching is based on the principle of fostering the student's personal musicality and interpretation. By contrast, the training of the early musician, while not suppressing the student's natural musical urges, always balances them against the desire to find out how the music originally sounded.

But how can one discover how it sounded? Many people are only faintly aware of what is involved in reviving the link with the past: so let us consider the processes, and some of the problems. I do not wish to give the impression that historical performance is a complex mystery; it is exciting, rewarding, and endlessly fascinating. Nevertheless, there are snags of which you should be aware.

In re-creating early music, at least five kinds of activity are involved: the efforts of the composer, scholar, player, instrument maker or *luthier*, and finally the listener. (Sometimes one person may wear two hats, for instance by being both performer and scholar, a desirable combination.) These activities form a chain that is both complex and potentially fragile. We shall more readily appreciate the miracle of communication that takes place in a successful performance of early music if we look more closely at the links of the chain, starting with the last one.

The Listener

Can we listen with historical ears? You probably have a sympathetic attitude toward old instruments in general, and the harpsichord in particular: but you still cannot hear harpsichord music as it was originally received, even when it is played on an appropriate type of harpsichord. You have experienced a great deal of post-baroque music; your ears are attuned to a greater degree of dissonance, and to a system of tuning not in use at the time the music was written. You are the product of a modern world, with its accelerated pace of life, its materialist philosophies, its enormous possibilities for choice and change; your preconceptions are not the same as those of the original audience. There is some danger that you will either look back on the music of past eras as quaint and limited, or venerate it purely as an antique. I point out all these differences simply to remind you where you stand.

You may already love the sound of harpsichord music, but you will come to love the harpsichord for more specific reasons, and find new dimensions in its music, as your mental perspective enlarges and your ears become attuned to various modes of historical performance.

The Instrument Maker

It should be fairly axiomatic that music will sound best on the instrument for which it was originally conceived. Admittedly, Bach or

105

Scarlatti can be made highly acceptable on the piano, if played with an intelligent regard for the musical concepts of their day. But the music of composers such as d'Anglebert, Kuhnau, Sweelinck, or Frescobaldi has little or no chance on the modern instrument, since the textures of their compositions are acoustically unsuited to the nature of the piano. Let us assume that harpsichord music should be played on a harpsichord. The harpsichord builder is then an important link in the chain of recreating the original sound of the music.

The reputable builder takes great trouble to examine historic harpsichords, to study their construction, dimensions, pitch, and stringing, and to assimilate a mass of other evidence. Some of the minute details that interest him may seem insignificant, but cumulatively they exert a great deal of influence on the eventual sound of the instruments he builds. He is knowledgeable about wood, and has learned to work with rediscovered technical skills. His work can sometimes throw light on the way the instrument was originally played. Conversely, it is much easier for performers to evolve a convincing period performance style when they feel confident that they are producing the kind of sound that the composer would recognize. (Harpsichord builders, however, will never cease to speculate exactly how and at what pitch such-and-such an old instrument was originally strung—facts which are extremely difficult to determine.)

The Scholar or Musicologist

The scholar's first task is to establish a reliable text of the music, whether it is a previously unpublished work or music that has already been printed in the past—possibly with errors. Establishing a text is a fascinating process in itself, though one that is beyond the scope of this book to describe. Be warned, however: that "reliable text" may still be far removed from what is actually played. It certainly cannot be regarded as a blueprint for the eventual sound, since so much renaissance and baroque music calls for an improvisatory contribution from the performer.

So the musical text established by the scholar still needs to be brought into better focus: many decisions remain to be made. Non-musicians simply do not realize how little, in effect, mere printed notes can tell us. But, just as neither a Shakespeare Folio nor its modern edition can convey to us exactly how the words should be delivered, or dictate a style of production, so there are large areas of performance practice that musical notation simply does not, and cannot, cover.

In the case of older music, there are also two further problems. The first of these is caused by the evolution of musical notation, many symbols having changed their meaning. Over the centuries there has been a progressive devaluation of note values; for instance, a breve, which was once a *brief* note, is now an extremely long one, twice a whole note in duration. Conventions of notation that were once instantly understood are now unfamiliar; for example, in the sixteenth century there was a widely prevalent (though even then archaic) custom of writing triple-meter movements in relatively longer note values than duple-meter ones. This fact could easily mislead modern players into thinking that, for instance, an Italian sixteenth-century dance movement in triple meter should be played much slower than was actually the case. Some time-signatures and tempo indications have also changed their meaning and can be potentially misleading[1]; for example, *Adagio* and *Largo* are not absolutely slow in Purcell's music—they are relative terms, and if they occur at the end of a movement they may simply indicate a slowing down. All such problems will have to be addressed by the scholar when editing music for practical use, and it must be made absolutely clear whether (and if so, how) the original has been modified.

The second problem of dealing with older music stems from the fact that the chain of tradition, which formerly governed the many unnotatable details of performance, has been broken, making it very difficult to know exactly how the music was originally played. The scholar can be instrumental in helping to bridge this gap, and his advice will encourage the player to approach certain technical matters historically: in particular, to discover what ornamentation style, articulation patterns, and conventions of rhythmic alteration (all of which are discussed in other chapters) relate to the music in question. Generally speaking, the scholar who is also an experienced performer will offer the soundest advice.

It might seem that no direct evidence about historical performance style could survive from periods prior to the invention of recording; but one voice from the past can actually resurrect eighteenth-century music for us—a well-pinned barrel-organ still in working condition. A few of these exist in museums, and the way they are pinned can give valuable hints about general musical style, for instance the treatment of dotted notes. Unfortunately, however, there is little they can tell us specifically about how to play the harpsichord repertory.[2] The scholar may help bridge the gap by directing us to other, more circumstantial types of evidence. Modern investigative scholarship has reached impressive levels, and it is becoming very adept at interpreting minute fragments of information, including evidence that may have previously been disre-

107

garded. Academics usually disagree about the results, especially if the evidence is obscure or conflicting. But nevertheless, the scholar can usefully point players toward a variety of sources: contemporaneous writers on music, paintings, and other general information about the artistic taste of the period. Pictorial evidence needs to be evaluated with a little caution, but evidence offered by writers and composers (in prefaces, etc.) is usually of primary importance. Analogy with trends in other arts can also be illuminating.

The Player

Many professional players of early music like to specialize in one period or nationality to some extent. Steeping themselves exclusively in its atmosphere and technique brings obvious rewards. Others, however, may live a more varied musical life—perhaps by being involved with contemporary music—thereby keeping an active sense of musical perspective.

As mentioned earlier, players need to know when to treat the musical text literally, and when to use it as a basis for further input. They will read widely and consult other music of the period or source material, and may do some research of their own; they will certainly attend to the consensus of other musicians dealing with the same historical style. They need to experiment with unfamiliar techniques of playing and with details of ornamentation, articulation, and so on. The actual process of playing on period instruments is in itself highly instructive and formative, although absorbing period style is an ongoing process and cannot be hurried.

Assimilating historical evidence and integrating it into one's technique admittedly takes a level head. Fashions and ideas about historical interpretation come and go, and it is not surprising that players occasionally stray into excess or mannerism (just as the original performers must occasionally have done). The general aim of players, however, is to work toward a balanced and coherent performance style that, while based on evidence from the period, is personally satisfying to them as musicians.

Because various players may draw different conclusions from historic evidence, and react differently to the music itself, markedly diverse readings of a work may result. It is however important to understand that, unless historic evidence has been distorted to the point of travesty, none of these versions has more authority than any other, and no single version can ever claim to be uniquely correct. Indeed, the concept of a

sole correct version is a delusion, since, even within appropriate para-
meters of period style, there is so much room for artistic maneuver and
individuality.

Unfortunately, the recording industry, by embalming performances
in a spurious permanence, tends to encourage the promotion of certain
versions as "authoritative" or "authentic"—possibly on the strength of
one isolated feature, such as a newly researched tempo, or the use of a
particular instrument. This is a dangerous accolade: in fact, those are
doubtful and illusory words, since there is always more to be learned,
and performance practice itself never stands still.

The Composer

We now turn to the fountainhead of the music, the composer himself. We may have made a genuine attempt, using our twentieth-century faculties and the great armory of resources available to us, to penetrate his world and discover how his music should sound. But there is
little doubt that he would be divided between amusement and amaze-
ment if he knew what was happening. He would be amazed, in the first
place, to find that his music had outlived him at all. Most music before
1800 was written for immediate use, and then discarded; no expectation of artistic immortality would have occurred to him, since the use of
music by composers of previous ages (with a few notable exceptions,
such as Palestrina) was virtually nonexistent.

Even when he had accepted that his music was being artificially res-
urrected, complete editions and icon-like Urtexts would astound him.
He would probably be amused to find that scholars were spending much
time discovering which manuscript of his works bore the latest water-
mark, or which copyist (using which ink) had added certain correc-
tions—all in an attempt to establish a text nearest to his final intentions.
In an impish moment, he might well confound them all by saying, "but
I think I prefer the *earlier* version now!" He might feel that we did not
understand what led him to write his music, or what its underlying
assumptions were. He would be ungracious, however, not to be warmed
and flattered by the realization that he had written music that interests
us, and which twentieth-century players may be keen to perform.

You are now perhaps better able to appreciate how many processes are
involved in playing old music. It is certainly not simply a matter of using
an appropriate instrument, or of treating the ornaments correctly,
although these matters are important. At the end of this chapter, I rec-

ommend some manageable books that will give the beginner an entry into the world of source materials, so that you may embark on your own investigation of the world of Couperin or Purcell, or the performance of baroque chamber music.

I must add a caution: most early treatises are unmethodical by modern standards. *L'art de toucher le clavecin*, for example, is fascinating and immeasurably valuable, but Couperin's layout and his rather rambling style is hardly a model of pedagogy. Other theorists sometimes offer little more than instruction in the rudiments of music, or strings of random, even inconsistent remarks. Their ideas may have been eccentric or atypical; their expositions may be unduly rigid, because of their efforts to make something that is complex to explain (although easy to demonstrate) look tidy on paper; and their remarks were often addressed to musicians in a specific situation, with different habits, problems, and preconceptions than those of our own day. Do take this into account when looking at old sources.

I have still done no more than scout around this controversial word, authenticity. Common sense recoils from the idea of a unique, definitive version of any piece of music, let alone those from periods of musical history in which the performer's input was so great. What does it really mean when we say that we want to "get back to the original?" (Would we have liked it if we had heard it?) Do we simply want to recapture a suitable performance style for a particular work? Or do we want to recreate, as exactly as is humanly possible, an actual historic event?

And if so, how far should we go in reproducing the original conditions? Today a player will naturally use a historic instrument (or a copy of one), a reliable text, and an informed performance style; and the performance will reflect a reasonably ideal set of conditions. But what about the hard realities of the past—the less-than-perfect performers (remember Bach's grumbles about his Leipzig scholars), the candlelight, the inaccurately copied parts, and the four-foot that on a particularly humid day would not stay in tune? No-one in their senses wants to recreate the adverse conditions. Candlelight looks romantic, but musicians hate to play by it.

Yet apparently adverse factors can have unsuspected importance. Consider the matter of organ design. It is obvious that no one today would wish to go back to the sheer physical labor of blowing an organ by hand, a task that, in the case of a large instrument, takes two or three men: we gratefully accept electric motors. But the uniform sound of pipes served by an electric blower that produces a rock-steady wind pressure is not quite the same as that of pipes fed from a hand-blown windchest: the subtle differences of tone that result from the slight fluctuations of the original winding are lost. To simulate that original effect, some historically oriented organs now have random computerized variation built into their electric blowing systems. This extreme but highly interesting case shows technology being used to conceal the effects of technology; in other words, if we wish to regain the original organ sound it is necessary to camouflage some of the mechanical advantages that we now enjoy.

No ingenious camouflage of this kind is possible, however, if one attempts to modernize the much simpler working of the harpsichord. One cannot, for example, lengthen the short keys of the virginal without changing its design and key action, and encouraging the player to adopt an unhistorical playing technique. In chapter 4, I pointed out how revival builders in the early part of the twentieth century sought to improve the tuning stability of the harpsichord by using an iron frame, and how this radically spoiled the resonance of the instrument and indeed affected its very nature. We must remember the axiom that one interferes with a closed system at one's peril.

The harpsichord is undeniably a closed system: an entity whose apparent limitations are integral to its being. They are limitations no longer once we view them philosophically in a positive, rather than a negative, light, and with a proper respect for the achievements of the past. The tone of the harpsichord is not limited—rather, it is proportioned to the size of the rooms for which it was intended. Its range of nuance and accent is proportioned to the idiom of its repertory. Knowledge dispels misconceptions—or, as often painted on the lid of Flemish harpsichords, *Scientia non habet inimicum nisi ignorantem.*

Unfortunately the word "authenticity" has become entangled with the equally emotive word "purism." This word also covers a multitude of ideas. It may simply mean care over exact detail—which is always worthwhile. For example, faithfulness to the exact type of instrument needed for a particular purpose brings great benefits, and professionals go to great lengths to ensure it. Lute players may own over a dozen instruments in order to be able to do justice to different types of music. Even if you, personally, may never be able to afford a French-style harpsichord, your first experience of Rameau's music played on a real Taskin will be unforgettable.

Few people would quarrel with this type of purism. Most of us, however, have come across other less attractive forms. For instance, there are people who, when confronted with anything novel or daring in a performance of early music, will say "that will upset the purist!"

111

This "purist" is probably no more than a scapegoat, an embodiment of extreme conservatism; but although he is faceless or even imaginary, he can nevertheless be a great critical nuisance. He has an exaggerated reverence for bare, well-behaved bones, and gets upset when someone presumes to clothe the bones in warm and possibly wayward flesh. He has his ears attuned to an abstract ideal of the music, which he fancies to be laid up in some Platonic heaven.

Bach has suffered in this century from a particularly tiresome kind of purism. In the 1950s there was a vogue for playing his music (on the piano) with immaculate, machinelike evenness. It is difficult in retrospect to say where this idea came from; it was certainly not founded on any knowledge of period style. Possibly it sprang from a high-minded, rather dehumanized veneration of Bach's music, and from a reaction (reasonable in itself, but carried to extremes) against the romanticized Bach style of the nineteenth-century pianist. The infection of this mechanistic manner of playing also spread to other kinds of baroque music, such as the concertos of Vivaldi.

I am by no means belittling impeccably regular playing, which has an important place in the spectrum of musical effects. But to exalt it to the status of an artistic code was both absurd and dangerous. The dehumanizing tendency was even more damaging. All period music was once new and instinct with life; a straitjacketed, impersonal performance reveals only that the player has not yet really penetrated its world. Period performance should have nothing to do with dullness or inhibited playing.

Yet, as a harpsichordist, you may still come across the old-fashioned notions that period music should be played literally and clinically, and that rubato is quite inappropriate. This is therefore a good place to discuss the role of flexibility and rubato in baroque music making.

Rhetoric, Gesture, and Rubato

From the broad aesthetic viewpoint, we should certainly expect that the baroque period, which produced flamboyant, passionate architecture and sumptuous painting, would be unlikely to favor prim, rigid musical performance. At the very beginning of the period, Caccini, writing in 1603 about vocal monody, puts forward the idea of a "noble neglect [of the written meter]," and describes his recitative style as "talking in harmony."[3] This idea of flexibility is developed strongly in the famous Preface to Frescobaldi's toccatas, as we shall note in chapter 13; it sets the tone for much baroque music.

112

From the purely practical viewpoint, music—like a tree—must be flexible if it is to survive. Baroque musicians wrote little on this elusive topic, but they must have been just as likely as performers of any other period to invoke the general principle of rubato. This means an elasticity between fixed points, an ebb and flow in the music, an easing of the meter at cadences: Roger North's wonderful definition of "breaking, and yet keeping, the time"[4], which he borrowed from the Italian singer Tosi, can hardly be bettered.[5]

If one attempted to distinguish between the familiar romantic rubato and that of the baroque period, one might say that whereas the romantic type was prompted by sentiment, baroque rubato sprang from gesture and rhetorical modes of speech. Gesture, rhetoric, and even a certain theatricality were the mainsprings of most baroque music. This means that the ability to see beyond the exactness (and even the baldness) of the notation and convey these qualities is vital to the performer. Baroque music can reveal a wealth of pride, tenderness, pathos or bravado—but only if it is played with flexibility and imagination. Purist notions of rhythmic severity cripple its emotional range.

The importance of rhythmic freedom manifests itself in several distinct ways. First and most obvious is that fairly small category of rhetorical music where meter is laid completely aside: for instance in the unmeasured preludes of Louis Couperin and later French composers (see chapter 14). Then there is a larger category of music in which, although the notation is conventional, a rhetorical and free delivery needs to be superimposed. François Couperin asks for several of his preludes in *L'art de toucher le clavecin* to be played freely in this way. He writes intriguingly: "Music has its prose . . . and its verse."[6] The preludes to many suites, including those of Handel, were written to allow the player to test the touch and tuning of the instrument and to establish the tonality; their textures invite an improvisatory style. Toccatas and *stylus phantasticus* passages were always intended to be played rhetorically. Bach's E Minor Toccata (BWV 914) and his great Chromatic Fantasia (BWV 903) contain recitative-like writing that calls for impulsive, though disciplined, delivery. Such music bears interesting similarities to the art of baroque orators such as Jacques-Bénigne Bossuet, the seventeenth-century Jesuit whose eloquent yet formal *Oraisons Funèbres* enjoyed phenomenal fame.

Mostly, however, rhythmic freedom is concerned with those small elasticities about a fixed norm which distinguish the sensitively human from the mechanical approach: the "breaking, yet keeping, of the time." Intelligently used, they are an important source of expression in harpsichord playing, compensating for the unvarying dynamic of the instrument. Couperin's *Les baricades mistérieuses* (*Ordre* 6) may appear on paper to be made up of uniform patterns in a regular rhythm, but if it is played by the metronome it will die. It needs constant delicate adjustment, in order to propel or retard the harmony, or display its eloquent points. Scarlatti's music demands a well-developed sense of dramatic timing. A *tendre* or *affectueusement* marking in French baroque music invites the yielding rhythms of sensuous languishment. Humor, in the quirky music of C. P. E. Bach or the burlesque movements of Couperin, depends on finely calculated bending of the rhythm. In fact, rubato, correctly understood, is as vital to a baroque score as to a romantic one.

Because you can only make the adjustments so vital to expressive playing within the context of a secure and steady beat, it is essential that you first cultivate a strong sense of regular rhythm. But once this is established, rubato should also become a natural part of your technique. Chapter 8 shows how controlled rhythmic displacement can contribute to expressive playing, by simulating dynamic accents and shadings.

Dance music can throw interesting light on the history of "playing in time." Movements written for actual use in dancing had obviously to be played in strict metronomic rhythm. There has, however, always been a tendency for dance music to become stylized—that is, to outgrow its functional role and to be listened to for its own sake. In the process, it tended to become more elaborate and flexible in style. One has only to compare the complex allemande from Bach's Fourth Partita with one of primary simplicity written seventy years earlier by Froberger to recognize the change that has taken place. In addition, the more refined aesthetic of the late seventeenth and early eighteenth centuries brought the concepts of taste and expression into focus. Kirnberger, one of Bach's pupils, held that the aim in playing dance movements was an *"expressive* performance" (my italics).[7]

In the same way, gesture, vividness, and flexibility have become the hallmarks of any worthwhile historical performance today. So much lies beyond the mere dots on the page.

After this long but needful digression, it is time to try to put historical performance into perspective. On one hand we have, for the first time in musical history, an extraordinary urge to recreate the music of the past, and to interpret it fairly. By adventuring into the musical thought of the past, we are constantly enlarging our vision and discovering fresh and revealing ways of performing old music. Not long ago, violinists using short baroque bows and bow strokes were thought eccentric; now, every back-desk player in a period orchestra takes them for granted, and the sheer freshness of sound and articulation can be breath-taking. The prim, rather "churchy" way of singing medieval music has been replaced by a more uninhibited and colorful approach. Organists have rediscovered the straight pedalboard, which was dismissed early in the present century as outmoded and inconvenient; and the different technique that it demands gives clarity and definition to the pedal part. Such experiments have brought a clearer understanding of how the historic instrument (or a copy of it), the way of playing on it, and the music itself are indissolubly linked.

Yet, on the other hand, we are twentieth-century people, and cannot recreate the original impact of the music. Neither can we entirely escape from our own culture. Certainly, we do better than the nineteenth-century virtuosi who rearranged Bach in their own style, because we have a clearer concept of cultural integrity and much greater opportunities to evaluate evidence from the past. They repainted the picture; we have superb cameras. Yet a filter may sometimes be a legitimate item of photographic equipment.

All these thoughts, and many more that will occur to you as your acquaintance with early music deepens, go to show that our relationship with old music is, perforce, complex. Nevertheless, we might now attempt to define that phrase *historically oriented performance*. My own definition might read: "Performance for twentieth-century people, by twentieth-century musicians, who want to play period music in a style that is meaningful and congenial to them. This will have been arrived at by sensible study of the music and the period documentation, and through close experience of period instruments."

Responsible performers will have thought about

- the general character and purpose of the music, as revealed by contemporary writers;
- how the music was phrased and articulated;
- the probable tempos intended, especially in the case of dances (although there are never universally right tempos; so much depends on the instrument, the occasion, and the building); and
- the treatment of the ornaments, and extra improvisation.

In addition, they will have equipped themselves with as good a period instrument as circumstances allow, and taken a lively interest in performances of period music in general.

Above all, they will play with love and enthusiasm. Nothing destroys natural musicianship more surely than an anxious approach, or a labored attempt to obey precepts from a historic treatise that was addressed to circumstances differing from our own.

The eighteenth-century musician laid great stress on the idea of pleasing the audience. Burney's repeated use (in his *History of Music*) of adjectives such as "agreeable" may strike us as rather tedious and even superficial, but it can help remind performers to be kind to their audiences. It is possible to become too intent on a mission of edification and instruction. Efforts to popularize period music, however worthy, will convince and convert others only if the players themselves really enjoy what they are doing. And the search for a more "authentic" performance style should be a part of the process of making the music pleasurable.

So if you are a player, try to keep a certain balance between past and present; between what the scholar says and how you feel the music might go. Cultivate an inquiring mind, read about the music you play, and find out how it was composed. What you learn about its harmony, counterpoint, and formal construction can often be turned to account to make your performance more vivid.

You will get great help from listening to reputable players as they set about bringing early music to life. If possible, see what they are doing: and above all sharpen your ear, so that you can hear what they are doing and understand how they get their effects. Where appropriate, try out ideas that appeal to you and apply them to your own playing—this is how professional musicians develop their own feeling for style. In this way, you will be able to participate in a great and fascinating quest. But always feel that there is room for your own contribution; your personality need not be obliterated by the sheer weight of history.

Integrity of performance, which is your ultimate objective, comes only from experience and a capacity to select and digest the results: but you are starting now.

A Short List of Further Reading

Oliver Strunk, *Source Readings in Music History* (New York, 1950). Reprinted as separate volumes in 1981, of which volume 2, *The Renaissance,* and volume 3, *The Baroque Era,* are especially relevant.

Robert Thurston Dart, *The Interpretation of Music* (London, 1954). An epoch-making book that, in spite of a few passages that reveal its date, is still very valuable. It has been updated and expanded in Howard M. Brown and Stanley Sadie, eds., *Performance Practice* (London, 1989).

Robert Donington, *Baroque Music: Style and Performance* (London, 1982). The shortest and most manageable of this writer's three classic studies. It provides and evaluates historic evidence about time signatures, tempos, articulation, ornamentation, rhythmic alteration, and much else.

Nicholas Kenyon, ed., *Authenticity and Early Music, a Symposium* (London, 1988).

Mary Cyr, *Performing Baroque Music* (Portland, OR, 1992).

Peter Williams, ed., *Bach, Handel, Scarlatti: Tercentenary Essays* (Cambridge, 1985). Williams's preface contains three pages of concise wisdom.

In addition, I suggest three famous source books that strike me as the most accessible and useful to the harpsichord beginner. Of these, Saint-Lambert's remarks relate to the first generation of French clavecin music, Couperin's to that of the eighteenth century. C. P. E. Bach's monumental work spans the gulf between the baroque and galant style, but his stylistic sympathies are with his own age, and his interpretation of ornamental practices should not be applied uncritically to the music of his father's era. His account of continuo playing is, however, full and useful.

Michel de Saint-Lambert, *Les Principes du Clavecin* (Paris, 1702). English translation by Rebecca Harris-Warrick, *Principles of the Harpsichord* (Cambridge, 1984).

François Couperin, *L'art de toucher le clavecin* (Paris, 1716). English translation by Margery Halford, *The Art of Playing the Harpsichord* (New York, 1974). This edition is preferable to others available.

Carl Philipp Emanuel Bach, *Versuch über die wahre Art, das Clavier zu spielen* (Berlin, 1753–1762). Translated and edited by W. J. Mitchell, *Essay on the True Art of Playing Keyboard Instruments* (New York, 1949).

Notes

1. Time-signatures in, for instance, the music of Frescobaldi are fraught with inconsistency; confused thinking, resulting from the change-over from the medieval proportional-based system to a more modern one, is apparent in the metrical marking of much seventeenth-century music, driving one writer of the time (Kircher 1650) to describe it as a "farrago" (a complete muddle). Donington (1982) and some editors offer helpful advice.

2. The limitations of barrel-organ pinning become very obvious when dealing with subtleties of ornamentation or articulation. A barrel-organ whose pinning

was supervised and approved by Handel nevertheless gives improbably simplistic, mechanical renditions of ornaments. Engramelle's *La Tonotechnie* of 1775 attempted to reproduce in barrel-organ notation the precise effects of harpsichord articulation, but the results are not exactly convincing. See le Huray 1992, 13.

3. Caccini, in the foreword to *Le nuove musiche* (1602), as quoted in Strunk 1981, vol. 3, 29–31.

4. Wilson 1959, 151.

5. The literal meaning of rubato, "robbed time" should strictly refer to adjustments of meter that cannot be paid back within the confines of the phrase.

6. Couperin 1716/1974, 70.

7. Ulrich Mahlert, ed., ca. 1777 *Kirnberger: Recueil d'airs de danse caractéristiques* (Wiesbaden: Breitkopf, 1995) 4 ff. The topic is developed in his *Die Kunst des reinen Satzes*, pt. 3 (1776–9).

— 11 —

Discovering the Repertory:
How to Choose and Buy Music

There is not always a clear line of distinction between music intended for the harpsichord (and virginal) and music for other keyboard instruments—organ and clavichord. This is particularly true of the earliest music in the repertory, which consisted largely of arrangements, or *intavolature*, of vocal music, either sacred or secular; but it can apply equally to English eighteenth-century music, some French and Austrian baroque music, and even certain preludes and fugues of Bach's *The Well-tempered Clavier*. Here, however, I concentrate on music that can be played effectively on the harpsichord by those wishing to know the main repertory.

Admittedly, the earlier in the repertory one explores, the more specialist knowledge one needs to perform the music enjoyably. For example, many of the *intavolature* and even some of the pieces in the *Fitzwilliam Virginal Book* appear at first sight to be dreary wastes of notes; one needs skilled understanding of the construction and ornamentation of the music, plus an appropriately tuned harpsichord, to restore the full color to these compositions. This can be done—with impressive results—but it is not really beginner's work.

The *Fitzwilliam Virginal Book*, however, also has plenty to offer the less proficient player, and you should certainly not pass it by. Among its 500-odd pieces are many dance movements and sets of variations that are a joy to play (see chapter 12). But the bulk of the music that the aver-

119

age beginner encounters originates from about 1660–1760. Minuets are a particular favorite in anthologies, because these are often written in an obligingly simple texture, with one part in each hand and not too many ornaments.

It would be impossible in a book of this scope to cover the entire repertory, listing composers and commenting on their output. I must be content with a slightly simpler approach. At the ends of several of the following chapters, you will find lists of composers, some with a brief commentary. Major composers also have some of their works discussed in the text.

Editions are recommended where possible. One should always try to acquire modern, scholarly editions that establish a reliable text. Ideally, an edition should contain no phrase marks, dynamics, fingering, etc., that are not the composer's own, as such guidance is at best spurious, at worst injurious. An acceptable compromise, however, is an edition where the editor makes suggestions about fingering and phrasing using a convention of print that clearly differentiates these additions from the composer's own markings (for example, italic for editorial fingering; a small vertical cross through editorial phrase marks). Other points of style should be relegated to prefaces and footnotes. Add your own fingering as you work; see the advice in chapter 9.

Complete Editions

Many composers have achieved the status of having an authoritative complete edition (often referred to as an *intégrale* or *Gesamtausgabe*) that can be bought volume by volume. These editions, however, are often expensive, especially the French series. But if you intend to pursue the instrument seriously you should make the hard decision, as early as possible, to start collecting the complete keyboard music of the composers that interest you. If you do not do this, you will find that you end up with an awkward miscellany of volumes and much duplication of items. Some recommendations about complete editions are made in the following chapters.

For practical purposes, Bach and Handel are served fairly well by various **Urtext** (original text) editions, such as Bärenreiter or Henle Urtext, which are available worldwide and reasonably priced—although only an Urtext of fairly recent date should be trusted.

Anthologies

Beginners, however, who might need only one piece out of any particular volume, will not find complete editions an ideal answer. They should turn instead to the numerous anthologies available; these contain many short pieces by various composers. The excellent series of *Early Keyboard Music*, edited by Howard Ferguson and published by Oxford University Press, can hardly be bettered. There are two volumes devoted to each of the national schools—French, German, Italian, and English. The selection is comprehensive, varied, and reasonably easy, and each piece has an excellent commentary. In addition, there is an extremely good general preface dealing accessibly and authoritatively with performance practice. Ornaments are interpreted by being written out, where necessary, above the staff, but sensible page layout has reduced the consequent clutter and visual distraction to a minimum. This series was published in the 1960s and 1970s, when the general availability of the harpsichord was still quite limited, and Ferguson's aim at that time was to open up its repertory to the pianist. In spite of this, what is written in the prefaces about articulation and so forth is in no way invalidated. The series is available in the United States through Oxford University Press, 200 Madison Avenue, New York, N.Y. 10016.

Also recommended are the following:

- the Associated Board of the Royal Schools of Music's *Baroque Keyboard Music* series, edited by Richard Jones (available in United States through Theodore Presser, United Music Publishers, 1 Presser Place, Bryn Mawr, PA 19010-3490)
- Stainer and Bell's *Early Keyboard Music* series, many of which were edited by Thurston Dart (available in United States through Galaxy Music Corporation, E. C. Schirmer, 138 Ipswich Street, Boston, MA 02215). As well as volumes devoted to many individual English composers, such as Tomkins, Locke, and Arne, the series contains the whole of *Musicke's Handmaid* and *Parthenia*, and selections from the *Mulliner Book* and *Fitzwilliam Virginal Book*. The musical text is generally extremely reliable, although there are a few minor modernizations; some advice about performance is (economically) offered.
- Ricordi's volumes of *The Belgian/Dutch/English/French/German/ Italian/Portuguese/Spanish Harpsichordists* (available in the United States). The text of these is not so authoritative. There is little editorial material, but at least there are no misleading markings.

Editorial phrasing and dynamics—although of a quite intelligent kind—slightly spoil the otherwise good and inexpensive *Early Keyboard Music* series edited by Eve Barsham and published by J. W. Chester. Again there are volumes devoted to the French, Italian, English, and German schools. If you use these, try always to discover (and distinguish between) what the composer wrote and what the editor added.

Facsimiles

One way around the problems of editorial intervention is to use facsimiles, which are now becoming popular. These are modern photographic reprints of original published editions or of manuscripts. Facsimiles may at first look slightly alarming, but one soon gets used to the various conventions of earlier musical typography, and in fact you will experience a much closer sense of the composer than can be had from even the best Urtext edition. As they contain no modern commentary, however, you will have to study the conventions of the period in order to make your own musicological decisions. Also, you are deprived of editorial guidance about possible alternative versions of the text.

Facsimiles can be bought from specialist music dealers, and because there is no editorial involvement they are usually relatively inexpensive. Look for the Minkoff Edition, the Italian *Studio per Edizioni Scelte* (S.P.E.S.), the Fuzeau Edition, and Broude's *Performers' Facsimiles*, a comprehensive range published in New York. Facsimiles of eighteenth-century English music are the easiest for the beginner to tackle, being generally written in familiar clefs. Other music may use less familiar clefs, so check before you buy: watch out for the C clef on various lines of the staff, or the F clef on the middle line. I hope you will want to learn these clefs eventually—they are not really difficult—but the beginner has enough to think about at first without bothering with unusual clefs. Be careful of facsimiles of early baroque Italian harpsichord music and English music before about 1700, which may use a staff of up to eight lines.

Some guidance about playing from facsimile is offered at the end of chapter 12. The addresses of facsimile publishers and specialist dealers in early keyboard music are given in appendix B.

In conclusion, one should note that, although anthology volumes divide composers by national schools, the music itself cannot be assigned quite so tidily. For example, Froberger, born in southern Germany, wrote his toccatas in Italian style, but his partitas (suites), which were influential throughout Europe, in a style that rests on a fusion of

French lutenist and Italian idioms. The Italian Domenico Scarlatti spent his working life in the Iberian peninsula, where he developed a highly individual style that drew on the idioms of Spanish folk music. Sweelinck, in Amsterdam, shared the idiom of the English virginalists. J. S. Bach achieved an unparalleled fusion of elements of the great national styles of the eighteenth century—French, Italian, and German—but different elements preponderate in certain works, such as the French Suites or the Italian Concerto.

For this reason, the following chapters (12 through 17) contain characterizations of these national styles as much as studies of individual composers. An awareness of the difference between the French and Italian style is particularly important to the performance of baroque music and is also of considerable interest to the listener. For reasons of space and convenience, ornamentation is considered separately in chapter 18, but it is nevertheless another important aspect of national style and performance that reflects this French-Italian divide with great clarity. The selection and notation of the ornaments used varied according to national usage, and the performer needs to become familiar with, and gradually absorb, these distinctive conventions. But please forget those abstract ornaments that one wrote out laboriously in music theory examinations. The real thing is much more interesting, and in chapter 18 you will find a functional, pragmatic approach to the subject, which should dispel many of the problems.

We now know a great deal about the way national traditions of performance varied: so cultivate your curiosity. Listen—with score in hand if possible—to recent recordings of good players, and study the historical evidence (some sources are given in chapter 10). The radio can also be useful; listen not only to harpsichord music but also to other period instrumental music. Gradually you will be able to build up distinctive profiles of the various national styles.

12

The English Style

Although the *Fitzwilliam Virginal Book*, whose manuscript dates from between 1609 and 1619, is the greatest keyboard collection from Tudor and Jacobean England, it had several predecessors, of which the *Mulliner Book* and *My Lady Nevell's Book* are perhaps best known. *Benjamin Cosyn's Book* also contains much charming music. Virginal books usually contain a medley of many kinds of items. The chief types are as follows:

TRANSCRIPTIONS OF VOCAL MUSIC

Keyboard music took some time to develop its own style. At first this was done by transcribing, for example, a well-known chanson, such as Lassus's *Margot Labourez,* and adding written-out trills at the cadences, and other keyboard flourishes or filling in of texture. Transcription of vocal music onto two lines of staff was known as **intavolatura**, and was often done by players for their own use. The *Mulliner Book* contains numerous transcriptions of Latin motets; the *Fitzwilliam,* transcriptions of Italian madrigals—all in an elaborately stylized texture best avoided by the beginner.

PIECES WRITTEN AROUND A *CANTUS FIRMUS*

Compositions on a *cantus firmus* were based on a preexisting fixed part such as a piece of liturgical chant. These pieces generally bear the Latin title of the chant; *Gloria tibi Trinitas* is one of the most common and famous. Bull, in particular, excelled in this type of writing, and he deploys scale passages of ever-increasing rhythmic complexity against the plain whole notes of the chant. *Ut, re, mi* pieces (written on the notes of the sol-fa scale) also fall within this category. Interesting but highly abstract in style, this music depends heavily on knowledgeable articulation to achieve the best effect in performance. On the whole it sounds better on the organ than on the harpsichord, because the *cantus firmus* can be sustained.

PRELUDES AND FANTASIAS

Influenced by the Italian writing of the sixteenth century, preludes often contain rapid passagework, and display the excitement and sparkle of which the virginal is capable. At this time, the word *fantasia* merely meant that some contrapuntal imitation was present—it had no connection with the evocative fantasy developed in the romantic period. Giles Farnaby's fantasias in the *Fitzwilliam* start with miniature fugal expositions, and only gradually expand into a typical keyboard idiom.

DANCE FORMS

The dance category is more accessible to the beginner. The main dances of the period were the **pavan** (in duple meter) and **galliard** (in triple meter). These were often composed as a pair and linked by common musical material, especially in the opening phrase. Byrd's pavans and galliards in *Parthenia* and the *Fitzwilliam Virginal Book* are especially fine. From the former, try the famous *Earl of Salisbury* pair: from the latter, try no. 166 (CLXVI: volume 2, page 202, of the Dover reprint). The **alman** and **coranto**—brisker versions of the later baroque dances—and the **gigge** can also be found in the *Fitzwilliam*, as well as two settings of the **lavolta** (a notorious jumping dance) by Byrd.

SETTINGS OF POPULAR OR FOLK TUNES

In the rich and worthwhile category of popular or folk tunes, one finds settings of many splendid traditional melodies: *The Woods so Wilde, O Mistrys Mine, Callino Casturame, Fayne would I wedd* and numerous others. The famous *Lachrymae* melody, originally by Dowland, enjoyed exceptional popularity, and Byrd, Morley, and Giles Farnaby all contributed a setting of its melody, with variations of texture, to the *Fitzwilliam* book.

Sets of variations on popular melodies were written by many Jacobean composers; those by Byrd and Morley are charming, resourceful, and delightful to play. Byrd's *O Mistrys Mine* set makes a good introduction to the genre and is not too difficult. Both Byrd and Bull wrote famous and extensive sets of variations on *Walsingham*. Bull's set is particularly brilliant and ends in an astonishing display of rhythmic complexities.

CHARACTER PIECES

Character pieces appear to be an English innovation, and they are a testimony to the freshness and vitality of the English idiom in the early seventeenth century. Farnaby's work is outstanding here: his miniatures, such as *His Humour, His Rest*, or *A Toye*, make an excellent introduction to virginalist style. *The Goldfinch*, by Benjamyn Cosyn, is another good piece for the newcomer to the style, while Martin Peerson's *The Fall of the Leafe*, with its almost programmatic descriptiveness, is also recommended. Byrd's *The Bells* is a magnificent piece of musical description whose technical demands are much greater. It evokes the sounds of traditional English change-ringing on church bells.

From this account, you may see that there are a great variety of idioms waiting for you to explore. As I have indicated, the pavans and galliards and the character pieces are both typical of the English virginal school and likely to appeal to the beginner. Remembering the nature of the virginal—its crisp action, its forthright tone—one may say that subtlety of touch and shading are less important in performance than rhythmic, clean delivery. Articulation and change of hand position must be carefully controlled, avoiding bumps of emphasis in unwanted places by placing the accents correctly.

Giles Farnaby's Dreame shows the typical keyboard texture of the period, with varying densities, ranging from two-part writing to a strong seven-note chord near the end: a texture often called *freistimmig*, i.e., free-voiced. This short piece, a three-strain pavan without repeats, is a good study in fingering, articulation, and the management of the instrument; it is studied in detail in chapter 7.

Pavans and galliards are often written in a fairly chordal style. Basically, their strains or sections have even numbers of measures, multiples of four or eight, although stylized pieces not intended for dancing can be more irregular. Each strain usually has a decorated repeat, which fitted the original dance figures: these decorated repeats offer useful models when you are ready to improvise your own **divisions**—running figures or other decoration—later on. The pavan is slow and stately, but galliards are quicker; do not let the rather long note values characteristic of the period mislead you into thinking that they are solemn. The robust rhythmic nature of the galliard should encourage you to make the most of any syncopation.

As with all dances of this period, the extra final chord (separately written in square notation) is intended for the final courtesy, and it should be spread in a deliberate, dignified manner. Incidentally, take any opportunity of attending a session devoted to historical dance: this will teach you a great deal about how the music should be played.

Virginalist Ornaments

Only two kinds of ornaments were used by the virginalists: oblique single or double strokes, which were drawn through the stem of the note if it had one, otherwise placed above or below the note. Because no contemporary ornament table or written description containing these ornaments survives, our interpretation must be based on conjecture, combined with some extrapolation back from the written ornament tables of Purcell's time. The general consensus of scholars is that the single stroke means a rapid slide up to the written note from a third below, while the double stroke may be rendered by either an upper or lower shake: the upper in a rising passage, the lower in a descending. Either ornament may be performed before or on the beat.

Sometimes, however, it looks as if the signs are merely intended to indicate prominent notes, such as the notes of a plainchant *cantus firmus;* or they may possibly suggest spread chords or other subtleties of performance. Furthermore, the ornament signs are not always placed identically in different manuscripts of the same piece. This suggests that although their presence was vital, their position was less important. You can therefore experiment, never losing sight of the idea that ornaments should add sparkle and even swagger in vigorous music but provide expressiveness in slower pieces. If necessary, don't hesitate to leave out ornaments for which you can feel no musical purpose, or that are beyond your technical ability to blend naturally into the texture.

The virtuoso John Bull was perhaps the most brilliant member of the virginalist school and a major contributor to *Parthenia*, the first printed collection of virginal music (the other contributors were William Byrd and Orlando Gibbons). *Parthenia* was published in 1613, and contains some magnificent music. Later in that year, Bull was forced by scandal and political difficulties to flee to Antwerp, where he had Catholic friends, and where an English colleague Peter Phillips (several of whose pieces are found in the *Fitzwilliam* book) was already working. The music of the Amsterdam organist Sweelinck is another instance of the close stylistic links that existed at this time between both the Protestant and Catholic Low Countries, on one hand, and England on the other; Sweelinck is represented in the *Fitzwilliam* book by a substantial (although rather inaccurately copied) fantasia. Even his sets of variations for organ—such as the beautiful *Mein junges Leben*—are entirely virginalist in style. Sweelinck is also significant, however, as a herald of the baroque idiom: he was the teacher of the majority of the north German organists of the next generation.

In England, things moved more slowly, and the virginalist style persisted well into the mid-seventeenth century, up to and during the Commonwealth of 1649–1660. *Priscilla Bunbury's Virginal Book* (belonging to two successive Priscillas of the family) is a typical collection of the 1630s. The contents are not so high powered as those of the great Jacobean collections, but there is some original fingering. A few of the *Fitzwilliam* categories are still represented (chiefly folk tunes), and its humbler domestic outlook was well suited to the troubled days of the Civil War. Roger North, writing in about 1700, said that it had been better during that period to stay "fidling at home, than goe abroad and be knock'd on the head."[1] In rural Worcestershire, the ultraconservative Thomas Tomkins continued to write in the virginalist style until the late 1650s. His *Sad Paven for these distracted times,* written in 1649, refers to the execution of Charles I in that year.

A new spirit is evident in *Musicke's Handmaid,* a famous collection of "new and pleasant Lessons for the Virginals or Harpsycon," which gives the beginner a good introduction to the music of the Restoration period. Part I, which first appeared in 1663, contains music by Lawes, Locke, Benjamin Rogers, and others. The influence of France is beginning to be felt, in titles such as *Corant—La Mounseer* (Monsieur) and in the use of such structural devices as the *petite reprise*. Charles II's triumphant return from France at the Restoration in 1660 brought about a new degree of openness to French culture, and the influence of keyboard writers such as Chambonnières was soon felt, although English composers handled keyboard textures with much less sophistication than the French. Locke's *Melothesia* (1673), *Musicke's Handmaid,* Part II (1689), and Purcell's keyboard suites show a fascinating tension between the essential Englishness of the older style—its characteristic melodic turns of phrase, brisk rhythms, and expressive if sometimes gauche harmony—and the newly imported French suite forms. Titles such as *Motley's Maggot, Old Simon the King,* or *A New Irish Tune* (the famous *Lilliburlero*) rub shoulders with French dances—riggadoons, gavottes, sarabandes—and a "Chacone." The French style of ornamentation also gained ground, particularly the use of the expressive appoggiatura and its compounds. One of Locke's preludes, which is studied in chapter 7, is obviously trying to convey, in conventional notation, the effect of the unmeasured preludes of Louis Couperin.

Purcell's *Lessons for the Harpsichord* (1696) are pleasing works whose quality is only now, through the recovery of an appropriate performance style, becoming fully appreciated. Good editions include that by Christopher Kite (Chester), which prints and elucidates Purcell's original—if not entirely unambiguous—directions for ornamentation. The *Prelude for the Fingering* in *The Harpsichord Master* of 1697 is also attributed to Purcell, and has authentic fingering; this piece appears in several anthologies, and *The Harpsichord Master* (a useful collection of twenty-one pieces) is published in its entirety by Faber/Schirmer (1980). Besides Purcell, one might investigate the erudite but slightly awkward work of Blow and the amiable music of Croft. The French elements in the work of this period call for the kind of rhythmic inequality described in chapter 15.

Jeremiah Clarke's sprightly collection of *Choice Lessons for the Harpsichord or Spinett* (1711) still retains many of the older English forms and styles, but nevertheless has a more typical eighteenth-century look about its facsimile. Significantly, it uses the modern five-line staff, instead of the six-line that had persisted in England throughout the seventeenth century. In the following decade, England increasingly forgot its insular musical heritage as the craze for Italian music, particularly for opera and the concerto, swept the country. In keyboard music, this Italian influence was most noticeable in the use of busy arpeggiated figures, which in the hands of a mediocre composer such as John Loeillet (the London member of a widespread musical tribe) could amount to much ado about nothing. His "Suits"—a common English spelling of "Suites"—appeared in 1723, and their title revealingly mentions a "variety of Passages and Variations throughout the work." The title of Sir Henry Burgess's *Collection of Lessons for the Harpsichord Compos'd in an Easy and Familiar Style* (1725) promises much the same kind of rather insubstantial fare.

Handel's unmistakable vitality, however, shines through even the minor items of his extensive keyboard output. His towering personality, both musical and human, gave him an effortless grasp of the diverse styles that were current, and a winning way of expressing himself through established forms. He could also display that understanding of England's own musical heritage that has endeared him to his adopted nation. To play Handel's music intelligently, you need to be aware of its widely spreading roots. For example, the second of the eight great Suites of 1720 is in the Italian style—a four-movement *sonata da chiesa*, which opens with a cantabile melody and accompaniment that could form the slow movement of a violin sonata. It continues with a typical Italianate *moto perpetuo*—the epitome of sunny straightforwardness, a quality shared by many of his other allegros. Some of the other suites are basically French: the allemandes have the flowing contrapuntal manner typical of the high baroque style, the courantes display the requisite rhythmic ambiguity. Yet Handel, never totally orthodox, delighted in introducing extraneous movements—the famous Air and Variations in the Fifth Suite, or the great Passacaglia in the Seventh. Fugues, on the Italian model yet quintessentially Handelian-English, occur in the Second, Third, Fourth, Sixth, and Eighth Suites, while the Seventh has a fugato as part of an overture in the French style, a form that German composers were particularly fond of transferring to the keyboard. Indeed, these suites could be regarded as some of the most cosmopolitan in the repertory.

Handel's keyboard music was not a central part of his output, but it nevertheless had few rivals during his lifetime; his friend Mattheson's *Pièces de Clavecin*, published in London in 1714, and Roseingrave's *Eight Suits of Lessons* might be the exceptions. Roseingrave is also remembered for publishing forty-two of Domenico Scarlatti's sonatas in an English edition of 1739. They made a great impression, and though they provoked no direct imitators, Arne commended them to his pupils.

I might add that the organists of the Georgian period—Stanley, Walond, Greene, Heron, Boyce—wrote a large number of voluntaries that are inscribed "for organ or harpsichord." As the English organ of the period had no pedals, these pieces can readily be used as harpsichord music. Greene also wrote suites for the harpsichord, and arranged some of his overtures for harpsichord or spinet "to Improve the Hand" (1745), while Stanley and the resident Italian Francesco Geminiani arranged some of their own concertos as music for solo harpsichord.

Even before the death of Handel in 1759, a new generation was emerging, whose musical language showed a gradual transition to the galant and early classical style. The many Italian musicians working in London, such as Geminiani or Paradies, set the pace; Paradies's so-called Toccata in A, beloved of pianists, comes from a set of *Sonate di gravicembalo* published in London in 1754. Arne's eight Sonatas, or Lessons (1756), are typical of this period; they show a few vestigial remains of the now outmoded French forms, but are chiefly full of easy Italianate grace. Arne, together with Roseingrave and other composers such as Chilcot and Nares, also wrote harpsichord concertos, although they are modest works, in which the harpsichord alternates between display passages and a continuo function. Such concertos were being written as late as the 1780s[2] and would have offered a fitting use for the splendid English instruments that, even at this late date, continued to be built.

The anonymous *A Collection of Favourite Lessons for Young Practitioners on the Harpsichord* (ca. 1776), edited by Gwilym Beechey and published in facsimile by Oxford University Press, shows the sort of staple diet a pupil could expect in the late eighteenth century: minuets, marches, and airs, plus the occasional burlesque or other character piece. The increasing use of facile Alberti-bass textures is a symptom of the demise of the linear contrapuntal style: and if any harpsichord music ever deserved the epithet of "tinkly," it might well be the rather shallow Italianate allegros. At least one of the minuet pairs in this collection, however, is delightful (see figure 8).

Playing from Facsimile

Of the music mentioned above, many examples are published in facsimile. Broude Bros. of New York currently offers *Parthenia*, the second part of *Musicke's Handmaid*, Purcell's *Choice Collection*, Clarke's *Choice Lessons*, Loeillet's *Six Suits*, Mattheson's *Pièces de Clavecin*, Roseingrave's *Suits*, and works by Geminiani, Burgess, Felton, and others. *The Harpsichord Master*, with the Purcell *Prelude for the Fingering* and his ornament table, is published by Price Milburn and Faber Music. Arne's Sonatas, edited by Gwilym Beechey and Thurston Dart, are published in facsimile by Stainer and Bell, who also offer the *Collection of Lessons* (1750) of Greene, edited by Davitt Moroney. Oxford University Press publishes facsimiles of many Georgian organ voluntaries and the anonymous *Collection of Favourite Lessons* referred to above.

The first three items of this list, on six-line staff and in extremely cramped format, are best left for the experienced player (*Parthenia*, indeed, strikes one as a score made for the purpose of record rather than performance) but the other examples are quite easily approachable. This might therefore be a good place to offer a few hints on playing from facsimile.

• Don't expect the vertical alignment always to be correct. Printers spaced the left-hand and right-hand parts independently, so you will sometimes need to work out for yourself what notes should sound simultaneously. A single note that lasts a whole measure tends to be

placed in the middle of the measure, rather than at the beginning: symmetry was evidently preferred to ease of sight reading.
• Scan the key signature carefully. Note that either sharps or flats may be indicated twice; for instance, G major may have its F-sharp both in the bottom space and on the top line of the treble staff: E major may look as if it has six sharps, because the F-sharp and G-sharp occur in two positions. Because of this, do not jump to premature conclusions about the key of the piece.
• Even when you are satisfied about the true number of accidentals, you should bear in mind that much minor key music of this period is written with one flat too few by present-day standards—e.g., G minor with only one flat. This is to avoid the constant use of the raised sixth of the scale (E-natural in G minor) in melodic contexts, but watch out for its effect on the harmony, too: for instance, C *major* chords in the key of G minor.
• Use common sense about the repetition of accidentals. There were varying conventions at different times. Throughout the seventeenth century, accidentals are generally repeated every time the same note is affected later in the bar. *Be warned*, however, that they are rarely canceled if the same note is *not* intended to be affected: they are simply absent. The use of the natural sign was not standard until the second half of the eighteenth century. (Before that date, if it was used at all, it was more often to sharpen a note that had been flat than to flatten a note that had been sharp.)
• Proofreading at this period was rudimentary. If you find a note that simply does not make harmonic sense, try moving it up or down one line or one space. This simple procedure will solve many problems.
• A whole note straddled across a bar line means a half note in the first measure tied to another in the second: look ahead as you play. A dot after a bar line was often used where we would today use a tied note of the value of the dot.
• First- and second-time measures are more economically indicated than is now the case, and you may need to use common sense to work out the composer's intention. Look out for symbols similar to the modern *dal segno* sign, which may be used as a guide to the place where the repeat begins.
• English eighteenth-century keyboard music is helpful to the beginner, since it does not often use unfamiliar clefs; but earlier music, and music in the French tradition, may well do so. As you progress, you should begin to learn to play from C clefs; viola play-

ers will already know the C clef on the middle line (alto or C3), and this symmetrical clef is a good one for other players to start with. As well as being commonly used for higher lying left-hand parts in French clavecin music, it may occur in the ensemble music you meet as a continuo player. Then tackle, in order, the C clef on the bottom line (soprano or C1) and the F clef on the middle line (baritone or F3). Once you view these clefs in their relative positions on a larger grid of horizontal lines (the "great stave") they will become progressively easier.

Early seventeenth-century Italian music such as that of Frescobaldi commonly uses a six-line staff for the right hand and an eight-line for the left. These large grids are rather confusing to the eye (for which reason they eventually dropped out of use), but reading becomes easier when you appreciate that they are simply extensions of the modern five lines. For instance, the right-hand staff may have incorporated the middle-C leger line (in which case, notes near the top of the staff will be the easiest to identify); or it may have added the upper leger line above the treble staff (now, notes in the bottom half of the staff will be the easiest). The eight bass lines are an overlapped version of the F and C clefs, and both clefs are usually indicated. With practice you will soon learn to concentrate on one portion of the staff at a time, and to ignore the rest.

Notes

1. Wilson 1959, 294.

2. Rishton 1992, 121. This is a very good account of eighteenth-century British keyboard concertos after Handel.

2

Figure 8. Minuets from *A Collection of Favourite Lessons for Young Practitioners on the Harpsichord* (anon., ca. 1770). Note the independent spacing of upper and lower staves, which does not always ensure perfect alignment. In m. 10 of the first minuet, the sharp sign for the A in the left hand, clearly necessary to the harmonic sequence, has been squeezed in, very small, after the normal key signature. Various commonsense adjustments are needed: for example, in m. 16, the G-natural of the preceding bar must obviously be repeated. The appoggiaturas in mm. 5 and 6 make triplets with the following figure: the one in m. 6 appears to be a C-sharp, but could be a misprint of B: leger lines were frequent casualties. In m. 6 of the second minuet, the third note in the left hand should probably be A. *Reproduced by permission of Oxford University Press.*

134

13

The Italian Style

Toccata, canzona, sonata, concerto—Italian words for the Italian way of making instrumental music. Yet in the period covered by this book, Italy did not exist as a nation in the modern sense. The output of Frescobaldi, Corelli, Vivaldi, and their contemporaries was produced within the complex and shifting boundaries of Papal states, duchies, and principalities, and in a miniature republic, Venice.

Moreover, although Italy was the birthplace of so many musical forms and styles, both vocal and instrumental, its keyboard music never attained any particular importance. The harpsichord, to the Italian composer, was primarily a continuo instrument, an accompaniment for the first loves of his life—voice or violin. After Frescobaldi, no Italian harpsichord composer of international distinction emerged, with the exception of Domenico Scarlatti, who must be considered a Spanish composer on several stylistic grounds.[1]

Nevertheless, much typical keyboard figuration originated in Italy. Renaissance composers transcribed vocal **canzonas** and transformed them into keyboard music by simply adding brilliant runs and the characteristic fully-notated cadential trills (example 13-1). (Such trills can be added in similar contexts even if they are not indicated.) The **toccata** is built from primary keyboard material—scales and chords. A player when improvising will naturally use such figuration, and more toccatas must have been improvised than were ever written down. In fact, a player who could improvise toccatas was esteemed far above one who had to be content with playing a composed piece.

Example 13-1. Typical cadential trills.

The toccata is above all a "touch-piece"—a vehicle for virtuosity and rhetorical skill. (Virtuosity is itself an Italian concept, born of the ebullient Mediterranean temperament and flourishing in its climate.) The dry and incisive sound of the Italian harpsichord, which makes it so suitable for continuo playing, is even more effective in toccata style. Rapid sixteenth-note passages, played with gusto (another Italian word), evoke a characteristic and spine-tingling rustle from its strings.

Frescobaldi's own Preface to his *Partite e Toccate; primo libro* (1637) gives clear suggestions for the performance of toccatas. "This way of playing is not subject to the beat . . . sometimes languid, sometimes swift . . . pausing according to the mood." "The openings of the toccatas should be played slowly and arpeggiated," with tied notes and long notes in chords freely repeated. When playing rapid runs in both hands, one should "pause . . . then attack the passage resolutely, so as to display the agility of the hand."[2] Main sections of the composition, he adds, should be clearly separated by pauses.

This spontaneous creative approach calls for a confident player, although it is never too soon—through the medium of recordings—to make the acquaintance of this highly seminal style, with its blend of virtuosic passages and learned fugal passages in stricter time. (Frescobaldi's description is "furnished with diverse sections and moods."[3]) The toccata style was absorbed by Froberger and Georg Muffat, and through their influence it spread widely through mainland Europe. Buxtehude and Bach, for instance, owe much to its idiom: in fact, the only places seemingly unaffected were the Iberian peninsula and, apart from a few exceptions, England.

It is probably easier, however, for the beginner to approach Frescobaldi's output through his balletti and correnti, his variations *(partite)* such as the delightful *Ruggiero* variations on *Fra Jacopino*, or his smaller *passacagli*. The early baroque period perpetuated the renaissance dance forms of the passamezzo and romanesca—fixed harmonic sequences around which divisions were improvised—by absorbing elements of their style into the **passacaglia**. The passacaglia structure involves characteristic harmonic phrases (usually four or eight measures of triple time) that can be freely extended into large and imposing, although not necessarily showy or difficult, pieces. Frescobaldi's monumental *Cento Partite sopra Passacaglia* contains passacaglia and ciaccona sections in alternation. (Notwithstanding rigid textbook definitions, the distinction between passacaglia and ciaccona becomes blurred in the seventeenth century. Although the typical ciaccona tends to be in the major mode and the passacaglia in the minor, Frescobaldi did not always observe this distinction strictly.) The sections of the *Cento Partite* may, as the composer hints, be played separately if desired: indeed, this work somewhat resembles a compendium—its tonality changes as it progresses, and it even contains a corrente.[4]

This remarkable piece is nevertheless unified by its consistently noble and elevated tone, and it offers fine examples of the expressive power of early baroque writing. Frescobaldi often invokes minor-key harmonies with particularly poignant effect (example 13-2). Later in the work, strong chromatic threads are woven in opposing directions through the textures, and by the end of the piece an almost visionary intensity is achieved. The pleading effect of inverted pedals, where the same note is repeated in the top part over changing harmonies, reinforces this impression. As noted above, the composer specifically encourages the player to repeat any long notes that fail to sustain on the harpsichord: one may take advantage of this to give extra point to a dissonance, or to underline a rhythm.

Mention should here be made of **hemiola**, a term that will recur in other chapters. Hemiola is a rhythmic feature based on the principle that six beats can be grouped either as 2×3 or as 3×2. Many people will be familiar with hemiola from the *intermedi* in Monteverdi's opera *Orfeo*, but those dances used the simpler renaissance form of the device, namely measures of 3/4 and 6/8 which alternated throughout the movement. The characteristic baroque hemiola is rather different: the rhythmic shift does not follow a regularly recurring pattern, but mostly falls just before cadences. It involves merging two triple measures into one long measure whose beats are of double length, or regrouping the beats within a six-beat measure. This conspicuous feature serves to delineate musical sentences or paragraphs.

Frescobaldi's correntes and passacagli are full of this device. In example 13-2, I have marked two of the hemiola groups with square brackets: one could well identify others. In playing this example, relish and emphasize the supple way in which the beat is constantly regrouped—sometimes into twos, sometimes into threes. (The tempo in

Example 13-2. Girolamo Frescobaldi, *Cento Partite sopra Passacaglia*, mm. 111–130.

this section of the piece moves at about half note = 132; do not let the archaic notelengths mislead you into adopting a slower, stolid tempo.)

Pasquini, the most famous Italian keyboard composer after Frescobaldi, also enjoyed a European reputation. As well as writing toccatas and passacaglias, and variations on the ubiquitous *La Follia* theme, he consolidated the dance suite (usually consisting of allemanda, corrente, and giga) in Italy. Together with Corelli and Alessandro Scarlatti, he belonged to the Arcadian Academy presided over by Cardinal Ottoboni, which is where Handel met him when he visited Rome. Handel's keyboard music bears some of Pasquini's stamp, and the fine Passacaglia in Handel's Seventh (G Minor) Suite must have been conceived on Italian soil.

Although the **sonata** was so firmly established in the literature of the baroque violin, it bypassed Italian solo keyboard music almost entirely until well into the eighteenth century. You may come across sonatas by Marcello, Durante, Platti, Galuppi, Rutini, and others, dating from about 1730 onward.[5] By this time, Italian music was permeated by the language of opera buffa, and most Italian keyboard sonatas of this period are rather lighthearted works, full of short-breathed galant phrases and cheerful rattling textures. There is more physical animation than intellect in their makeup: but with spirited phrasing, they can be steered away from their latent triviality and prove good fun to play.

The clear strong light of Italy can offer us a valuable analogy for the performance of Italian baroque music. All is, more or less, as it seems. Except in the obvious case of the toccata, deliberate rhythmic alterations of the kind practiced by the French are almost unknown—a feature that Couperin noted approvingly.[6] Ornaments are few and simply notated, although this is balanced by the fact that the performer is expected to add generous improvised embellishment, especially in repeated sections and slow movements. Bold and brilliant in allegros, serene and elevated in slower movements, Italian music should always be played with luster and generosity. It is less subtle than French music, but manifests a straightforward delight in living.

Although Italy's keyboard repertory was relatively small, Italian contributions to the development of baroque instrumental style were of enormous general significance, and these fed back into European keyboard literature in a fascinating variety of ways. Chief among these contributions were the patterns of violin figuration, particularly the cross-string type (example 13-3) and the idioms of the baroque string sonata and concerto, which are now so familiar to us in the music of Corelli and Vivaldi.

Example 13-3. Typical cross-string figuration.

The ingredients of Italian string style were disseminated across Europe, largely through the influence of church or court, and composers were quick to incorporate them into keyboard music. Bach, who in his

Figure 9. Italian harpsichord by Giovanni Antonio Baffo, 1574. This picture shows clearly the robust, though decorated, outer case and lid within which the separate inner case, decorated with ivory studs, is housed. Note the sharp curvature of the bentside, as compared with the Flemish instrument in figure 5. The instrument could be laid on a table for playing, or have a stand attached to the outer case. *Photograph reproduced by courtesy of the Board of Trustees of the Victoria and Albert Museum, London.*

posts at the courts of Weimar and Cöthen came to know much Italian music, assimilated its style especially thoroughly. The D Minor Prelude in Book II of *The Well-tempered Clavier* (BWV 875/i) is an excellent example of how he could write a keyboard piece with all the *brio* and impact of the Italian string concerto. In this prelude, Bach evokes from the keyboard the sound of the orchestral tutti, plus the exactly observed figuration of the solo violin, all brilliantly compressed into a mere two-voiced composition (one part in each hand). His well-known Italian Concerto is a systematic essay in the Italian style, and it makes use of the important tutti-solo *(forte* and *piano)* contrast that was another of Italy's legacies to baroque style.

Frescobaldi's keyboard music contains much distinguished contrapuntal work; the ricercares in his *Fiori Musicali*, in particular, look forward to Bach's *The Art of Fugue* over a century later. Another crucially important contrapuntal idiom developed by the Italians in the seventeenth century was the **stile antico**—that language of *alla breve* half notes, tied dissonances, and quarter-note passing tones, which survived into the baroque period as a kind of retrospective idealization of Palestrina's style. The *stile antico* lacked the characteristic rhythms of genuine sixteenth-century polyphony, and it later acquired a formula-ridden textbook status at the hands of Fux, Martini, and other contrapuntal theorists, but it was nevertheless of enormous importance to European musical culture. Like Latin, it was the language in which serious formal matters were conducted, and many of the movements you may accompany as a continuo player are couched in this elevated language. "And with his stripes" from Handel's *Messiah;* "Cum sancto Spiritu" from Vivaldi's *Gloria;* and the "Dona nobis pacem" from Bach's B Minor Mass are three well-known examples.

This academic contrapuntal style spilled over into keyboard writing. Bach uses it in several organ works, where its essentially sustained style is very much at home. Although it is by nature less suited to solo harpsichord writing, there are nevertheless a few lovely examples, such as the E Major Fugue from Book II of *The Well-tempered Clavier*. Handel's second harpsichord Suite in F (an Italianate *sonata da chiesa*) contains an enigmatic second movement that, when viewed without its rather waywardly indicated ornamentation, proves a typical specimen of *stile antico* polyphony.

The *stile antico* has a particular claim on the interest and respect of all harpsichordists. This style is founded on an intense awareness of intervallic relationships between each of the parts and the bass line. The dissonant intervals—the second, the fourth, and the seventh—are regarded as sounds that require special handling in composition. This concept of dissonance runs as a unifying thread, almost as a moral principle, through practically all music written between about 1580 and 1800. It is strongly present, for example, in Mozart's music, and it has never totally disappeared even in the present century.

Suspensions of sevenths that resolve to sixths (figured as 7–6), of fourths to thirds (4–3), and of seconds to unison (shown as 9–8) are the staples of figured bass. One should also be aware of these intervals when playing solo harpsichord music. Even passages in Scarlatti's sonatas that seem cavalier and whimsical are based on a sure fundamental recognition of the principles of dissonance. Dissonant intervals between the left and the right hand that fall *on the beat* occur almost invariably as either appoggiaturas or suspensions. These intervals, which sharply enhance the flavor of the music, need appropriate articulation to make their true effect. The dissonance needs to sound stronger than the resolution (the consonant interval that follows); and it is normally connected to that consonant resolution by a slur. A gap between the two is uncomfortably like a full stop in the middle of a sentence.

Last but not least among Italian developments is the concept of tonality itself—a striking (if later) parallel to the Italian development of perspective in painting. Corelli was perhaps the purest exponent of the tonal style, which evolved in the second half of the seventeenth century, and which made possible the fluent grammar of standard harmonic progressions—the "circle of fifths" and many other common formulas—with which, consciously or unconsciously, all continuo players spend so much of their time.

Since so many vital musical resources owe their origins to Italy, it scarcely seems to matter that no truly great school of actual harpsichord composition evolved. Italian ways of thinking inescapably permeate baroque music, just as Italian musicians were active in every corner of Europe.

A Checklist of Italian Harpsichord Composers

Giovanni Maria Trabaci: capriccios, galliards, toccatas, etc. (1603).

Girolamo Frescobaldi: dances, variations, ricercares, toccatas, etc. (circa 1615; frequent reprints). Facsimile of 1637 reprint: S. P. E. S., Florence, 1980; modern edition: K. Gilbert, Padua, 1979.

Giovanni Picchi: *Intavolatura di balli,* or dance movements (1621).

Michelangelo Rossi: *Toccate e corrente* (1640).

Bernardo Pasquini: dance suites, variations, toccatas (including *Toccata con lo Scherzo del Cuccu*), passacaglias, and several sonatas for two harpsichords, written entirely in figured bass (from circa 1690–1700).

Antonio Poglietti (working in Vienna): toccatas, ricercares, suites, *Rossignolo* (1676). Some notable capriccios based on bird calls.

Alessandro Scarlatti: partitas and toccatas, including *Toccata per studio di cembalo* (1716). Some fine variations on *La Follia* (1715).

Francesco Durante: six *Sonate per Cembalo* (1732); Harpsichord Concerto in B-flat, (circa 1750). The sonatas are in two movements, a contrapuntal *studio* being followed by a *divertimento*.

Domenico Cimarosa: sonatas.

Leonardo Leo: toccatas.

Domenico Paradies/Paradisi (working in London): twelve *Sonate di Gravicembalo* (1754), which enjoyed an enormous vogue.

Baldassare Galuppi: six *Sonate per Cembalo*.

Francesco Geminiani (working in London): two sets of pieces (1743, 1762) mostly arranged from other works by himself. Also various important theoretical works, including *The Art of Accompaniament* (circa 1754), written in English.

The work of the last six composers shows the gradual absorption of galant and early classical styles into harpsichord composition.

Notes

1. The work of Domenico Scarlatti is considered in chapter 17.

2. See Preface to S. P. E. S. facsimile edition. (The present translation is by the author.)

3. As note two.

4. The varying time signatures in this piece offer an excellent example of the confused situation referred to in chapter 10 (note 1). Some of the signatures bear their modern significance; others that are relics of the proportional system of notation were meant to give guidance about relative tempo and the subdivision of the measure. In fact, they work out much better in practice than in theory: do not be deterred.

5. Much keyboard music was also written by Italians working in London (probably stimulated by the greater resources of the English harpsichord; see chapter 12).

6. "We write differently from the way we play. . . . On the contrary, the Italians write their music in the true note values in which it is to be played" (Couperin 1716/1974, 49).

14

The French Style

There is a tendency to refer to the French music of the *grand siècle* as classical, rather than baroque. Although this is unfortunately rather confusing from the reader's point of view, there is no doubt that the music itself wears an aura of unassailable inner certainty, which gives it a good claim to this label, using the word "classical" in its Augustan rather than its Viennese sense.

To understand this music, we must begin by realizing how profoundly it was conditioned by the character of the seventeenth- and eighteenth-century French court. French music was highly distinctive and to a large extent self-contained (although other nations were keen to imitate its features) throughout the reigns of three monarchs, Louis XIV, XV, and XVI, that spanned an astonishing total of 150 years. Of these, Louis XIV, *Le Roi Soleil*, set the seal upon the unified cultural tone of the court from the outset. Etiquette and entertainment, architecture and art all ministered to the monolithic French political system and helped to glorify the image of the absolute monarch. The ballets of Lully united music, dance, and drama to this end, and Louis himself participated in the masques in his personal character of the Sun King.[1]

Although order and stylization were paramount elements of French civilization at this time, this does not imply that all music of the French baroque school is grand or formal. Even in the seventeenth century, French style became concerned with the delicate and the intimately

144

expressive. By the time of Louis XV, the salons of eighteenth-century Paris were ousting the court of Versailles as the chief place where music was to be heard, and sensuous charm began to vie with formal dignity. Colorful character pieces became very popular: a handful of these, such as Daquin's *Le Coucou* or Couperin's *Les petits moulins à vent*, remained well-known as piano pieces even during the general eclipse of the French baroque school in the nineteenth century. Indeed, it is often necessary to point out to the average music lover that the clavecin output of Couperin ranges far wider and deeper than mere elegant rococo works. It would be hard to exaggerate the variety and richness of the whole French keyboard tradition, and I hope this chapter will whet your appetite. There is so much music of exceptional quality waiting for you to explore.[2]

The Evolution of French Clavecin Idiom

The texture of French seventeenth-century keyboard writing owes a great deal to the style of lute music and rivals its subtlety of nuance.[3] The lutenists' ornamentation, their development of the eloquent improvisatory prelude, and their use of fascinatingly impressionistic "broken" textures, which can suggest a polyphonic web, all influenced the early work of the clavecinistes. The actual indication *luthé* can still be found as a reminder of this source in several pieces by Couperin that use broken textures, e.g. *Les charmes* (*Ordre* 9) or *La Mézangére* (*Ordre* 10).[4]

Dance music was the other parent of French keyboard style. Here again the lutenists had already led the way, but the dance forms were taken up strongly by French keyboard composers. The spread of French cultural influence ensured that the keyboard suite of dance movements became an important component of baroque music throughout Europe. Its core dances—the allemande, courante, sarabande, and gigue—enjoyed a classic status. On the other hand, clavecin composers were not greatly interested in formal contrapuntal procedures, and seldom went to the trouble of writing actual fugues.[5] This in no way implies that French clavecin textures lacked contrapuntal interest: the player will discover much exquisite voice-movement woven into the fabric of the music. But the rhythms and gestures of baroque dance lay deepest, and welled up most consistently, in French musical consciousness.

Most French harpsichord music was engraved or printed, often ornamentally and beautifully; but notable exceptions are the Bauyn manuscript, a late seventeenth-century source of great importance, and the Parville manuscript, now in the University of California at Berkeley.

145

These manuscripts contain work by the composers of the first *clavecin-iste* generation; Jacques Champion de Chambonnières, Louis Couperin, and Henri d'Anglebert. All three were in their different ways extremely influential. Louis Couperin's eloquent music, although written as early as the 1650s, displays the quintessence of the mature clavecin style, while d'Anglebert expands its ornamental aspect. Their music shares the atmosphere of dignity and formality that marked the reign of Louis XIV—although one should never ignore the strong, if controlled, element of passion that is also emerging. Indeed, the tension between formality and passion is one reason for the extraordinary fascination of all French baroque music.

The elevated tone that one soon comes to recognize in the output of the first generation never totally deserts French clavecin music throughout its entire history. However, in the work of the second great generation—François Couperin, Daquin, and Rameau—this tone is joined by new and seductive sounds. The character piece, with its rococo elements of charm and picturesqueness, comes to the fore, and we find an increasing sensuousness of style, which forms a perfect counterpart to the paintings of Fragonard and Boucher. The work of Couperin le Grand is divided fairly equally between the formal traditional manner and the novel decorative style—although as one might expect, the decorative style is more prominent in the later of his four books of pieces. Both manners are still represented in the music of the final generation of Duphly, Balbastre, and Armand-Louis Couperin.

The harmonic language of French music is outstandingly expressive, deserving much more attention than it normally receives. This expressive element began to emerge strongly in the second half of the seventeenth century: for example, there was often an emotive tension between major and minor modes, which is well illustrated in the piece by Chambonnières studied in chapter 7. Even before 1700 this passionate language had attained great heights of eloquence, with two further notable features. The first was a poignant use of harmony drawn from the melodic (as well as the harmonic) minor scale; this frequently shows in the use of a *major* subdominant triad in the minor key (see the F major chord in example 14-1). The second was a love of rich suspended dissonances—single, double, or even triple. These dissonances were used in characteristic ways, as in this sarabande by d'Anglebert (example 14-2), where an appoggiatura—the C-sharp—creates a highly expressive augmented triad against which the E in the tenor range is suspended. (Augmented triads were widely used by the French: Louis Couperin even used one as the opening chord of a sarabande in D minor.)

Example 14-1. Louis-Nicolas Clérambault, *Sarabande Grave* in C Minor, mm. 5–8.

Example 14-2. Henri d'Anglebert, *Sarabande Grave*, from Suite No. 3 in D Minor, mm. 20–22.

These sumptuous harmonies still permeate the later French style, whether in the solo clavecin music or in the very beautiful chamber music of the period by Leclair, de la Barre, Marais, and many others. The lateral influence of this French musical language was also great: for instance, some of its elements had spread into the music of Purcell as early as the 1680s. Above all, the harmonic language of J. S. Bach would have been immeasurably poorer had he not studied and absorbed the work of Couperin and the French organ school.

Patterns of Construction

In such a formalized cultural regime, it is not surprising to find highly stylized patterns of musical construction. The binary dance forms may head the list, but the **rondeau** pattern (a main theme, often of eight measures, alternating with contrasted episodes) was also prevalent. Gavottes en rondeau were a typical application of this pattern.

The triple-meter **chaconne** or **passacaille en rondeau**, whose refrain often featured massive and dignified harmony, was one of the longest and most imposing instrumental structures of the baroque period.[6] Notable examples include the sonorous Chaconne in F in the Bauyn manuscript, usually attributed in anthologies to Chambonnières but almost certainly by Louis Couperin; and the great, heart-stirring B

147

Minor Passacaille in François Couperin's Eighth *Ordre*. The chaconne was chiefly used by the French as a large dance movement to round off an act of an opera or a *comédie-ballet*, but it was taken over with conspicuous success by keyboard composers.

The magnificent Passacaille in d'Anglebert's G Minor Suite is not actually in rondeau form, but it shows a similar method of building up a lengthy piece from repeated eight-measure phrases, interspersed with choruslike refrains. It is easy to imagine this splendid music as an accompaniment to monumental baroque dance.

The Dance Idioms

The French court imbued dancing with great cultural and even political significance, and many dances had their distinctive characteristics honed and standardized at Versailles. You should aim to become familiar with these idioms, since dance characteristics permeate many movements even when not indicated in the titles. There is scope here for some enjoyable detective work.

Bear in mind, however, that dances became liable to **stylization** with the passage of time: their distinctive features of rhythm and texture became exaggerated or even overlaid, and movements became more complex and lengthy, once music was no longer intended for dancing, but for listening. This stylization particularly affected dances such as the sarabande and courante, which had traditionally been mainly danced by professional dancers (although Louis XIV's favorite dance is said to have been the courante). The social dances, such as the minuet and gavotte, retained their essential simplicity longer.

Some modern time signatures are used in the following summary, since these are often found in modern editions; but it should be noted that in the baroque period 2/4 and 3/4 were Italian time signatures, only hesitantly introduced into French practice. French composers clung to the old binary and ternary signatures that simply used the single figures 2 and 3. The binary 2 seems to have indicated a lively tempo, but the ternary 3, often used for courantes and sarabandes, is less brisk than the Italian 3/4.

ALLEMANDE (C, 2, OR 4/4)

In the first generation, allemandes tend to have fairly simple, chord-based textures, but the mature eighteenth-century allemande usually features continuous sixteenth-note motion somewhere in its texture. This motion passes from one part of the keyboard to another, although there is never a strict number of voices, and it suggests rather than states an interesting contrapuntal activity, which the player should project appropriately. Some of Couperin's most elevated movements are in the allemande style—for example *La castelane* in *Ordre* 11, *La superbe ou La Forqueray* in *Ordre* 17, or the touching and possibly autobiographical *La convalescente* in *Ordre* 26, which is in the anguished key of F-sharp minor.

COURANTE

Most students are aware of the two types of courante, the **French** (in 3, 3/2, or 6/2) and the **Italian** (in 3/4). The nomenclature is, however, not strictly limiting—both types were used by composers of several nationalities. The simpler Italian corrente, written in a fairly chordal texture with a melodic bias, presents few problems to the player: but the true French courante is full of subtlety and rhythmic ambiguity, deriving from its six-beat measures, internally grouped (and articulated) as either 2×3 or 3×2. There is a fascinating tension between the twos and the threes—indeed, different groupings occasionally occur simultaneously in the two hands. Pay particular attention to the way the eighth notes are beamed together: a good edition will reproduce the original groupings shown by the composer, which (according to some authorities) may reveal how he wished the measures to be subdivided. Aim for flexibility of phrase within a regular overall pace: a courante should never sound stiff. A courante by Chambonnières is studied in detail in chapter 7. Bach's courantes, incidentally, are carefully inscribed *courante* or *corrente* according to their type—a symptom of his meticulous awareness of stylistic roots.

SARABANDE (3, 3/4)

One of the many dances that started life as a quick movement, the sarabande gradually became stylized into a slower tempo, as the music ceased to be used for actual dancing. The mature French sarabande is the jewel in the crown of dances, being conspicuous for its nobility and expressive gravity. There is a tendency for long notes to occur on the second beat, reflecting a physical movement in the dance itself. More melodic in character than the preceding dances, the sarabande may be sumptuously ornamented and supported by sonorous chords. Many composers used a particularly rich harmonic palette for this dance, drawing on minor-mode harmony at poignant points, such as just before the first double bar. Hemiola may also be found, especially in precadential measures.

The sarabande was in fact the *last* movement of the archetypal Froberger partita, and it occasionally occupies this position in the suites of Louis Couperin and Chambonnières. (Purcell also adopted this practice.)

GAVOTTE AND BOURRÉE

Both the gavotte and bourrée are 2/2 movements, but the gavotte has two quarter note upbeats and the bourrée only one.

MENUET (MINUET)

The minuet (3, 3/4) was the commonest of all the French dances, and its texture was generally simple, often consisting largely of one note in each hand. In the eighteenth century there was an increasing tendency for minuets to appear in pairs; or an alternating minuet and trio may be indicated. The **passepied** (3/8) is a quicker version of the minuet, and also often appeared in pairs.

GIGUE

The tradition for this dance seems to have originated in England rather than on the continent, and there is a continuous, if tenuous, strand of development from the virginalist jigg. There is always an element of triple rhythm, although the *moto perpetuo* gigue (as commonly found in eighteenth-century music, such as Handel's suites or Bach's Fifth French Suite) is basically an Italian type. One thinks of this dance as having the characteristic lilt of compound rhythm, but this is not a constant feature: in fact, some of the gigues by d'Anglebert and Elisabeth Jaquet de la Guerre are so crowded in texture as almost to defy a lilting style of performance.

An imitative, quasi-fugato element made its appearance in the baroque gigue from the outset: it can be observed in the work of Froberger, while the gigue in the G Minor Suite of Chambonnières contains an actual canon. In addition, composers often inverted the fugato motif, or introduced a new motif, in the second half of the binary structure. This can be seen in the 6/4 gigue in Couperin's Eighth *Ordre*. (Bach built on this idea: the gigue in his Fourth Partita has a new second-half motif that is eventually combined contrapuntally with the original motif from the first half.) Whatever motif or rhythmic pattern the composer is using, the player should project it as clearly as possible.

OTHER DANCES

The **loure** (slow 6/4), **rigaudon** (2/2), **canaries** (6/8), and other occasional dances may also be found in the work of many composers. The **pavan** and **gaillard(e)**, although by then archaic, were still occa-

150

sionally found in the later part of the seventeenth century. Chambon-nières has a splendidly old-fashioned three-strain pavanne in his Suite in G Minor; Louis Couperin's gaillardes are full of rhythmic interest.

Any one of the entire range of French dances may have written-out **doubles**—variants of the original statement of the dance, with some elaboration of texture, especially in the right-hand part. Doubles offer interesting evidence about how musical material can be decorated in improvised variants.

Suites and Ordres

The first generation of French composers usually included in their suites the core dances of allemande, courante, sarabande, and gigue, plus possibly one or two extra movements, particularly the chaconne. There might, however, be more than one specimen of any particular dance, or it might not be represented at all. In the eighteenth century the scope was widened considerably, and the galant, lighter-textured dances such as the minuet, passepied, bourrée, and gavotte, and the newly-evolved character piece, became popular. The grouping of all these movements into suites was a fairly arbitrary matter—it was often done by key rather than with any clearly defined notion of artistic unity, and there was (and is) no obligation to play all the items at any one time.

Couperin used the term *ordre* rather than *suite*, and this distinction may refer to the fact that his collections of movements, especially in his first book of 1713, are sometimes large (*Ordre* 2 has twenty-two items) and frequently unorthodox. His character pieces usually bear the title "La *xxx*" (not necessarily a reference to a female person—it may simply be an abbreviation of "La pièce *xxx*"). As noted above, these character pieces may themselves be in concealed dance idioms; for instance, *Les moissonneurs* in Couperin's Sixth *Ordre* is a gavotte en rondeau. Couperin's movements owed their origin to a rich variety of personalities and sources; the ascriptions of the pieces in all his twenty-seven *ordres* are discussed in Mellers (1987). The composer was also greatly fascinated by the theater and by the Parisian street fairs, and many of his pieces are related to their picturesque activities.[7]

One isolated type of movement, not a dance but of particular interest, is the **tombeau**—a piece usually written by a pupil as a tribute to his departed teacher. Tombeaux were more common among lutenists and gamba players than among the *clavecinistes*, but d'Anglebert's lament for his master Chambonnières (which concludes his Fourth Suite) is a magnificent, eloquent example that needs the ability to sustain a very slow tempo in a richly ornamented style. Both Froberger and Louis Couperin wrote a *Tombeau pour M. Blancrocher*, a notorious Parisian scapegrace; the descending scale that concludes Froberger's clearly bears a symbolic significance. Louis Couperin's is a piece of great originality.

Keyboard Textures and Timbres

The French have always been masters of instrumental timbre, and their interest in the picturesque both stimulated and was served by the use of harpsichord color. Clavecin composers reveled in the qualities of the instruments at their disposal, and the sumptuous sonority of the Taskin or Hemsch harpsichord in its lower range gave rise to some particularly fine pieces. Incidentally several composers, including Gaspard le Roux and Couperin (Allemande, *Ordre* 9), wrote pieces for two instruments.[8]

The rustic **musette** inspired a colorful style of writing that is particularly easy for the beginner. Such pieces borrow the drone idiom of the bagpipe (musette), which is expressed in the left hand by some such repeated figure, as the one in example 14-3. The key of A was particularly favored for this device, since the low A on the keyboard lies very near to the natural resonance frequency of the French harpsichord's cavity. In his Fifteenth *Ordre* Couperin writes two musette movements in this key, where the carefully written left-hand part elicits a progressive build-up of tone that can be most impressive. A simpler but very effective musette, often quoted in anthologies, is found in *La Malesherbe* of Balbastre. Musettes will leave you plenty of attention to spare for the artistic articulation of the right-hand part: however, you can also break up the resonance of the left-hand *bourdon* (drone) if you wish by dividing it into phrases.

Example 14-3. François Couperin, *Muséte de Taverni* (*Ordre* 15), ostinato left-hand figure.

Most musettes are hypnotic and hurdy-gurdy-like, but they could also be delicate and expressive, since the instrument was taken up by ladies of the French court in a fashionable idealization of the rural idyll. This type is illustrated by Rameau's musette in his E Minor-Major Suite (1711), which is marked *tendre*—a typical and significant French mark-

Figure 10. Harpsichord by Jean-Antoine(?) Vaudry, 1681. An early French double with reversed keys (i.e., black naturals). Notice the empty space below each manual: the key dip is limited by a rack at the back of the key (not visible). The knob above the left-hand end of the upper manual controls a register by sliding right or left. The painted soundboard and the chinoiserie of the case and lid could be found on any French harpsichord, but "barley-sugar" (as opposed to cabriole) legs indicate a seventeenth-century instrument. *Photograph reproduced by courtesy of the Board of Trustees of the Victoria and Albert Museum, London.*

ing, unique in European music at this time. **Tambourins**, by contrast, are cheerful and boisterous. Here, the repeated left-hand figure is usually a chord pattern that simulates the rhythmic drumming of Breton folk music. A good example is found in Daquin's G Major *Ordre*.

In the **pièce croisée**, the hands are not so much crossed, as in a Scarlatti sonata, as superimposed: this involves a double-manual instrument, with two uncoupled eight-foot registers, the two hands playing in the same part of the keyboard (usually the middle) but on separate keyboards. This arrangement, as well as being comfortable to the player, is interesting to the ear, as the different tone colors of the two eight-foots entwine. Couperin's *Le tic-toc-choc ou Les maillotins* (*Ordre* 18) and *Les bagatelles* (*Ordre* 10) are well-known examples. The composer indicates that these pieces may be played on a one-manual harpsichord by playing certain marked left-hand passages an octave lower, although something is inevitably lost in the process.

No account of French clavecin style would be complete without mention of **style brisé**. "Broken style," which suggests mere arpeggios, is a misleading translation that does not convey the great expressive potential of this texture. Rather, chords are fragmented and selectively sustained to suggest contrapuntal interest. Example 9-3 illustrates how the unique *brisé* sonority is created by carrying over certain notes of a chord into the next harmony. This enriches the texture with dissonant suspensions, or creates evocatively melting effects. Keyboard notation is able to show *style brisé* with precision: this gives it the advantage over lute music, in which this style was pioneered. (Lute notation can show the point at which each note begins, but not its duration. In *brisé* lute textures, each note is left to resonate as long as the instrument permits.)

Couperin's first prelude in *L'art de toucher le clavecin* (from which Example 9-3 is taken) is a valuable piece for the beginner to study. Although the harmony is divided among four parts, only one note (occasionally two) changes at any time: the other notes are held down, contributing to the halo of sound. Because of this, the piece is technically easy, but one needs to be meticulously careful to sustain all the overlapping notes for their entire length, as the complete harmony can only sound when the correct dampers are off the strings. Couperin developed a system of finger substitution—i.e., changing fingers while a key is held down—to promote this sonority and ensure a resonant legato. (Organists will be familiar with this technique, but it is not generally appropriate to the harpsichord.)

Pieces in *style brisé* tend to be concentrated in one area of the keyboard—often a low one, but occasionally in the treble. *Les baricades mis-*

térieuses from Couperin's Sixth *Ordre* is one of the most famous pieces in *style brisé*. Hardly penetrating the top two octaves of the keyboard, this piece has the capacity to conjure a rich sound from even a mediocre instrument. There are many theories to account for the title, an evocation of the Maze at Versailles being perhaps the most plausible; but whatever its intention, it remains one of the greatest baroque keyboard pieces, its impressionistic texture revealing new facets with each playing.

You should become thoroughly at home with the *style brisé* before attempting any of the amazing **unmeasured preludes** that stand at the head of suites by Louis Couperin, d'Anglebert, Clérambault, Marchand, and Rameau.[9] These unique movements are written in a stylized notation without bar-lines, and the composer invites the player to realize them according to his taste and fancy. Those of Louis Couperin are written entirely in whole notes, with beautifully engraved slurs *(tenues)* to suggest how these notes should be grouped into melodic phrases or sustained in harmonic progressions. Eloquent appoggiaturas, suspended dissonances, and strands of melody can be teased out of this impressionistic web of notation by a skilled player who can sense the drift of the music. To coax these elements into a convincing sequence is one of the most stimulating challenges in the entire harpsichord repertory.

The other composers mentioned above offer a little more help to the player; they indicate recitative-like melodic phrases in normal note values, as well as chord sequences, although the structure is still unbarred. When you feel moved to explore this esoteric corner of French keyboard culture, Clérambault's unmeasured preludes in his two suites are quite approachable examples. In fact, Clérambault's suites as a whole offer the beginner an easy introduction to French baroque style.

These improvisatory preludes had, like all preludes, a practical function. They enabled the performer to warm up, assess the tuning of his instrument, and outline the tonality in which he would play. They might also have a deeper rhetorical significance, however, suggested by the lute preludes of Gaulthier and the toccatas of Froberger, on which they are partly modeled.

Couperin indicated that all the preludes in *L'art de toucher le clavecin*—including the first prelude, referred to above—should be played in a similar improvisatory style, unless they are marked *mesuré* (measured).

The Later Use of the Clavecin

The composers of the first generation, and even to some extent Couperin, had tended either to confine themselves within one distinct area of the keyboard—upper, lower, or middle—in each piece, or to juxtapose different registers deliberately in repetitions or echoes. This disciplined approach suggests a parallel to the doctrine of the unities (of place, of time, of action) observed in the classical French drama of Racine and his contemporaries. Rameau's clavecin textures, however, were more ambitious and varied. His movements often range continuously and fluently over the entire five-octave keyboard and display highly imaginative writing. The innovative *Les Trois Mains* features a roving left hand, which can serve as either bass or treble. He also divides long arpeggiated figures between the two hands, by marking *d* (*droit*, or right) and *g* (*gauche*, or left). Sometimes, as for example in *Les Tourbillons,* this is done in a novel and challenging fashion.

All these features can be seen in Rameau's superb *Pièces de Clavecin en Concert* (1741), which were the first French ensemble pieces to have a fully notated keyboard part. Indeed, the keyboard is the main protagonist; the role of the other instruments (violin or other melody instrument, gamba or other bass instrument) is often merely to fill out the exquisite textures. Rameau himself arranged some of the contents of the five *Concerts* as pieces for harpsichord solo.

Daquin's work shows a similar desire to exploit interesting keyboard textures: *Les Trois Cadances* makes a feature of simultaneous triple trills, and the rushing scales of *Les Vents en Courroux* give a splendid impression of boisterous, angry winds. Both these pieces demand considerable virtuosity. Much of Daquin's charming writing is, however, accessible to the less advanced player.

The way was now open for the final generation of writers—in particular Duphly and Balbastre, who also commanded considerable keyboard virtuosity, and whose music often shows the unmistakable influence of Rameau. The work of this final generation of *clavecinistes* is full of interest, displaying a strong tension between the remains of the traditional French style and the rise of the early classical idiom and pianistic style. Many composers use both styles: one can observe the contrast between Duphly's *La Forqueray*, an example of the old French idiom, and his *La de Drummond* (possibly a spiritual ancestor of Beethoven's *Für Elise?*), which prefigures early pianistic style. The great chaconne from his third book of pieces shows the typical chaconne spirit and the harmonic types of the old language, yet combines these convincingly with some pianistic textures near its end.

In general, however, it has to be admitted that the musical matter of the later *claveciniste* works is not always worthy of the brilliance of their manner. A fatal fascination with Alberti-bass textures and a tendency to indulge in showy but mechanical sequential writing becomes disturbingly apparent. One sometimes feels of this music that—like the *ancien régime* itself—the nearer its impending doom advances, the more hectic and trivial its round of pleasure becomes. The music of Armand-Louis Couperin, grandson of François, clearly displays this easygoing hedonism—it is agreeable music, but totally devoid of any spiritual depth. Armand-Louis deserves mention for his *Simphonie de clavecins* (1773) for two harpsichords with the new Taskin knee-levers, which facilitated changes of registration; his obvious interest in such technical innovations stems from his marriage into the Blanchet family of harpsichord builders. This type of development, however, can be seen in retrospect as decadent, and in any case it came too late to help avert the incipient decline of the instrument.

Duphly's chaconne, or Balbastre's great *La d'Héricourt*, may be viewed as epitaphs: final, passionate assertions of the nobility of the departed *grand siècle*. Duphly died, symbolically, on July 15th, 1789, the day following the outbreak of the French Revolution. By then, the great era of clavecin composition had closed; there had been no important publications for almost thirty years. New musical interests, emanating from Vienna and the south, were ousting the old idiom. The child Mozart played in Paris in 1764; the piano sonatas of Schobert and Eckhard captivated audiences at the increasingly popular public concerts, and a Haydn symphony was first heard at the Concerts Spirituels in 1773.

As far as the keyboard sonata was concerned, there was inevitably a period during which both piano and harpsichord were current, and during this period composers naturally tended, for commercial reasons, to describe their compositions as suitable for either instrument, and to write with a certain elasticity of style. This might be the place to point out that an Alberti bass is not totally incompatible with harpsichord style, as is sometimes stated. Other features of the classical idiom, however, favor the piano more exclusively. The firm of Érard began making pianos in Paris in 1780, and this proved the most popular way forward during the years immediately preceding the Revolution.

The music of revolutionary France—much of it grandiose outdoor music for enormous forces—opened up still further avenues, foreshadowing the romanticism of Berlioz. And yet, the era of Liberty, Equality, and Fraternity never produced music that understood itself so well as that of the *grand siècle*, or could express itself with such civilized elegance, economy, and clarity of focus.

Checklist of the Main French Clavecinistes

This list is arranged chronologically by dates of publications. Editions are listed below. The list should rightly be prefaced by the name of Froberger, who, though a German working in Vienna, did so much to promote the French suite style. He died in 1667, and his partitas date from around 1650.

> Louis Couperin (died 1661), undated MS sources only
> Jacques Champion de Chambonnières, 1670
> Nicolas le Bègue, 1671 and ?1687
> Jean-Henri d'Anglebert, 1689
> Charles Dieupart (mostly in London), 1701, 1705
> Louis Marchand, 1702
> Louis-Nicolas Clérambault, 1704
> Gaspard le Roux, 1705
> Elisabeth Jaquet de la Guerre, 1707
> François Couperin, 1713, 1716–1717, 1722, 1730
> Jean-Phillippe Rameau, 1706, 1724, 1731, 1741
> Jean-François Dandrieu, 1724, 1728, 1734
> François Dagincour, 1733
> Michel Corrette, 1734
> Louis-Claude Daquin, 1735
> Jacques Duphly, 1744, 1748, 1758, 1768
> Armand-Louis Couperin, 1751
> Claude-Bénigne Balbastre, 1759

RECOMMENDED EDITIONS AND FACSIMILES

> Froberger: Bärenreiter, Le Pupitre
> Louis Couperin: Oiseau-Lyre, Le Pupitre
> Chambonnières: Oiseau-Lyre, Fuzeau facsimile
> d'Anglebert: Le Pupitre
> Clérambault: Oiseau Lyre, Performers' Facsimiles
> Dieupart: Oiseau-lyre (with facsimile of his own arrangement of the suites for flute and harpsichord)
> de la Guerre: Oiseau-Lyre
> Couperin le Grand: Oiseau-Lyre, Fuzeau facsimile, Schott (specially recommended; the fingering is editorial, but there is a good fold-out chart of *agréments* and many facsimile pages). The old Augener edition by Brahms and Chrysander is far more reliable than its date would suggest and can certainly be used if necessary.

Beware only of the misprints in *Les tours de passe-passe*, (*Ordre* 22), where a clef has been mistranscribed.
Daquin: Faber Music
Rameau: Bärenreiter, Fuzeau facsimile
Duphly: Le Pupitre
Armand-Louis Couperin: Performers' Facsimiles
Balbastre: Le Pupitre, Performers' Facsimiles

Notes

1. Mellers 1987 gives an exceptionally good account of the ethos of French classical music.

2. Gustafson and Fuller 1990. A comprehensive catalog.

3. Ledbetter 1988 offers a full study of this influence.

4. I have preserved the original French of Couperin's day, including his capitalizations and accents, for the titles of his pieces. The acute é was in the eighteenth century often used instead of the grave è.

5. Organists were different: both François Roberday and Louis Couperin pursued distinguished contrapuntal paths in the seventeenth century. The Oldham MS, now released for publication by Oiseau-Lyre, contains many fine fugues by the latter.

6. The seventeenth-century French passacaille and chaconne, like the Italian passacaglia and ciaccona, discussed in chapter 13, did not differ greatly except in mode. The passacaille favored the minor mode, whereas the chaconne favored the major and had a subtle but unmistakeable aura of confidence and well-being.

7. Jane Clark's article "Les Folies Françoises" in *Early Music* (April 1980): 163-169, is well worth reading for its insight into this aspect of the life of the period.

8. Sloane 1995 catalogs works for two harpsichords.

9. Tilney 1995 offers a comprehensive study of the French unmeasured prelude, in three volumes: facsimile, suggested modern transcription, and commentary. The harpsichordist Davitt Moroney has also identified himself thoroughly with this style in broadcasts and lecture-recitals.

15

French Baroque Style in Performance

The musical style described in the previous chapter was unique in Europe throughout the baroque period. France's isolation in political matters, particularly under the reign of Louis XIV, was reflected to a large extent in its musical outlook, and to some extent the French set themselves up in deliberate opposition to their neighbors. After the death of *Le Roi Soleil* in 1715, a more liberal spirit in artistic matters gradually began to emerge, but the French continued to feel, or feign, indifference to the brilliant instrumental style that was sweeping in from Italy. They also conducted vigorous polemic wars about the relative merits of French and Italian opera, with foreseeable results. Perhaps the verve and virtuosity of Italian music, both vocal and instrumental, was simply too extroverted and direct for refined French taste, which under the influence of seventeenth-century court formality had tended to favor the subtle and understated. Couperin's deliberate essays in the Italian style in his chamber work *Les Goûts Réunis,* or his occasional use of Italian idioms in his harpsichord work (e.g., *Les papillons, Ordre* 2), only serve to emphasize that his Italian still bears a French accent.

France's musical insularity naturally went hand-in-hand with idiosyncracies of notation. For this reason, it is worth devoting a separate chapter to the way French baroque music is written and performed.

Inevitably, the absolutism of the court of Louis XIV was reflected in its musical life. For instance, the detailed organization of the court's string ensembles was famous and envied throughout Europe; the *Vingt-quatre Violons du Roi* boasted a highly refined style of execution, in which particular attention was paid to neat and uniform bowing and to different types of bow stroke. The great subtlety and panache they achieved can now be savored once more in the performance of period orchestras, and as a harpsichord player you can apply much of what you observe to making your own performance equally vivid. You can learn a great deal about articulation by observing the bow strokes of the baroque violin: you can also aim to imitate, in harpsichord terms, the way the string player conveys arresting gestures by means of varied shading, attack, and release. Indeed, to think of all French music as consisting to some extent of **gesture** will bring many useful insights to your playing.

To my mind, however, the most exciting development in present-day historical performance practice is the increasing awareness of the tremendous expressive potential within eighteenth-century French style. As performers explore deeper below the polished surface of the music, unlocking its sheer passion and sensuousness, they discover a new dimension in a style that once had a reputation for mere rococo prettiness. To listen to good performers of French chamber music, on viol, baroque flute, or violin, can be a revelation. The *enflé* of the viol player—a bow-stroke that starts with a crescendo and leaves the string vibrating—or the nuances of the Hotteterre flute can inspire you to search for equally seductive sounds on your harpsichord: through subtleties of spread chords, through sensitive shading of appoggiaturas, or through sumptuous sostenutos. If your playing of French music sounds pale or prim, be assured that there are a few more expressive effects waiting for you to discover.

Ornamentation

Ornaments—called *agréments* by the French—are dealt with in detail in chapter 18, but a few important observations about French usage follow.

- There were two basic methods for notating ornamentation. Most composers used the Chambonnières symbols, as amplified by Couperin, but a few people (including Rameau) preferred d'Anglebert's, which derive more closely from the lute symbols. Consequently, different composers may use different signs for the same purpose. It is always advisable to look at the composer's ornament table if possible, even if you come back to this book afterward.

• The nuances of French ornamentation take a little time to master, but you will get a lot of help from listening to good harpsichordists. Viola da gamba playing also offers an excellent model—look for performances of viol music by Marin Marais or Forqueray. Many ornaments have their roots in gesture and expression. As befits a style with origins in lute music, French ornamentation is as often tender and pensive as it is brilliant and assertive. Rapid or aggressive performance of ornaments is clearly out of place in a movement marked *languissament.*

• You will gradually build up an awareness of the kind of mood and context appropriate to particular ornaments, and this will ease your way through the confusing maze of symbols. For instance, upper-note shakes tend to occur in descending passages, lower-note ones in ascending. This awareness will also ensure that eventually your ornaments blend naturally and expressively into the textures, instead of sounding like uneasy excrescences. (Incidentally, ornaments flow easily on a good French style harpsichord action.)

• Couperin laid special emphasis on the importance of performing the *agréments* in his music exactly as indicated, without addition or alteration. This might be taken to imply that some performers graced what they played in accordance with their own taste.

Rhythmic Conventions

The gap that lies between notation and actual performance in so much baroque music is nowhere more apparent than in the French treatment of rhythm. A full study of the way in which rhythmic patterns were modified by the French might be a little daunting for the beginner, and it is only fair to say that certain points are the subject of considerable controversy. You can sample the arguments in, for example, Neumann's *Essays in Performance Practice* or Donington's *The Interpretation of Early Music.*[1] These two giants of the performance practice scene have for over two decades honed their ideas by the amicable hurling of polemical rocks in each other's general direction. There is no need, however, to be deterred by the subtleties of their arguments, interesting as they are to the specialist. In practice, you will find that a few simple observations based on the general consensus will suffice.

• One kind of rhythmic alteration about which there is little disagreement is the practice of playing **notes inégales**. This was an established part of the French musical scene for well over a century, and a convention that was understood by all practical musicians.[2] It meant that, in situations where there are pairs of conjunct notes of half-beat duration (for example, sixteenth notes in 3/8 or 6/8, eighth notes in 3—the French equivalent of 3/4—or quarter notes in 3/2), the two notes of the pair were not played quite equally. The same effect may occasionally apply to notes a quarter beat in duration, e.g., sixteenth notes in 4/4 or C—although not generally in allemandes.

The first (main) note of each pair is lengthened slightly, and the second (which is usually a passing note) is shortened, to give a gently lilting effect. The inequality is not so extreme as a dotted rhythm—more like a lazy, sinuous triplet: the sources stress this mildness of effect. (*Inégalité* may even strike the listener as an alternation of heavier and lighter, rather than of longer and shorter, notes.) Within this general range, experiment with different degrees of *inégalité;* discover how it brings suavity and elegance to the most routine passages.

The composer may or may not indicate *inégalité:* if he does, the words *notes inégales, lourer,* or *pointer* will appear. It is not, however, applicable if the composer writes *notes égales, marqué,* or *mesuré,* or if the movement of the half-beat notes is spread out into arpeggios or large leaps. Also notice that dots over notes are another eighteenth-century method of showing that *inégalité* is not to be used: take care that you do not equate them with the modern staccato sign.

The best way to learn the feel of this rhythmic alteration is to listen to recordings (which should be fairly recent ones) with a score in hand. Many editions now give sensible advice on when and how to apply the convention. Apply your own common sense, too. For example, if a few disjunct notes appear in a mainly conjunct phrase, it will sound ludicrous only to apply the inequality to the conjunct notes. Be guided by the overall character of the passage.

• Occasionally, **inverted inégalité** is effective; that is, pairs of apparently equal notes are played short-long, giving the effect of slightly exaggerated, swaggering appoggiaturas. Composers were not consistent, or even clear, about the way in which this kind of inequality was indicated, but marks that we would assume to show ordinary phrased pairs may in suitable contexts be treated thus; when in doubt, be guided by the editor of your music. If you decide to use inverted inequality, do it with style. Conviction covers a multitude of sins, but if you sound doubtful no one will be impressed, even if you are theoretically correct.

163

- A further kind of rhythmic alteration, often referred to as **double-dotting**, is more familiar. In strong, stately movements containing many dotted rhythms, the dots are exaggerated, so that the shorter notes become very short. If there are two values of shorter note in different parts, play them simultaneously at the last possible moment. It is quite in order to sharpen the effect by including some silence between the long note and the short one(s) that follow.

Where there are flourishes or runs leading up to the beat, treat these in the same manner by leaving them as late as you can, so that speed gives them maximum brilliance. You need not worry about playing the rhythm of flourishes precisely—they were not always notated exactly, or even mathematically correctly. Many of Couperin's flourishes have no less than six beams, the engraver's wonderful calligraphy conveying a sense of sweep and urgency far more effectively than any literal rendering of the rhythm could ever do.

Movements written mainly in dotted rhythms can pose problems on the harpsichord, and they need to be played with particular confidence and cleanness. There is a temptation always to slur the short note to the long one, because it is easiest to do: but if done constantly this tends to impart a lurching effect to the music, whereas poise and buoyancy is more likely required. Distinguish clearly between the floating effect produced by example 15-1a; the sharp rhythmic effect gained by articulating each note and substituting a rest for part of the value of the dot (as would a good period orchestra playing a French overture), as in example 15-1b; and the arresting effect produced by slurring across the beat, as in example 15-1c. The latter should only be used where indicated: for example, in *L'olimpique,* in *Ordre* 9, where Couperin's detailed marking shows the (relatively few) places where he wants the shorter note slurred to the longer.

Example 15-1a, b, c.

- A further rhythmic convention that should be noted is **hemiola**, which originated in Italian music of the late renaissance but is widespread in French baroque style. Hemiola implies the merging of two 3/4 bars into one long 3/2 measure, or the regrouping of a 6/8 measure into 3/4. Sometimes the composer signals the presence of hemiola beyond all doubt by omitting the middle bar line, but generally you must look for typical rhythms in the melody, or the kind of shape in the bass-line shown in example 15-2. Here the bass should be clearly slurred in pairs. Hemiola causes a shift of accent that points elegantly to the cadence. It often takes the place of a big ritardando before the final cadence, which most performers now consider foreign to baroque performance style.

Example 15-2. François Couperin, *L'artiste* (*Ordre* 19), m. 36. Typical hemiola formation.

Although this rhythmic regrouping is usually said to be typical of the courante, it is common in all French triple-meter music. For instance, in many seventeenth-century gigues, with six quarter notes to the measure, the triple rhythm can operate at quarter- or half-note level in different measures. The buoyant rhythmic effect of hemiola in quick movements can be further sharpened by making distinct gaps in any dotted rhythms (example 15-3).

becomes approximately

Example 15-3. Élisabeth Jacquet de la Guerre, Courante in G Major, mm. 17–18.

Conventions of Repetition

Practically all French dance movements are in binary form, with two double bars and repeats (many earlier composers wrote *reprise* after the double bar, to clarify the middle point to which one should return). Movements such as the passacaille have internal repeats, especially for the rondeau section. In all these cases the repeats should ideally be observed; to do so will reveal the true proportions of the work, and give time for its ideas to make their full impact. Some performers reduce the scale of French baroque music to a minimum by omitting repeats and then wonder why it sounds slight.

In binary movements, one can often with advantage change manuals for the repeats. Consider the schemes I, II, I, II or I, II, II, I, or II, I, I, II. (In all these schemes, the lower manual, I, could optionally be coupled to II.) In rondeau movements, the episodes (**couplets**) can often be played on a different manual. Consider, too, I+II for the rondeau, II for the couplets. The ease with which one can contrast the full tone of I+II with the more acute tone of II alone is a feature of the French harpsichord that should not be overlooked.

Originally a variety of decorative signs indicated the points to which one returned in a rondeau: these of course are preserved in facsimile editions. Matching the pairs of signs poses a fascinating challenge to the player, particularly when one is sight reading.

When there is a **petite reprise**—a procedure whereby the last strain, or few bars, of the piece are repeated a further time—this should certainly be observed. Composers use it sparingly, but tellingly: it can form an elegiac or wistful coda, or serve to balance the proportions of the piece. Return to the point at which *petite reprise* is marked, or to where there is a *da capo* sign in the music (figure 11). In *La rafrâichissante* (*Ordre* 9) Couperin writes out a decorated *petite reprise*, which offers useful ideas about how one can improvise varied repeats.

White Notation

A few select movements by Couperin and other composers are printed in white notation—that is, an open-headed font of print lacking the black coloration. Eighth notes, for instance, look like half notes, although they may be beamed together in a group. There is no certain reason why composers should have perpetuated this convention, which is an obscure relic of pre-1600 notational usage. Perhaps it sprung from a desire to mystify the uninitiated by using an apparent trade (or guild) secret. Although this description sounds complex, a little common sense applied to the score will soon sort out how the rhythms function in practice.

A good example of white notation is found in the great set of character pieces that conclude Couperin's Eleventh *Ordre*. Here, the notation may visually underpin his references to the ancient "Ménéstrandise" of Paris (the minstrel's guild: thinly disguised by the composer as "Mxnxstrxndxsx"). By Couperin's time, this guild had degenerated into an association of rather disreputable street musicians, jugglers, and their picturesque hangers-on. In the fourth *Acte* of the *ordre*, which is in white notation, the dotted rhythms of the right hand represent "les disloqués," while the halting rhythms of the left hand portray the limping "boi-teux," worn out in the service of their guild. The fifth *Acte* depicts the

Figure 11. Sarabande in C Minor by Clérambault, from *Premier Livre de Pièces de Clavecin,* 1703. (mm. 5-8 of this piece are transcribed in music example 14-1). There are several features to note. The key signature has two flats for C minor instead of three, in spite of appearances, the E-flat being repeated in the upper octave. This is typical of baroque practice; beware of supplying A-flats (e.g. m. 10, where both hands have A-*natural*). The baritone clef, F3, is used for the left hand—the top line is middle C. Half and quarter notes are superimposed where parts coincide (mm. 3, 4, 7). The sharp is used to cancel the flat of the key signature (mm. 2, 4, 7). Note the wavy tie-mark in m. 13; the *petite reprise,* whereby the last part of the second strain is repeated again—the second-time measure leads back to the sign in m. 18; and the *hemiolas* in mm. 18–19 and 22–23, of which the first has an eloquent diminished third in the bass. *Reproduced by arrangement with Performers' Facsimiles, New York (in vol. 22 in the series).*

whole shabby troupe being driven away, pursued by "drunkards, monkeys and bears." Couperin's brilliant musical satire is given extra edge by the fact that Louis XIV had, in an unwise moment, proposed that Parisian harpsichord teachers should be required to be members of the minstrels' guild. Court musicians understandably objected to being classed with street hurdy-gurdy players and near-vagabonds, and many petitions and even lawsuits ensued before the king's order was eventually rescinded. Trade union problems are nothing new.

Suggestions for Further Reading

Michel de Saint-Lambert, *Les Principes du Clavecin* (Paris, 1702). English translation by Rebecca Harris-Warrick, *Principles of the Harpsichord* (Cambridge, 1984). Valuable for study of French performance practice before about 1700.

François Couperin, *L'art de toucher le clavecin* (Paris, 1716). English translation by Margery Halford, *The Art of Playing the Harpsichord* (New York, 1974). This edition is preferable to others available.

Howard Ferguson, *Early French Keyboard Music* (Oxford: Oxford University Press, 1966). The preface to these anthology volumes is excellent, giving useful guidance about *notes inégales* and ornaments.

Wilfred Mellers, *François Couperin and the French Classical Tradition* (London, 1987). This revised edition by Faber and Faber is preferred.

Notes

1. Neumann 1982; Donington 1974.

2. There are many primary source references to *inégalité*. (Fuller's article in *The New Harvard Dictionary of Music*, 549–51, has no less than 85.) The two following may be taken as typical: "In melodies of which the sounds move step-wise, sometimes the first half beats are made a little long" (Loulié 1696). "We dot several eighth notes in succession moving by conjunct motion, [although] we write them in equal time values" (Couperin 1716/1974). "Dot" is here used approximately.

16

The German Style

To understand the Germany of the seventeenth and eighteenth centuries, we must imagine a vast patchwork quilt of small units, ruled over variously by princes, dukes, bishops, counts, electors, town councils, and so on. It would be fruitless to look for the kind of cultural unity that existed in France. Nevertheless, once they had recovered from the devastating ravages of the Thirty Years' War, many German rulers looked enviously at Versailles and sought to model their much smaller courts on its prestigious style. French music thus came to have a profound formative effect in Germany; so, a little later, did Italy, whither ambitious princes sent their musicians for training, and from whence they eagerly imported opera and the concerto style.

Many elements of German style, then, are derivative. What is left that is distinctively German? More than one might suppose. In the first place, the **chorale** heritage, which was naturally the pillar of church music, also made itself felt in domestic music making. Family music was an officially encouraged part of the Lutheran tradition and has always been a strong German characteristic. Buxtehude, Walther, and many others wrote harpsichord partitas on chorale melodies for domestic use as a matter of course; although these could also be played *manualiter* on the organ, they are nevertheless genuine items of the harpsichord repertory. Kuhnau, in his ambitious *Biblical sonatas* of 1700, could include a movement based on the Passion chorale in his *Sickness and Recovery of King Hezekiah* (a sonata well worth investigating) without doubting that the melodic quotation would be understood.

A further Germanic characteristic was a decided taste for writing **fugues**; not the serenely elevated counterpoint of the Italian *stile antico* as noted in chapter 13, but fugues with busy, rambling subjects, which fill page after page with exuberant sixteenth notes. The fugues in Bach's youthful but very fine harpsichord toccatas show him flexing his contrapuntal muscles, and drawing on his knowledge of Froberger, Böhm, and Buxtehude. It was only after his arrival in Weimar that this copious flow of notes yielded to other, more mature influences, including the streamlining discipline of academic Italian counterpoint. The end product was the greatest fugue writing ever known—the fugues of *The Well-tempered Clavier*. In these independent keyboard fugues, musical expression reaches a philosophical stature.[1]

The procedures of fugue can also be applied in other musical contexts, one of which is the **overture**, whose second section is fugal. The French orchestral overture entered German culture by way of the ducal courts, which were keen to imitate the instrumental style fashionable at Versailles. Transcriptions of orchestral overtures became a popular keyboard genre, and composers also produced original keyboard works in this style.

The French **suite**, originating in the work of the French lutenists and developed for keyboard by Froberger, was also disseminated through the German courts in the later part of the seventeenth century. Under the aegis of the courts, the keyboard suite enjoyed a lengthy vogue, and German composers often used the fashionable French title *Pièces de clavecin*. Georg Böhm and J. C. F. Fischer were notable exponents of the French style: their suites contain some charming movements and are well worth playing. As well as his earlier *Pièces de clavessin* Op. 2 (1696), Fischer wrote nine *Parnassus* suites, each bearing the title of an Olympian deity. Written in 1738, they are ambitious and interesting works. As late as 1777, the theorist Kirnberger was still extolling the qualities of the suite: his *Recueil d'airs de danse caractéristiques* shows a Germanic view of the typical French dances, inevitably somewhat metamorphosed by the passage of time. This is nevertheless a pleasant collection, composed as a linked keyboard sequence and fairly easy to play. It is available in several modern editions.

French influence came from the west; Italian influence filtered naturally into Germany from Austria and the south, and first took root in the Catholic areas of southern Germany before spreading north. It is not surprising to learn that the ubiquitous Italian **toccata** had an important impact. Frescobaldi's toccatas inspired the fine toccatas of Froberger and in turn those of the Viennese Georg Muffat (although Muffat's toccatas fall on the organ side of the line that divides harpsichord and organ style—a line which in Catholic areas tended to be vaguer than in Protestant).

The chief musical ingredients of the toccata, apart from the fugal sections, were darting scale passages and recitative-like phrases interspersed with massive chords. Using the terminology of the Austrian Jesuit Athanasius Kircher, the Germans referred to this style as the *stylus phantasticus:* they made it very much their own, both in harpsichord and organ writing. Such flamboyant keyboard flourishes appealed greatly to Buxtehude, and it was possibly his organ music that commended them to Bach. In Bach's E Minor Harpsichord Toccata (BWV 914) we find a crowning example of the effects sparked by this incandescent style as it spread across Europe. Bach reveled in its impetuous declamatory phrases with built-in continuo punctuation, and its exciting tremolando chords (example 16-1).

Example 16-1. J. S. Bach, Toccata in E Minor, BWV 914, mm. 49–52.

In the eighteenth century, the musical language of Italy, especially the forms and idioms of string writing, swept through Germany, offering a strong challenge to the French style. The driving ostinato rhythms and lucid harmonic sequences of the Italian style disciplined and helped every German composer who came in contact with them: as pointed out above, they tightened up even the youthful Bach's prolix outpourings. Bach transcribed and arranged Vivaldi's concertos, and himself enriched the harpsichord repertory with both a concerto for solo instrument (the Italian Concerto) and the first real specimens of concertos for harpsichord and strings. In doing this, however, he was only giving particularly deliberate expression to tendencies that were widespread in German music. As well as the concerto, the four-movement Italian *sonata da chiesa* also attracted German composers, although naturally it had less effect on solo keyboard music.

In spite of these waves of foreign influence, Germany nevertheless managed to keep its own artistic head above water. For example, it was foremost in the development of the **praeludium**, a genre that reached its greatest heights in *The Well-tempered Clavier* but is found in the work of many other composers. The German type of prelude is not improvisatory like the free unmeasured French prelude: instead, it systematically explores a single motive, texture, or **affekt** (emotional characteristic)—a logical, typically Germanic procedure. Kuhnau's G Major Praeludium (an excellent piece for beginners, which appears in many anthologies) is an obvious essay in the patterned style that was later used by Bach for the first prelude in Book I of *The Well-tempered Clavier* (example 16-2).

Example 16-2. Johann Kuhnau, Praeludium in G Major, mm. 19–24.

Even in Kuhnau's small piece, one can see the particular Teutonic harmonic genius; it is rich in implied suspensions, marked as asterisks in the example. Playing a piece of this kind as block chords (i.e., not arpeggiated) will help you to work out which notes are essential to the chord and which are foreign (i.e., dissonant notes suspended from the preceding chord). The ones marked with a double asterisk in this piece—suspensions in the highest or lowest part—can be highlighted by holding them down slightly.

Bach's wonderful harmonic style was built on three foundations.

Much of its expressiveness derives from the eloquent harmony that he encountered in his study of French music. The architectural sense of key balance that characterizes his style is developed from the Italian concerto idiom; while the strength and seriousness of his harmonic language owes at least something to the German inheritance of the chorale. Indeed, practically every element in his mature work represents a crowning of his predecessors' achievements, a consummation of all that the French, Italian, and native German styles had developed during the previous century. It is consequently difficult to write about Bach without implying that all the music that preceded him was in some respect inferior, although I have tried to avoid giving any such impression. The sheer magnitude of his genius, however, needs to be emphasized to every new generation of harpsichord players and listeners, and it is therefore right to end this section with a summary of Bach's harpsichord output. It should by now be evident that any French or Italian elements in the music call for appropriate treatment in performance, and identifying these elements can offer you another good opportunity for detective work.

A Checklist of Bach's Harpsichord Music

Numbers, where given, are from Schmieder's thematic catalogue of Bach's works (BWV). The Neue Bachausgabe (NBA) Bärenreiter, Kassel (1984) is the standard text of Bach's music: reprints of individual items and sets are made from it by Bärenreiter and Breitkopf. Henle Urtext is an acceptable edition with editorial fingering. The Associated Board of the Royal Schools of Music produces editions of many standard works, including an excellent recent edition of *The Well-tempered Clavier*. For addresses of suppliers, see appendix B.

- *Clavierbüchlein für Anna Magdalena Bach* and *Clavierbüchlein für Wilhelm Friedemann Bach*. These instruction books for Anna Magdalena Bach and Wilhelm Friedemann Bach offer useful material for the beginner, and sometimes contain Bach's original fingering. The **Anna Magdalena** book contains music by Couperin, Böhm, and C. P. E. Bach as well as by her husband. The **Wilhem Friedemann** book contains the **Kleine Praeludien und Fugen** (BWV 924–930), the twelve two-part **Inventions** (BWV 772–786), which originally bore the title *Praeambulum*, and the twelve three-part **Sinfonias** (BWV 787–801), originally titled *Fantasia*. Both two-part and three-part sets are usually referred to as *Inventions* today; they are studies

173

in part-writing, extremely valuable for both technical and musical purposes, and quite searching to play. The *Kleine Praeludien und Fugen* and the other small preludes (BWV 933–943) are delightful little pieces, useful for the less experienced player.
- Seven **Toccatas** (BWV 910–916). These lengthy and often brilliant works incorporate fugal sections and sections in *stylus phantasticus*. They date from Bach's early years in Weimar.
- Six **French Suites** (BWV 812–817). This title is not Bach's, and numbers 1–5 had previously appeared in the Anna Magdalena instruction book, with some interesting manuscript additions of ornamentation, etc. The movements are largely French in style, although there are Italian *correntes* as well as French *courantes*, and a few exotics—for example the polonaise in the Sixth Suite (Polish dances were fashionable in the period after the unification of the Saxon and Polish monarchies). The gigue in the Second Suite, and the anglaise in the Third, actually exhibit some of the rhythmic qualities of English music of the period, such as the tendency to cadence on the last beat of the bar: how this came about is uncertain. The easier movements—minuets, gavottes, etc.—make a good introduction to Bach's style.
- Six **English Suites** (BWV 806–811). Again, the name is not Bach's, and there are no particular stylistic grounds for it, although many commentators note similarities between the First Suite in the set and the A Major Suite of Dieupart, published in England and copied by Bach. The grand first movements of these suites are cast in some of the major forms of the period—Italian concerto-ritornello form in numbers two and three, for example. The sarabandes are particularly rich and eloquent, some having fine written-out *doubles*. In general, all the movements tend to be more complex than the compact movements of the French Suites.
- Six **Partitas** (BWV 825–830). (Partita is another word widely used for suite in Germany.) These were published in 1731 as Part I of the *Clavierübung* (keyboard exercise). The Partitas are the most lengthy and highly stylized of all Bach's works in suite style, the furthest removed from functional dance music, and the most complex in texture. Again, the opening movements are on a monumental scale, with French overture, toccata, and concerto-ritornello represented.
- **The Well-tempered Clavier, Book I** (BWV 846–869, 1722); **Book II** (BWV 870–893, 1742). Written partly with the intention of demonstrating the merits of certain types of keyboard temperament (see

chapter 20; the didactic urge lies behind much of Bach's work). The preludes are self-consistent explorations of various idioms; the fugues display a wide range of devices and procedures, and breathtaking contrapuntal skills, but this work as a whole is not a compendium of fugue in the sense of *The Art of Fugue*. Nor is it exclusively intended for harpsichord—*Klavier* is a generic term for keyboard in German, and some of the items work well on organ or clavichord.

- The **Italian Concerto** (BWV 971) and the **French Overture** (BWV 831). Forming Part II of the *Clavierübung* (1735), the intention of these works is to display the two main national styles in conscious juxtaposition—though again, mere national characteristics are transcended. The French Overture is, like orchestral works of the period with the same name, an actual overture (dotted-rhythm opening, fugal section) followed by a suite of dances, including the lighter galant type. The Italian Concerto is notable for a first movement in ritornello style and an eloquent slow movement in which a wonderfully ornamented melody unfolds against a Vivaldian ostinato bass.

- The so-called **Goldberg Variations** (BWV 988). These form Part IV of the *Clavierübung* (1741): thirty variations on a sublimated sarabande theme that is first found in the Anna Magdalena book. The variations explore a variety of styles; some of them are very ambitious in texture, and require two keyboards as well as a formidable technique. Every third variation is in canon—first at the unison, then at the interval of the second, and so on.

- The **Chromatic Fantasia and Fugue** (BWV 903). The Fantasia is a wonderful piece of keyboard rhetoric, involving the player in many creative decisions: how to realize the arpeggiated chords, how to time the rapid 32nd-note interjections to best effect, and so on. It is definitely a work for the professional in performance (as are many of the great pieces), but is endlessly interesting to hear and explore.

To this list might be added:

- Many miscellaneous fugues, suite movements, and arrangements.

- The famous **Capriccio on the departure of his beloved Brother** (BWV 992)—an enjoyable youthful piece, with an exuberant fugue typical of Bach's early fugal style.

- Four **Duetti**, included in Part III of the *Clavierübung*, which is an organ collection; but these Duetti seem better suited to the harpsichord. They are rather esoteric but fascinating studies in two-part writing. There is a viable theory that they are musical illustrations of the Lutheran catechism,[2] which would place them in the domestic-religious tradition.

Ensemble Music with Harpsichord

When Bach was working as a Kapellmeister in Weimar, he came in contact with the practice of arranging Italian instrumental concertos for solo keyboard instrument, and the sixteen such arrangements he made himself (BWV 972–987) are important milestones in Bach's mastery of the Italian style. These arrangements led naturally to the writing of his own **concertos** for harpsichord and string ensemble—eight (BWV 1052–1059) for a single harpsichord, three (BWV 1060–1062) for two harpsichords, two (BWV 1063–1064) for three harpsichords, and one (BWV 1065) for four harpsichords. In this field, Bach was an undoubted pioneer, even though some of these works are still arranged from other music, either by Bach himself or by other composers such as Vivaldi. To this list should be added the famous Fifth Brandenburg Concerto (BWV 1050), which has an extended virtuoso cadenza in the first movement. This work was the result of Bach's visit to Berlin in 1719 to buy a new harpsichord for the Duke of Anhalt-Cöthen's musical establishment from the Berlin builder Michael Mietke. Bach himself played the solo part, which was obviously designed to show off the merits of the new acquisition.

Harpsichordists are also privileged to play a fully notated concertante part, rather than a continuo part, in much of Bach's **chamber music**. Six of the violin sonatas (BWV 1014–1019), two of the flute sonatas (BWV 1030, 1032), and all three sonatas for viola da gamba (BWV 1027–1029), have a concertante part. The quick contrapuntal movements are almost all written as trios, with two very active parts assigned to the two hands of the keyboard player and one part for the solo instrument; but the slow movements often have more individual textures.

Isolated works by other German composers also have written-out parts for the harpsichord: for example, Telemann's engaging trios in *Essercizii Musici* (1739–40), which combine concertante harpsichord with a variety of other instruments. The trios and other pieces are now available in a volume published in Broude's *Performers' Facsimiles* series. They are not so complex or demanding as those by Bach, but are written in a lighter galant idiom.

Telemann's music is typical of that of the new generation of composers influenced by the rationalist outlook of Enlightenment philosophy. Written for amateurs rather than professional court musicians, it shuns complexity of style and contrapuntal procedures, and its outlook is overtly relaxed and pleasurable. It makes copious use of the easily marshalled patterns of the Italian idiom—in fact, without such patterns, Telemann would never have achieved his prodigious output. This observation is not meant to disparage his generally delightful music: rather, it demonstrates how a composer with a capable technique and an adaptable ready-made idiom is enabled to work extremely quickly. Telemann's best-known works for solo harpsichord are the thirty-six *Fantasies pour le Clavessin*, suave two-movement pieces that are written in either the French or the Italian style. He also wrote some small fugues, and—inevitably—several suites, which contain many delightful movements for the beginner.

Bach's Sons

Not surprisingly, there is a good deal of keyboard music by Bach's sons Wilhelm Friedemann, Carl Philipp Emanuel, and Johann Christian, who received a thorough musical education from their father. All of their work, however, lies near the stylistic dividing line between the harpsichord, on the one hand, and the fortepiano and clavichord on the other. Johann Christian's music is pre-Mozartian in style, with considerable use of Alberti-bass figures. Carl Philipp Emanuel wrote numerous agreeable harpsichord concertos, designed for use in his post as court cembalist in Berlin. Those of his sonatas that are specifically designated for harpsichord—as distinct from fortepiano—show a Scarlattian brilliance of texture coupled with his own inimitable quirks of style. He chiefly deserves, however, to be remembered for his famous *Essay on the True Art of Playing Keyboard Instruments,* which appeared in two parts (1753–1762). This monumental and systematic treatise covers the development of fingering technique, the performance of ornaments, and the art of continuo realization, as well as containing many comments on taste and aesthetics. Particularly in the latter respect, he is already moving sharply away from the baroque period, and his remarks on every subject need to be seen in their transitional historical context. The treatise is nevertheless of enormous interest and value.

Influential as Carl Philipp Emanuel was, Bach's eldest son Wilhelm Friedemann is considered by many to have inherited the greatest share of his father's genius. He wrote several harpsichord sonatas, and a *Concerto a duoi cembali concertanti* in F major which, because it was copied by his father, was for a long time attributed to him. It does not need orchestral parts and can be played as a delightful duet for two harpsichords.

The fortepiano reached the Potsdam court of Frederick the Great in the 1740s: J. S. Bach tested a Silbermann instrument there while on a visit to Carl Philipp in 1747. The clavichord, which had flourished quietly in Germany as a domestic practice instrument for many years, came into greater prominence at about the same time. Its special genius—a capacity for intimate dynamic nuance and expressive vibrato (*Bebung*)— seemed tailor-made for the artistic ideals of the emerging *empfindsamer Stil*, of which Carl Philipp Emanuel was a leading exponent. This "expressive style" looks forward in certain respects to the classical style of Haydn, but has its own particular vein of pathos, and is often full of abrupt and rather mannered contrasts of mood and texture. The deliberate emotionalism of the style points the way to a new and potentially dangerous aesthetic, whose exaggerated tendencies threatened the contained integrity of existing harpsichord idioms. Certainly, the harpsichord had little part in this new scene.

Notes

1. Other composers had preceded Bach by writing didactic sequences of fugues in all or most of the twenty-four keys; Fischer's *Ariadne Musica* of 1702 is a well-known example. Fischer's concise pieces, however, are more in the South German style, influenced by the Italian tradition, and are intended specifically for organ.

2. Humphreys 1983, 11–18.

17

The Spanish Style

Most exotic, most poignant, and capriciously brilliant, the sonatas of Domenico Scarlatti are loved by every harpsichordist. They escaped the nemesis that obscured much eighteenth-century music during the romantic period, and earlier in the present century they were commonly encountered as the opening items of piano recitals. Some pianists certainly perform them with crisp and exciting results; but only the rich harmonic structure of harpsichord tone can fully reveal the true colors of this music and suggest its inscrutable yet beguiling mixture of aristocratic poise, mercurial wit, and wayward melancholy.

The sonatas seem to have sprung from no obvious parentage. The Italian keyboard music that Scarlatti encountered in his youth, particularly the work of Francesco Durante, must have formed his general style, but once he settled in Iberia, there was no local tradition on which he could build. Spanish composers before Scarlatti had preferred the native vihuela (a type of lute) and guitar for secular music. Admittedly, there had been a harpsichord tradition among Spanish renaissance composers such as Bermudo and Cabezón;[1] but during the seventeenth century, Spanish keyboard music seems to have been mostly inscribed for organ. Not that it was entirely sacred in style; there are numerous battle-pieces, galliards, and passacaglias in the organ output of Cabanilles. Martin y Coll's great *Flores de Musica* collection of 1706–1709 is also full of cheerfully naive organ music; but it is all relatively old-fashioned and provincial, and would have provided little substance for Scarlatti's development.

179

As the son of a famous opera composer, Scarlatti had experienced an eclectic musical upbringing in Naples, Venice, and Rome before making his momentous decision in 1719 to leave Italy for the royal service in Lisbon. There he became the harpsichord tutor of the gifted Princess Maria Barbara of Portugal, who later ascended the throne of Spain after marrying the heir apparent. At first, Scarlatti revisited Italy several times, but after 1728 he apparently remained in the relative cultural isolation of Madrid until his death in 1757. For the music-loving court of Maria Barbara he wrote entertainment music, including some splendid solo cantatas, and the 555 sonatas for harpsichord.

These biographical details are bare: they will, however, suffice as a framework for our understanding of Scarlatti. They account for his wide musical expertise and its subsequent canalizing into a narrow but deep channel. His cultural isolation in Spain meant that he was, in a sense, preserved from the distraction of novel musical developments around him; like Haydn at Esterházy, he was forced—or enabled—to create his own.

As far as formal structures are concerned, Scarlatti was notably unadventurous: practically all the sonatas are in one movement, which is in Italian binary form with the usual double bar. What happens within that conventional framework, however, is another matter. The dramatic transitions from one theme or texture to another, and the relationship between pure passagework, sequential development, repetition effects, and so on, are extremely original, relying for their effectiveness on surprise and a sense of musical humor.

Because a tiny proportion of the sonatas happens to follow the textbook sonata-allegro form, early twentieth-century writers tended to depict Scarlatti as a precursor of classical sonata form; but this is completely misleading. Kirkpatrick's important study of Scarlatti (1953–1968) gives fresh and sounder insights by analyzing the internal organization of the sonatas, with particular emphasis on the way many of the works progress toward a dramatic **crux**—a point, often associated with a pause, at which the sonata crosses, as it were, a watershed (of tonality, theme, or texture, or all of these). Kirkpatrick supports the theory that the sonatas were intended to be paired, for purposes of contrast or complement, although some writers now dispute this view. His catalog numbering (the K or Kp numbers), however, is universally used, and supersedes the old Longo L numbers.

Although the famous *Essercizi* (K. 1–30) were published in London in 1738, the overwhelming majority of Scarlatti's sonatas are only known from the sumptuous sets of manuscript volumes now preserved in libraries in Venice and Parma. These were written by a copyist. No sonata survives that is indisputably in Scarlatti's hand, and the overall scarcity of copies is often explained by the assumption that Maria Barbara wanted to keep her ownership exclusive.

There may not have been any obvious Iberian precursors of the sonatas, but the influence of Iberian musical life on their idiom is crucial. Here again Kirkpatrick extended our understanding, focusing attention on the characteristic flamenco turns of phrase, the guitar timbres, and the cyclical harmonic progressions of Spanish folk music, which emerge time and again from the sonatas. It is remarkable how evocatively these sounds can be drawn from almost any type of harpsichord, although the Spanish instrument for which Scarlatti composed was near to the Italian type in its scaling, and often had only one manual with two eight-foot registers. Some examples, however—notably three harpsichords in the Queen's possession—had a long compass of 61 notes. (One of these harpsichords was kept at each of the royal residences of Buen Retiro, Aranjuez, and Escorial, so that all the sonatas—even those containing high Gs—would have been playable wherever the court was in residence.)

Since Scarlatti quite commonly uses these high notes, the first thing you must do before playing a sonata is to check whether your instrument will accommodate them. If your harpsichord stops at D, it is sometimes possible to adapt a little by transposing odd notes or phrases down an octave, but it is hardly ideal. The bottom end of the compass presents fewer problems; low notes usually form part of octave leaps or doublings that can be discreetly modified or omitted.

Some of the sonatas are well-known as tremendous virtuoso pieces, exploiting the techniques of crossing hands, big leaps, and rapid repetitions.[2] If Maria Barbara played all these herself, she was clearly a formidable player. However, a great many sonatas are approachable by the beginner, and almost every one of them is, at its own level, delightful and stimulating to play. Complete editions of Scarlatti are mentioned later, but there are several alternatives for the beginner. The Associated Board of the Royal Schools of Music publishes a graded series; Stainer and Bell publish a collection of easy pieces; and most of the anthologies of Italian keyboard music mentioned in chapter 11 contain a few sonatas. The Chester *Early Keyboard Music* series includes in its Spanish volumes the splendid K. 380 in E, which when played with taut rhythmic control and *brio* can give even a modest player an immense thrill. This piece brilliantly evokes the sound of tympani and trumpets of an eighteenth-century court: Scarlatti's other musical world (example 17-1).

Example 17-1. Domenico Scarlatti, Sonata in E Major, K. 380, mm. 65–74.

Many other sonatas can similarly be made to suggest orchestral effects by subtlety of touch: this is an exciting challenge to the player. As you get to know Scarlatti's music, you will find that it stimulates imaginative response. Look at the massive left-hand chords in the Sonata in G, K. 105, which so splendidly evoke the sound of the strummed guitar by inserting an extra crushed note into the chord; or the gentler Sonata in E, K. 215, which *strokes* the guitar in the lovely passage after the double bar. (Both K. 105 and K. 215 are in the Schirmer *Sixty Sonatas* edition.) Your ear must decide whether you should release the crushed notes before the essential notes of the chord, or hold them all down together; some sound best one way, some the other.[3]

Scarlatti's music appeals to the ear, not the eye. In terms of musical grammar, his writing is full of loose ends—unresolved discords, parts that disappear, and so on. Like all Italians, he writes for immediate effect and does not worry about academic detail in situations that pass too quickly to be observed. What does matter to him is the musical argument, and in particular the way the music progresses toward the salient structural cadence points. Often these cadences are delayed, by Scarlatti's favorite device of triple repetition; and the performer needs to savor to the full these little dramas of expectation, deflection or frustration, and the final successful arrival, and convey their excitement to the listener. A sense of dramatic timing is essential: always aim to know where you are going, and to pace your travel and your arrival. Learn to distinguish, too, between those passages where you really are traveling and those where you are merely standing decoratively still (e.g., in brilliant dominant-tonic cadence passages). Scarlatti's telling manipulation of the rate of harmonic change is perhaps the feature that links his music most closely to the future classical style.

In their overall structure, these sonatas mostly use the conventional range of modulations, reaching the dominant at the double bar, and so on; but in the section immediately after the double bar, Scarlatti often revels in a peculiarly Iberian feature. Taking a simple musical idea—perhaps a mere couple of melody notes (see example 8-6)—as his sheet-anchor, he embarks on magical voyages through kaleidoscopic sequences of keys. Harmonies gradually change color before our ears, as a note is changed here, an ambiguous step (e.g., from G-sharp to A-flat) is taken there: and our sense of forward movement is suspended, under the trancelike influence of these seductive maneuvers.

Scarlatti's style is also notable for its liberal use of appoggiaturas—especially in plangent, melancholy movements such as the Sonata in C Minor, K. 84 (also in the *Sixty Sonatas*), or the Sonata in E Minor, K. 232. The use of a slightly overlapping touch and a gentle roll of the hand will help you to deliver these appoggiaturas eloquently. In general, Scarlatti's use of expressive appoggiaturas, and his penchant for augmented seconds and other irrational intervals, which may derive from flamenco music, confers upon many of his sonatas the typical haunting sadness that characterizes so much Spanish art. Even a modest acquaintance with Scarlatti's output will soon dispel the image of a writer of innumerable brilliant allegros.

There is a complete Scarlatti edition (by Kenneth Gilbert, for Le Pupitre/Heugel), and a facsimile edition (edited by Ralph Kirkpatrick); but both are expensive, and contain far more material than the student requires. Apart from the three Associated Board volumes of his sonatas already mentioned and the Schirmer *Sixty Sonatas* (some of which are technically very demanding), students of moderate ability might investigate the *Hundred Sonatas* available in the reliable Japanese *Zen-on* edition (recently acquired by Schirmer). The *Hundred Sonatas* are well presented, with a minimum of editorial intervention.

Scarlatti's pupil Soler abandoned the idea of paired sonatas in favor of sonatas with three or four separate movements. His three-movement sonatas end with fugues, while those with four include minuets—another move toward the classical sonata layout. (Some of Soler's sonatas were published in London by Lord Fitzwilliam in 1796, and are clearly viable on the piano.) Like many Spanish composers of the eighteenth century, Soler was a monastic cleric with scholarly enthusiasms: he wrote a treatise demonstrating methods of modulating between any two keys, no matter how distant. Ambitious modulation tends to be a feature of Spanish music at this period; a factor that, in conjunction with the choice of remote keys by both Soler and Scarlatti for some of their sonatas (D-flat major or F-sharp major, for instance), suggests that some well-tempered tuning must have been in use.

There is little in Soler's musical language that had not been at least pioneered by Scarlatti; and the same is true of the sonatas of Albero, Anglés, Rodriguez, Cantallos, Matéo Albéniz (father of the well-known piano composer), and Gallés, who carried forward the school of keyboard composition amiably but without real distinction into the early nineteenth century. All this music is, however, enjoyable to play, and some of it is well within the capacity of the amateur. Soler and Albero have achieved their own complete editions, edited respectively by Rubio and Galvez for *Unión Musical Española*: some Soler sonatas are also available in Henle Urtext. There is a reasonable selection of the remaining composers in the Ricordi anthology *The Spanish Harpsichordists*, which is adequately edited and contains some enjoyable pieces.

For the sake of completeness, one should mention Portugal. Its chief composer was Carlos de Seixas, a contemporary of Scarlatti who worked alongside him in his Lisbon days. Seixas wrote charming and varied sonatas that range from one to four movements; he also wrote a concerto. The great Lisbon earthquake of 1755 destroyed much of his work, and of the 700 sonatas he is reputed to have written, less than a hundred survive. Some of these have been recorded by Robert Woolley on the Portuguese harpsichord in the Finchcocks collection, and make fascinating listening.

Notes

1. The work of Cabezon had a noticeable influence on English keyboard writing during the brief Anglo-Spanish era of Philip and Mary (1553–1558).

2. See Boyd 1986, 186. According to Boyd, these sonatas are mostly grouped within the numbers K. 44–65 and 95–145. Many hand-crossings also occur in the *Essercizi*. Some of these, such as the famous K. 27, seem to be done purely for

their own sake—although Boyd suggests the possibility of varied timbres on two manuals.

3. Again according to Boyd, these sonatas containing multiple dissonances are grouped mainly in the range K. 120–220, suggesting a particular phase of Scarlatti's output.

_ 18 _

A Commonsense View
of Ornamentation

> One must use with discernment certain ornaments making
> the pieces much more beautiful and agreeable, lighting them up,
> as it were, with sparkling precious stones.
> —GEORG MUFFAT, _Florilegium Secundum_ (Passau, 1698)

Ornamentation is usually a troublesome subject to the beginner, who has visions of complex, but inevitably approximate, illustrations that show how ornaments should be realized. Of course these may be helpful; but as they may generally be found in editions of music you are studying, I am going to take an unconventional approach and write this chapter without any realizations at all. This overview of the topic will give you a better understanding.

If you had to invent harpsichord ornamentation from scratch, what would you do? There are in fact relatively few things you can do to decorate a single harpsichord note. You cannot add vibrato, or a portamento; so what are the possibilities? Normally, the answer involves the addition of extra notes: you can

- _lean_ onto the note, from below or above;
- _shake_ on it, in alternation with the note below or above, or a mixture of both; or
- _slide_ to it, usually from a third below.

Additionally, in the case of two or more notes, you can _spread_ them in different ways, or add notes in between them.

That virtually exhausts the options; it is not a vast range. But I hope

186

you have already been prompted to wonder why composers should have used ornamentation at all—what is it there for? As you read this chapter, you might try to find the answers for yourself. At the end, see if you agree with C. P. E. Bach's definitions.

The Problems of Notation

Ornaments were not invented theoretically, but evolved in performance. They arose naturally from the player's observation of what could be elicited from the instrument and what created certain effects.

The process of writing down ornaments, however, causes much trouble. Many ornaments defy being expressed in notation at all. For example, the baroque trill should start rather slowly and accelerate: but how does one notate this in 16th and 32nd notes? Even in the case of a simple mordent, the notation of what one might reasonably play is cumbersome, approximate, and page-cluttering—a sign or symbol is much better, provided its meaning is understood.

Normally, the baroque composer relied on the traditions of live performance amid which he worked. His shorthand symbols served merely as approximate reminders of what everyone knew was required—pictorial mnemonics, like the neumes that preceded staff notation in early plainchant. Some symbols must have virtually devised themselves—a serrated line for a shake, a scrolled sign for a turn, and so on—although other symbols had to be more arbitrary.

Whatever signs were used, this approach sufficed when composer and performer were in close touch, or were the same person. But there could be problems when the composer wished to publish his music for the use of those beyond his immediate circle. A table of ornaments then became necessary. Further problems arose after the passage of time, when musical styles had changed and the performing tradition was broken. By then, even the ornament table might need some interpretation, and editors usually tried to bridge the gap. Today editors have a highly responsible attitude toward this task, and aim to show by one means or another exactly what the composer originally intended. If you come across late nineteenth- and early twentieth-century editions, however, beware: these tended to modernize the ornamentation by substituting a more familiar symbol (which could possibly mean something different), or even left out altogether any symbols that were considered puzzling or superfluous.

Systems of Ornamentation

Not surprisingly, the French of the *grand siècle* were the first to develop both an intricate and intimate style of ornamentation and also the means of notating it—although French composers were not unanimous in their use of the symbols. There were two main French traditions of notating ornaments: d'Anglebert's, which is set out in his *Pièces de Clavecin* (1689), and Couperin's, which is developed from that of Chambonnières and is set out in the *Premier Livre de Pièces de Clavecin* (1713). Of these, d'Anglebert's table of ornaments is particularly detailed, enabling subtle lute-derived nuances to be indicated: Rameau and other composers who followed his system tended to condense and simplify it slightly.

J. S. Bach's rather brief table of ornaments in his notebook for Wilhelm Friedemann, *Clavierbüchlein für Wilhelm Friedemann Bach,* used a selection from d'Anglebert's table. He made use of other signs as well, however; and his ornament symbols are not always as precise as one might expect from a composer with his didactic outlook. The reason for this is largely that, where precision mattered, he wrote the ornamentation into the notated rhythm of the music. Where this has occurred (e.g., in the slow movement of the Italian Concerto) his melodic lines have a uniquely complex appearance.

As I said, one ornament may be indicated in different ways, especially in the two French traditions: for instance, d'Anglebert's symbol for a lower-note mordent is a comma-like sign after the note, while Couperin's is a more elegant version of the sign we still use. But on the other hand, one symbol can sometimes bear different meanings, according to who is using it. A case in point is the + sign: Chambonnières and Elisabeth Jaquet de la Guerre used it to mean an appoggiatura from below, while to Duphly, it represented a lower-note shake. And again, this contrasts with the sensible pragmatic Italian approach, whereby a composer was quite capable of using the easily written + sign in an omnibus sense, meaning simply "put an appropriate ornament here." Perhaps this is the true essence of ornamentation—that the player should sense which ornament will best suit a given situation. In an ideal world, no other sign might ever be needed.

Most composers, however, did add tables of ornaments to their works, and if you are going on to do specialized work it is important to consult these tables. Admittedly, tables do not make everything absolutely clear—in particular, how and when the ornament ends. And nomenclature can be a nightmare. But the names do not matter greatly, and many names can be ignored for present purposes. By grouping the main ornaments under a few headings, the situation becomes more manageable. The rest is learned by listening to good players; stylish ornamentation is best "caught, not taught," and intelligent imitation is preferable to poring over masses of 32nd-notes.

So, although you must obviously learn the basic facts about ornamentation, please do not worry too much about so-called correctness, which can be illusory. It is more important that your ornamentation sounds spontaneous, as though improvised and flowing organically from the music. Ornaments laboriously executed (an appropriate word) defeat their own ends. The secret is to relax: try not to stiffen, both physically and mentally, when you see ornament signs. Ornaments do not always have to be played rapidly: the speed of an ornament bears a natural relationship to the speed of the music. Beginners need not be ashamed to leave out ornaments they simply cannot manage. With increasing experience, you will find that ornamentation follows clearly defined patterns in various styles, and it will in time integrate naturally into your playing.

Accidentals above or below an ornament inflect its upper or lower note. Their use, however, is neither consistent nor invariable, and generally speaking you should aim to play ornaments within the scale of whatever key the music is in *at that point*—not necessarily the key of the movement.

The Ornaments

Having cleared the ground thus, I shall consider the various family groups to which ornaments belong. The following account does not include every conceivable ornament, but should cover the majority of those you will encounter.

APPOGGIATURAS

There is a certain obliquity about these important ornaments. They strike me as the musical equivalent of calling a spade, not a spade, but a horticultural implement. One approaches the main point indirectly and rather ornately. The name appoggiatura derives from the verb "to lean," and there is a certain courtly suggestion of a gracious gesture or bow.

The musical essence of the appoggiatura lies in the initial dissonance with the bass part, which commands attention. The ear is then led to the main note, as the dissonance melts into consonance; the main note gains consequence and sonority as a result. C. P. E. Bach asked perceptively

189

"what would harmony be without these elements?"[1] Note that he did not write "what would *melody* be?" So I want first to alert you to the existence of this important harmonic crunch, by looking at passages in which appoggiaturas are present but hidden, because they are written out as normal notes. This happens commonly in melodic phrases covering a descending fourth, as in example 18-1. Here the first and third notes are appoggiaturas, leaning respectively on to the second and fourth notes. The outsiders to the harmony and their subsequent resolutions can be identified by counting intervals from the bass: 4, 3; 7, 6. (In all renaissance and baroque theory and practice, fourths, sevenths, and ninths (or seconds) were dissonant intervals if they occurred on strong components of the beat.) These intervals add the salt to otherwise bland harmonic passages. If you develop an ear for dissonance and its resolution, you will find that compositions acquire sharper relief and a greater sense of light and shade. Moreover, if you can spot appoggiaturas even when they are written in normal notation, this will often help you to decide how a phrase should be articulated.

Example 18-1. Typical appoggiatura passage.

It is perhaps puzzling that composers should sometimes write out appoggiaturas fully and at other times use small notes or ornament signs instead. The insouciant Scarlatti, for instance, may alternate for no apparent reason between the two methods, even within a single phrase (but you can turn this to useful account, by deducing from the fully notated version exactly how long the shorthand appoggiatura should be). Nevertheless, there is no doubt that distinctive notation helps to underline the special harmonic status of the appoggiatura, and that the use of the small notes or signs reveals what is structural (essential) and what is decorative.

In slow music, the appoggiatura should create an expressive, sighing effect. Overlap the two notes, and release the second soon after the first, to simulate a diminuendo (rolling the hand slightly in the direction of the second note). In allegros, the ornament should create a dissonant tang: again, this can be emphasized by a fleeting overlap. Occasionally, a short appoggiatura is squeezed in front of a group of sixteenth notes of which the first is already dissonant: here, the function is to create a "buzz" highlighting the initial note, and so the appoggiatura must be snappy, almost like an acciaccatura. Appoggiaturas, then, operate at different speeds in different rhythmic contexts.

Musicians generally understand that appoggiaturas are played on the beat and lean into the main note, stealing some of its written value. But they often worry unduly over what mathematical proportion the appoggiatura should deduct from the main note. In practice, this concern is generally unnecessary—play as it sounds best; and in expressive situations, err on the long side. C. P. E. Bach was emphatic that the ornament should never take less than half the written value, but his book reflects a relatively late view that does not always suit earlier music, even that of his father. (Historically, it appears that the duration of appoggiaturas tended to get longer as the eighteenth century progressed.)

Bear in mind that appoggiaturas need not resolve on a rational subdivision of the measure; for example, the vexed example of the E-flat Major Prelude (in 9/8) in Book II of *The Well-tempered Clavier* sounds much less arbitrary and angular if resolved as Donald Tovey recommended in his well-known edition—*between* the B-flat and A-natural of the bass. Just touch the note of resolution briefly in passing, so that the note sighs away: don't sustain it for its full written length.

Example 18-2. Girolamo Frescobaldi, *Partita sopra l'aria della Romanesca,* mm. 4–5.

Example 18-2a. Henry Purcell, Almand from Suite in C, mm. 8–9.

Appoggiaturas that are definitely intended to be short are often written out. You can find crisp appoggiaturas in Lombard rhythm (i.e., short-long) in the work of Frescobaldi (example 18-2). These may in turn

A Guide to the Harpsichord

show us how to stress phrases like this in the rollicking style of Purcell (example 18-2a). It also gives us a pointer to one of Couperin's signs—the slur over a pair of eighth notes, with a dot over the second ⏜ , which is rather ambiguously captioned in the ornament table of his *Premier Livre de Pièces de Clavecin* (1713): notes marked in this way may also be played in Lombard rhythm.

Before about 1750, appoggiatura symbols were only used for ornaments that approach the main note from the *same side* as the preceding note—that is, a lower appoggiatura if the melody is rising, and an upper one if it is falling (often involving a repetition of the previous melody note). Any exception to this principle was usually written out fully for clarity. Opposite-side appoggiaturas are more characteristic of a later musical idiom—that of the Viennese classics.

Signs (other than small notes) used for the appoggiatura:

from below: ♩ ♩ ♩

from above: ♩ ♩

undifferentiated: ♩

The appoggiatura is usually slurred to the note of resolution, although the slur may not be notated.

Note carefully that the modern sign used for an acciaccatura—a small eighth note with one or two strokes through its tail ♪ —was in the eighteenth century merely an alternative method of notating a single, *normal* sixteenth note. This sign occurs frequently in the work of Scarlatti, where it signifies, not an acciaccatura, but a short appoggiatura. (There is no eighteenth-century sign for an acciaccatura as such, though crushed notes are often written in—see below under Spread Chords.)

SHAKE ORNAMENTS, INVOLVING TWO ADJACENT NOTES

These may be of varying duration. Long alternations (trills), which are dealt with later, are not particularly common; but a short alternation of two notes is ubiquitous in music from about 1550 onward. Although the names and signs vary, the effect is constant, and it is important to be able to play these ornaments fluently. Shakes are classified according to whether they involve the upper or lower auxiliary note.

In the baroque period, shakes of both kinds start *on* the beat—not before it. There are possible exceptions, but the beginner should assume that this procedure is standard and invariable. One can easily relax it later if need be. Some students find it hard at first to start their shakes on the beat—they assent to the theory, but cheerfully carry on squeezing them in before the beat. Playing an ornament on the beat feels quite different; it may even upset your rhythmic balance at first, if you have become used to counting the time from the end, rather than the beginning, of the ornament. The ornament needs to overflow freely into the space/time after the beat, and this may mean that it ends somewhere irrational—neither a quarter of the way through the beat, nor a half, nor a third: yet it should still feel poised, as if you meant it to end where it did.

Since the ornament consumes some of the value of the note, it may be that, in the case of a short note, there is little or no time left after the ornament. Examples can be found everywhere (see, for instance, example 18-3, where the tempo is quite fast).

Example 18-3. Élisabeth Jacquet de la Guerre, Chaconne in D, mm. 50–51.

UPPER-NOTE SHAKES

All baroque ornament tables agree that shakes involving the upper auxiliary start *on the upper note*—the note above the written note. (This point has been seriously misunderstood in the past, due to confusion with Mozartian practice.) Again there can be exceptions, but it is best to start by assuming that this is the invariable practice.

Starting on the upper note has two consequences. First, it means beginning with, and continuing to stress, a note that is more dissonant than the main note. Relish the sparkle that this confers—it is much more interesting than the flat mechanical sound of a shake focused on the main note. Second, it means playing an even number of notes; the shake usually contains four, sometimes six.

If the note before the ornamented note lies a step above, which is very common, *the shake still starts on the upper note,* unless the tempo is so quick that you simply cannot realistically repeat that previous note. This can happen when the ornament occurs during a series of very quick notes, or in a particularly tight and unforgiving corner such as that shown in example 18-4, where an upper-note shake sounds forced. Then

193

the ornament may be better played as three notes (main note, note above, main note).

Example 18-4. Domenico Scarlatti, Sonata in D Major, K. 490, m. 66.

Signs used for upper-note shakes are: ⸿ ⸿ ⸿ ⸿ ⸿ .

The markings *tr.* and *t,* can also signify an extended **trill** when applied to a long note; or a longer serrated line may be used. As mentioned above, the trill in baroque practice tends to begin slowly and accelerate. It is not always merely a mechanical repercussive device; it can be capable of expressive inflection. Couperin writes out an expressive *tremblement* to evoke the song of the nightingale in his famous *Le rossignol-en-amour* (*Ordre* 14): he even makes a forlorn attempt to notate the required acceleration by progressing from 16th- to 32nd- to 64th-notes, and writing the indication *Augmentées par gradations imperceptibles.*

You are not obliged to add terminations to baroque trills, although a termination will sometimes make it easier to end comfortably and elegantly. If you are not adding one, decide exactly where you want to stop trilling, using the movement in other voices as a point of reference. In the case of a trill on a dotted note, it is often convenient to end at the point where the value of the dot begins.

Returning to upper-note shakes, there are certain important ways in which they can be modified.

• A composer may wish to make the first note of the upper-note shake longer for expressive purposes. Bach, for instance, sometimes prefixes his shake with the upper note written separately as an appoggiatura. Other composers, quite logically, add their usual upper-appoggiatura sign. The result in the d'Anglebert tradition was ⃒ᴡ . In the Purcell tradition, it was ⃒= . Shakes of this kind were specially typical of music influenced by the French tradition, and in slower movements they should be played with great feeling.

• In quick movements, if an upper-note shake occurs in this extremely common melodic formula at a cadence (example 18-5), it can also be effective to elongate the first note. A quick repercussion, and a snapped-off final note (probably coinciding with the place where the dot begins) follow. The "chirruping" effect thus produced is beloved of many baroque instrumentalists. (Incidentally, an ornament should be inserted whenever this type of cadential formula occurs, even if it is not expressly indicated.)

Example 18-5. François Couperin, *Les petits moulins à vent* (*Ordre* 17), m. 47.

• One may well choose to lengthen the first (upper) note of any shake even when it is not so notated. But don't make an invariable habit of it, or its expressive currency will be weakened. Neither should you apply it in the case of composers of the d'Anglebert tradition, who clearly distinguished the symbols for a shake with a long, leaning first note *(appuyé)* and for a normal shake: |ᴡᴡ and ᴀᴡ .
• If the previous note lies one step higher, the first note of the shake may be tied over. This cancels out the repetition of the first note, and the ornament therefore sounds fractionally *after* the beat. You will have no difficulty in playing these tied shakes when another part is sounding on the beat, so that you can push against it (as it were): if there is nothing else on the beat, it is not quite so easy, but by subtly delaying the ornament you may manage to convey a delightful hint of rubato. Sometimes to ignore subtlety is simplest: just play three notes starting *on* the beat—the written note, the one above, and the written note again. (You will probably now realize that the latter is what the ordinary shake symbol came to mean after about 1780, after a confused process of convergence in which theory lagged behind practice.)
• The ornament may be introduced by a flourish from below ʄᴀᴡ or from above ʅᴀᴡ . These flourishes are usually notated very graphically, and with a little thought the symbols will be self-explanatory.
• The ornament may have a termination. This may be written out as two short notes; their length is purely nominal, and they can be played as quickly as seems appropriate. Alternatively, one of the signs for the lower-note shake (see the next section) may be incorporated into the symbol to indicate the termination: ᴀᴡᴠ , ᴀᴡ) . This usage shows how readily the various components of ornament

shorthand can be combined. Note that, unless one of these indications of a final termination is present, none is expressly called for.

LOWER-NOTE SHAKES, OR MORDENTS

When the ornament consists of main note, note *below,* main note,
the most usual symbol is the serrated line with a stroke through it: 𝆮.
Couperin's engraver devised a beautiful variant of this—a sign derived
from the fleur-de-lys: 𝆮. The d'Anglebert tradition used a small
comma-like mark placed *after* the note: ♩, . Some later French composers used + . Purcell, confusingly, uses 𝅥𝅥𝅥, which—even more confusingly—he calls a *beat.*

Again, you should assume that in the majority of cases this ornament starts *on* the beat, although there are exceptions to every rule, and
occasionally playing the ornament just before the beat, or even straddled across it, sounds better.

The lower-note shake is rhythmic and emphatic if played quickly,
but can be eloquent and even languorous if played slowly. And it has at
least one coloristic use in Couperin's music. Couperin frequently writes
a bass in quarter-notes that alternates between two adjacent notes: the
upper note bears a 𝆮 , the lower a 𝅥𝅥𝅥 , and the notes are slurred
together. In *Le moucheron (Ordre* 6) this convincingly imitates the hum of
the mosquito (example 18-6). Couperin also borrowed the technique for
other contexts where he wanted to suggest hypnotic repetition.

Example 18-6. François Couperin, *Le moucheron (Ordre* 6), m. 22.

In the French tradition, it is common to precede the lower-note
shake with an expressive appoggiatura from below—the appoggiatura
duly falling on the beat, and the shake ending somewhere near the next
subdivision of the beat. To notate this combined ornament, both signs
are inserted; either a small appoggiatura note slurred to the main note
bearing the fleur-de-lys (in the Couperin tradition); or the comma-before
plus comma-after of the d'Anglebert school: ♩, . English keyboard
music of the Purcell period, which relies heavily on French influence,
uses the same combination of two ornaments; and in the music itself

(but not in Purcell's table of ornaments, which is unfortunately ambiguous on this detail) this is notated by a combination of the lower-appoggiatura stroke and the "beat": $-\stackrel{\text{\tiny www}}{\boldsymbol{\flat}}$.

TURNS

The symbol for the turn ∾ is a good piece of shorthand for the four notes required; note above, note, note below, note. In the baroque period, turns occur more often on the beat (for graceful emphasis) than between beats (for elegance of joining), although you may find either.

Many French composers, and Bach after them, combined the shake and turn sign: ∾̈. This simply means that you play a shake and round it off with a termination at the end; six or eight notes.

SLIDES

The slide may seem to resemble the appoggiatura in its gesturelike effect. It is, however, harmonically softer, since it runs up to the main note from a note three notes below, which is generally a consonant note, whereas the appoggiatura is inherently dissonant. Think of the slide as a rather expressive caress: it is seldom meant to be brilliant. Again, it is important to sound the first note *on,* not before, the beat, so that the ornament tails away from the stress.

Slides can also be combined with spreads: see below.

Signs used for the slide are: ♩ and ♪ .

CONNECTING NOTES

Sometimes composers, especially of the Couperin school, add small notes between melody notes lying a third apart, to connect them. It is a matter of debate whether these small notes—which should not be confused with grace notes—should be played as passing notes (between the beats) or appoggiaturas (on the beat of the second note). But as there is conflicting evidence on the matter, try both options and select which sounds most satisfactory. In French music, such small notes often occur in a specific context referred to as the *coulé de tierce.* The *coulé de tierce* is frequently found in a cadential situation, and it involves two melody notes that *fall* by a third, from strong beat to weaker beat. In this case, most authorities agree that an off-beat passing note is best (example 18-7).

In other contexts, no rule is infallible, and one should experiment to see where the small notes may best be played. If in doubt, consult the harmony of the passage. There are a few problematic places in Couperin's music where two such small notes appear simultaneously in dif-

Example 18-7. Louis-Nicolas Clérambault, Gavotte in C, mm. 1–5. (The slurs in m. 4 may indicate that the eighth notes should not be played unequally.)

ferent parts. If they do not sound satisfactory together, try putting one before the beat and one on it. *Les sentimens,* in the first *Ordre,* contains a particularly knotty problem of this kind. (This Sarabande is not a beginner's piece, but it is well worth looking at because it serves as a demonstration sampler for almost every ornament that Couperin used.)

SPREAD CHORDS (ARPEGGIATIONS)

As with other ornaments, the spread generally starts *on* the beat, not before it. This, again, is in contrast to later practice, and may require thought. Place the lowest note (or the highest, in a downward spread) on the beat, and feel the pulse from that point; let the remaining notes flow away from this first note into the space/time after it. The tightness (speed) of the spread may be varied: indeed, this is a valuable expressive resource.

Spreads can be applied with discretion in many places where they are not notated, as an expressive or softening device. This is discussed in chapter 8.

A stroke through the stem of the note is a common indication of a spread chord in the baroque period. (The similarly notated virginalist ornament possibly also indicates a spread chord[2]—you might experiment with this.) The stroke runs through a stem below the note for an upward spread ♪ , and through a stem that points up for a downward spread ♩ . Couperin and other baroque composers used carefully devised symbols for upward and downward spread.

upward: ♪

downward: ♪

Chambonnières used the second of these for both upward and downward, but positioned the sign below the chord for upward, above or

198

beside it for downward (see figure 7 in chapter 7). All of this is less complex than it sounds: the direction of spread is usually integral to the flow
of the music, so that one naturally approaches it from the right end. The
two effects are tellingly alternated in the sarabande of Couperin's Third
Ordre.

EXTRA NOTES IN SPREAD CHORDS

Two notes a third apart in a spread chord are often filled in with the
intervening note, which is played in passing and then released. The foreign note adds "buzz" and sonority to the chord. Couperin's symbol is
an oblique stroke between the notes, ⌡ , whereas d'Anglebert's is a little mark joining the notes vertically—on the left for ascending: ⟨⌡ ; on
the right for descending: ⌡⟩ .

The sarabande of Bach's Sixth French Suite is interesting, as one of
the source copies shows this type of ornament added afterward for the
instruction of a pupil, using Couperin's system of oblique strokes. The
one in measure 2 involves five notes—C-sharp, D-sharp, E, G-sharp,
and A. Caress the whole complex of notes, then release the nonharmonic
ones.

Extraneous notes were also added in other contexts. For instance, in
Italian continuo practice, where they were called *mordente,* quick "bit-
ing-notes" were crushed into chords for punch and brilliance, as
described by Gasparini and Geminiani.[3] These were not notated. Dissonant added notes were, however, so obviously effective as an emphatic percussive device that some composers began to notate them.
Even Bach added rumbustious extra notes to some chords in the *Burlesca*
of his Second Partita. The most obvious composer in this respect, however, is Scarlatti, who was a pupil of Gasparini. The striking crushed
notes in some of Scarlatti's chords, such as the opening chords of his
notoriously flamboyant Sonata in A Minor, K. 175, are a brilliant way of
evoking Iberian color. Today it is almost unbelievable that Longo's edition expurgated these imaginative dissonances and reduced the chords
to bland harmonic orthodoxy.

Experiment with different ways of playing crushed notes. In some
cases, they should be released quickly, as in these chords from Scarlatti's
Sonata in D Major, K. 490 (example 18-8). (In this example, the left-hand
A is the foreign note in the first measure, the D in the next, and the G in
the last.) Or they may be sustained to simulate the strum of an undamped guitar chord, as in the milder Sonata in E, K. 215 (in the passage
after the double bar).

Example 18-8. Domenico Scarlatti, Sonata in D Major, K. 490, mm. 80–82.

Since Scarlatti's crushed notes are not differentiated visually from the main notes, we are now passing beyond the sphere of literally notated ornamentation and entering that of creative performance. Another effect that, although common, was rarely notated was the convention that expressive notes in the right hand were played after the notes in the left hand. Couperin and Rameau called this effect **suspension** (not to be confused with the suspension of a dissonant interval), and Couperin actually gave it a special sign in his first table of ornaments: ⩗ . It is notable, however, that the sign seldom appears in Couperin's later work. Kenneth Gilbert offers the explanation, which appears likely to be true, that this expressive device became so much a normal part of harpsichord technique that it no longer seemed worthwhile to indicate it.[4]

A suspension can be effective even when there is only one note in each hand. The intended effect is a common feature of baroque musical rhetoric—the sigh, or catch in the voice. One can find prototypes in vocal music: short rests are often inserted to break the melody if sighs or pathetic interjections occur in the text.

OTHER SIGNS

Couperin pioneeered the use of a *large* comma to mark breaks between musical phrases. It is a helpful sign, although he does not use it consistently.

The wedge-shaped symbol ❜ may cause trouble; it signifies a strong *marcato* or *spiccato* to a modern player, but in the eighteenth century it was simply a staccato sign. Play the marked notes lightly but not too sharply. Normal staccato dots were also used occasionally (but beware—in some French music, dots can have a different significance, being an instruction to avoid *inégalité*).

D'Anglebert, whose symbols are very logical, uses a sign resembling a small eighth-note rest attached to the top of a note to show that it should be artificially shortened: ♪ . Signs of shortening were not used before the late seventeenth century, an interesting fact that may confirm the hypothesis that the touch norm before that date was already slightly detached.

Occasionally one meets a puzzling symbol—for instance, the long wavy lines that occur in Scarlatti's Sonata in D Minor, K. 52. These indicate the holding of notes beyond their written duration, although nothing in the music explains why this could not be shown by using normal note values. Such problems are happily rare. The majority of composers used a comparatively small range of signs, and you are unlikely to encounter symbols that I have not mentioned unless you are doing specialized work. Most good editions today have helpful tables: each of the Howard Ferguson volumes of French music (in the Oxford University Press anthologies mentioned at the end of chapter 15) has a particularly comprehensive table, which compares the notation of ornaments used by the major French composers. Your researches should be complemented by listening, with score in hand, to an accomplished and imaginative player.

Baroque ornaments were not inserted at random; they were generally placed according to context, and familiarity with a composer's music leads one to acquire an instinctive feeling for the kind of ornament that fits a given situation. Try to understand the purpose of each ornament: Is it for rhythmic incisiveness and brilliance, or for expression? Does it smooth out an angular corner? or does it introduce an interesting crunch into the harmony? Does it signal a cadence or structural point? With this approach, you will soon be able to stop worrying about the meaning of the symbols and play your ornaments in a free, almost improvisatory manner. Better still, you will know where and how further ornamentation can be applied.

Extemporized Ornamentation

I have not yet touched in this chapter on the kind of extemporized flourishes that the English sixteenth- and seventeenth-century composer knew as **divisions**, and the renaissance and early baroque Italian theorists called *groppi* and *tremoli*. These involved, for instance, the filling out of intervals larger than a fourth, or the breaking up of simple material into more elaborate figuration. Such divisions originated in the need to adapt vocal music, with its natural power of sostenuto on long notes, to the needs of the harpsichord: but it soon passed into the language of the instrument, and the extemporization of divisions was part of the

201

education of all players. Many treatises contained instruction on this point: samples can be studied in Donington's *Baroque Music: Style and Performance* (1982) or in the quotations from *Le nuove musiche* (1602) by Caccini reprinted in Strunk's *Source Readings in Music History* (1981). See also Howard M. Brown's *Embellishing Sixteenth-Century Music* (1976).

Further extemporized ornamentation can be observed in the playing of experienced specialists, particularly string players. Their usage is based on the numerous printed **graces** that appear in instruction books of the period, or in contemporary editions of sonatas. Composers in the Italian tradition were likely to present their music, particularly their slow movements, as unadorned melodies that invited embellishment. Corelli's classic violin sonatas were the subject of numerous printed embellishments by Geminiani and others. Improvised decorations of this kind do not involve the harpsichord player directly, but you should be prepared to accommodate them when you are playing continuo for a violinist.

A movement that ends with an imperfect cadence nearly always calls for extemporization from the soloist, and this needs to be worked out by both players together. In this context, the bass falls from the sixth degree of the scale, which is often figured with the suspension 7 6, to the fifth. A famous example is the connecting passage between the outer movements of Bach's Third Brandenburg Concerto, which calls for improvisation by one or more of the players.

In solo harpsichord music, Handel offers some good examples of musical elaboration in his Second Suite in F. Here the first and third movements are copiously decorated. Handel himself wrote out the graces in small notes; this is helpful, since it enables one to see the essential structure of the music. Bach's English Suites likewise present interesting and beautifully varied *doubles* of the sarabandes in A minor and G minor (Suites Two and Three). The A Minor Sarabande is particularly worth studying as a source of ideas about melodic embellishment suitable for repeats.

Practical Hints on Playing Ornaments

The required physical action is a mixture of delicacy and finely-focused strength. Even more care must be expended on releasing the keys than on depressing them.

The fingers most used are 3 and 2, or 4 and 3 in the right hand, and 2 and 3 in the left. Occasionally, in polyphonic music or chords before cadences, you will need to use 5 and 4 of the right hand. The following exercise will increase your facility and strength (example 18-9). It can be played in various keys: where a black key falls on 5, move your hand forward a little.

Example 18-9.

Long trills do not occur so frequently that you need to practice them specially. Do not try to play them faster than you can manage; stay relaxed and breathe *out;* and if you find you are becoming tense, then stop.

I mentioned above that some students find it difficult to feel the rhythmic placing of their ornaments. Ingrained habits of playing ornaments before the beat, or of excluding them from the rhythmic structure altogether, can lead to the practice of counting the duration of the main note from the end, rather than the beginning, of the ornament. To correct this tendency, think of some words with the right accentuation and say them to yourself while playing the ornament. The word HARPsichord, for instance, might be a pattern for the lower-note shake (three notes); MEMorable for the upper-note shake (four notes). The words are said quickly, with the accent as shown. You can even incorporate these words into sentences that will hold the rhythm of the whole phrase firm.

If you find it difficult to play a shake on the beat in one hand against a moving part in the opposite hand, identify the point in the moving part at which your shake will *end,* and coordinate your hands appropriately.

Some students have problems combining ornaments in both hands simultaneously. Couperin is particularly prone to combine a *tremblement* in one hand with a *pincé* in the other (example 18-10, measure 2). Here it is best to ignore one ornament completely at first, until the playing of the remaining ornament has become fluent and almost subconscious. Then reverse the procedure. Do not attempt to play both together for some time: and even then, don't try to *combine* them (in particular, don't try to end them tidily together). Rather, feel two independent ornamental actions flowing easily away from the beat.

In this example, the addition of the appoggiatura to the right-hand

Example 18-10. François Couperin, *La mistérieuse* (*Ordre* 25), mm. 1–2.

B means that the two ornaments at this point are in fact mirror images of each other, if the first note of the left-hand ornament is slightly elongated. This sounds neat, and makes execution easy. The little note in the second measure is another specimen of the connecting notes referred to previously (under *coulé de tierce*). It should be played as a sixteenth note.

In conclusion, what did C. P. E. Bach say about embellishments?

- "They connect and enliven tones,"
- "... impart stress and accent" (this is of course true, although it is irritating when people say that this is the only way the harpsichord can do it),
- "... make music pleasing, and awaken our close attention,"
- "... increase the weight and import of notes and differentiate them from others," and
- "expression is heightened by them: let a piece be sad, or joyful ... they will lend a fitting assistance."[5]

All these definitions are highly significant. Other observations in the same chapter of the treatise, however, show clearly how the taste of the mid-eighteenth century was parting company with that of the baroque period. In stressing how embellishments provide "opportunities for fine performance" and improve mediocre composition, C. P. E. Bach implies that extemporized ornamentation is almost an end in itself. He corrected this impression elsewhere, saying that one should not overdo the "spices, which may ruin the best dish."[6] Nevertheless, the proliferation of extempore ornament in his day was potentially decadent: we are reminded that "good taste" meant, to the English musician of Burney's day, not a refined cultural outlook, but merely the ability to grace a melody becomingly.

I leave you with an ongoing question: which composers seem to integrate ornaments most fully into their music?

Notes

1. C. P. E. Bach 1753/1949, 87.

2. The ornaments of the English virginalists are discussed in chapter 12.

3. Gasparini 1708/1963; Geminiani 1749/1969.

4. Kenneth Gilbert, ed. *F. Couperin: Pièces de clavecin.* (Paris: Heugel, 1969), preface, xvii.

5. C. P. E. Bach 1753/1949, 79.

19

First Steps in Continuo Playing

In writing this chapter, I have tried to keep in mind the needs of a variety of people in many different situations. Some of my advice relates to instrumental music, and some to choral work (including the special treatment of recitative). But, with the exception of recitative, the same principles apply throughout, and to discuss continuo playing in separate categories would involve a lot of repetition. I hope you will read the entire chapter and then select what you need.

About the Continuo

The majority of readers of this book will be familiar with the concept of the basso continuo—that harmonic foundation present in practically every concerted composition written between about 1600 and 1770. Many people even think that the term implies harpsichord by definition, although in fact the part was just as often played by organ, harp, or theorbo. The basso continuo was notated as a bass part with figures that indicate the required harmonies in shorthand form. Because this bass was present throughout the piece, English writers often called it **through-bass**, or **thorough-bass**: German writers may use the phrase **Generalbass**.

The figures refer to the intervals to be sounded above the bass. Modern editions of baroque music usually have a fully written-out continuo part in which these figures have been interpreted by an editor. These **realizations**, however, often leave much to be desired and may need to be modified. For this and other reasons, a professional continuo player frequently plays directly from the figured bass, although to do this fluently takes both natural ability and practice. (Musical common sense is also needed, for figuring is not always entirely logical, or even complete.)

Whether you use a realization or not, however, you need to be clear about the purpose of the continuo part. It is not there simply to fill out harmonies: indeed, in a full ensemble, this is hardly necessary. But at all times, it should be providing rhythmic propulsion, helping the ensemble, and generally shaping the music from within. Historically, many ensembles were directed from the keyboard—a method frequently revived today.

The Way In

Continuo playing is great fun, and being able to take part in ensemble music is a joy in itself. As soon as you begin to feel familiar with the harpsichord's action and can achieve light and shade in your playing, look around for opportunities of joining with instrumentalists. One excellent place to learn continuo skills is undoubtedly in a trio-sonata ensemble. The trio sonata was one of the classic chamber music forms of the high baroque, and it offers a splendid range of music. Italian composers of trio sonatas normally used two violins and continuo, and Corelli's fine works in this genre form the core of the repertory; they were imitated throughout Europe. Other composers—Telemann, Quantz, Handel, Hotteterre, Dornel, and many more—wrote for two recorders, flutes, or oboes, or optional combinations of instruments: so whatever your players, there is plenty of scope. Ideally, your ensemble also includes a cello or viola da gamba, or even (with wind instruments) a bassoon: a trio sonata should be performed by four people. Your collaboration with this bass player is of prime importance—cultivate a good rapport.

Little by little, you can extend your experience to include working with singers and solo instrumentalists, then to chamber orchestral music (concerti grossi, etc.) and choral works. Involvement with bigger ensembles often has a performance in view. It is a big responsibility to play continuo for choral works where you will be accompanying vocal soloists: do not take this on until you have acquired adequate performing experience.

When you play with a bigger group, make sure that your instrument is well positioned within the ensemble, near the bass instruments: you need to be where you can influence events. The siting of the harpsichord should be discussed with the director of the ensemble before the music stands are set out for the other players. If the harpsichord is to be in the center of the ensemble, the lid of the harpsichord should be removed so that it does not interfere with visibility. (To do this, close the lid and lay back the flap of the instrument; remove the hinge pins, putting them somewhere safe; then carefully lift the lid clear.) The advantages of being right at the center of the group generally outweigh the less focused sound of the instrument without its lid.

Different Types of Continuo Parts

Always try to use an edition that, although practical, is based on scholarly editorial principles. You and your bass player both need to be sure that any slurs or dynamic markings are original—or, if not, that they are clearly distinguishable as editorial. In your keyboard part, remember that only the bass is original: there can obviously be no definitive version of the right-hand part, as it was originally improvised.

A figured bass without realization is for the skilled player. But if you are serious about the harpsichord, you should start work on one of the various instruction books dealing with figured bass, and progress toward the ultimate, and liberating, objective of playing solely from figures. Many unrealized figured-bass parts can be found in facsimile editions (q.v.) of chamber music and other works. These are ideal for practice purposes.

There are various modern text-books on the subject of figured-bass playing. It is inevitably a far cry from the controlled safety of their exercises to the thrills and spills of real-life continuo playing, but they are nevertheless helpful as an introduction. Of the historic instruction books, the second part of C. P. E. Bach's *Essay on the True Art of Playing Keyboard Instruments* (1762) is a mine of information on the subject, but it contains no practical exercises. Two other treatises with exercises based on historic teaching practice are now available in modern editions: of these, the first is particularly recommended for the beginner:

- *Continuo Playing According to Handel* (Oxford University Press, Early Music Series no. 12, 1984). This concise treatise, which was designed by Handel for the instruction of a daughter of George II, is edited with an excellent practical commentary by David Ledbetter.
- *Precepts and Principles for Playing the Thorough-bass or Accompanying in Four Parts:* J. S. Bach. Translated with a commentary by Pamela Poulin (Oxford University Press, Early Music Series no. 16, 1994). This valuable historic document is discussed later in the chapter.

208

Both of these treatises are based on the working out of the figures into a four-part keyboard texture, because this norm is the most convenient to teach. (This four-part texture, however, is not always ideal, as we shall see.)

A written-out continuo part has certain disadvantages, as I hinted above. It is almost impossible to notate what a good player would actually play, and if it could be done, the result would often look untidy and odd. In any case, realizations should ideally be unique—tailored to meet the demands of individual circumstances. What is right for one performance or ensemble is not always right for another; and ideas about continuo playing are constantly evolving, in the light of research and practical experience.

Certainly, it is best to avoid the very intricate realizations, replete with countermelodies and ornament, offered in certain editions of French baroque chamber music; or Tippett's celebrated realizations of Purcell's vocal music, which have highly elaborate and idiosyncratic accompaniments loosely derived from the original figured basses. You are safer with conventional realizations that offer innocuous and fairly minimal keyboard parts. But even so, it is best merely to regard these rather neutral versions as a nucleus which you can adapt, or a safety net to fall back on if you are having difficulties. Always remember that the right-hand part need not be played literally—a tolerable result can even be obtained by hardly playing it at all. As you develop as a continuo player, you will understand the limitations of printed realizations, and move toward evolving your own parts. Some suggestions for doing this are given below.

An interim format. Some desk-top publishers, such as King's Music, are pioneering a highly desirable format—a score containing the melodic part(s), the figured-bass part, and a blank staff between, on which you can sketch in your own ideas. There may be a realization at the back of the copy, in small print, so that you can check the harmony. This format offers a flexible compromise between working from a realization and from a figured bass. You can cut and paste your own copy thus if no printed version is available.

A score of some kind. If you are playing continuo for an oratorio or other large choral work, it can sometimes be feasible to play from a vocal score, having someone to help you with the frequent page turns. You then have to extract the essential chord-patterns from the piano accompaniment (which is either a transcription of the instrumental parts, or a realization of the figured bass, or both at once). It sounds tricky, but students who have the knack of perceiving the musical structure often cope well. This method has the advantage of providing a good overall view of what is going on, and it enables you to do some tactful rescue work if one of the soloists goes astray. It can also be advantageous to play from a full score of an orchestral work such as a concerto, provided you have help with page turning.

If you want to know how to modify your score effectively, or how to shape your own realization of the figuring, you first need to understand what characteristics are desirable in continuo playing.

Continuo Textures

A good continuo player varies the texture—the number of notes in a chord, and other details—according to context. Full, strong chords call for notes to be doubled in the right and left hand, whereas a *piano* effect may call for the texture to be thinned down to three or even two notes, and a *pianissimo* often needs no more than the bass on its own. (This is sometimes noted for other special effects by the indication *tasto solo*, *tasto*, or *t.s.*)

You will notice that editorial continuo parts are often arranged in academically correct four-part harmony, with one note in the left hand and three in the right. The few eighteenth-century realizations of figured bass that we know were often written like this (for reasons explained later), and four-part realization has consequently been taken as an almost invariable precedent. This one-plus-three layout, the "bread-and-butter" of realization, is admittedly very practical. It has the advantage of enabling you to phrase the bass part sensitively with the left hand, which is important. Also, chords fall easily under the right hand, and it ensures an acoustic layout that suits the instrument—that is, with the notes closer together as you ascend the keyboard.

But there are many contexts—such as quickly-moving sequences of first-inversion chords, or quieter passages—where one-plus-*two* is preferable: while running eighth- or sixteenth-note basses often call for one of the classic effects of continuo playing, namely playing in tenths (octaves-plus-thirds) with that bass, giving a one-plus-*one* texture. It should be apparent, in fact, that an unvarying four-part texture, although it may look tidy, goes against the first cardinal point of continuo playing—flexibility. A good realization, even one suitable for a beginner, should incorporate an appropriate mixture of textures. As you gain confidence, try to modify the written textures you meet in this way.

Even when you are realizing in four-part harmony, do not worry too much about correct voice-leading. If a choice has to be made, fluent and rhythmic playing is far more important than a desperately anxious avoidance of consecutive intervals. Even so, sensitive players generally try to avoid consecutive (parallel) fifths or octaves, particularly between the outer parts of their realizations. Consecutive fifths and octaves feel messy and uncraftsman-like, and are best avoided by using plenty of contrary motion of right and left hands.

- As a general rule, keep the right-hand part below the top of the treble staff. If you are playing from a realization, you may find that the given chords lie rather high (they were possibly conceived as a piano part). They often sound better if moved down to a different position, as in example 19-1. Avoid a dense concentration of notes low in the left hand and a thin right-hand part, as this spacing conflicts with the natural acoustic layout of the instrument. But sonorous doubling and filling-out of triads in *both* hands, as shown by d'Anglebert in his *Principes d'Accompagnement* (1689) or Geminiani's *The Art of Accompaniament* (ca. 1754) can be extremely effective in grand, full passages.

Example 19-1.

- If the realization you are playing from is old-fashioned and has the left-hand part doubled pianistically in octaves, leave the lower note out, except perhaps for the occasional *fortissimo* chord.
- Do not play consistently above the melody, unless you are accompanying low-range instrumental solos, or bass voices.
- With increasing experience, you can experiment with coloring a few emphatic chords by using extra non-harmonic notes, as advocated by d'Anglebert, Gasparini, Geminiani, and other eighteenth-century writers.[1] This increases the sonority of the instrument (example 19-2). There are two ways of doing this—either treat the extra note as a scintillating crushed acciaccatura, which is released instantly (Geminiani says "as if it were fire"), or include it, in a more meditative spirit, in a slowly spread expressive chord. This latter can be useful for the final chord of a slow movement.
- As well as playing chords, it is sometimes good to add a certain

211

Example 19-2.

amount of part movement. Eye-witness accounts of Bach's continuo playing noted how he would introduce complete counter-melodies: but this technique is for experts, and needs discretion to avoid detracting from the solo part. However, short complementary or answering melodic/rhythmic fragments can sometimes be introduced in the rests of the soloist's part. A well-timed flourish, such as a brilliant scale sweeping up to a massive chord, can emphasize a salient point—for instance the re-entry of the orchestra after a solo passage. All these effects should of course be used sparingly, or mannerism will creep in.

Rhythmic Patterns

Whatever the context, beware of playing too many notes; an extremely busy continuo part nearly always defeats its own ends. But play with conviction and rhythmic vitality. Make your presence felt in the ensemble by elegance and suppleness, not by aggressiveness: Couperin warned the player against the dangers of a rigid continuo hand.[2]

- Use your musical discretion. For instance, if there are repeated notes in the bass, it is not necessary to harmonize or even to play all of them. Let the string bass take care of the repetition. To pound doggedly through passages of reiterated eighth-note basses, which are a feature of many Italian baroque concertos, can be a sure way to anaesthetize both the audience and one's fellow-musicians to the sound of the continuo. A few propulsive strokes at well-chosen rhythmic points are more elegant and effective. It is a useful exercise to go through some well-known piece, such as a choral movement from Handel's *Messiah*, and decide where the propulsive strokes should occur. Up-beat patterns are particularly important. For example, in the chorus "For unto us" from *Messiah*, two up-beat and down-beat patterns per measure will suffice in many passages to keep the rhythm buoyant.

- On the other hand, it may sometimes be desirable to restrike a chord, particularly a sustained one, using some pattern that reflects rhythmic movement elsewhere in the music.

• To discover good rhythmic patterns, imagine that you are playing a percussion instrument such as a tambourine. Indeed, the occasional use of discreet body language to express rhythm is not entirely ruled out in continuo playing, although you might enlist a candid friend to check that you are not falling into indiscreet mannerism. Aim to go with, and to some extent initiate, the rhythmic impulses of the music. If you are a beginner, you will achieve far more by playing a few well-chosen chords in an alert manner and omitting the rest than by playing a realization accurately but inertly, laboring in the wake of the rest of the ensemble. Remember that if you are behind the beat, even by a micro-second, you can no longer help to shape events, or correct bad ensemble in the group.

• In triple-time music, be on the alert for hemiola figures, especially just before cadences. Their presence in the bass part is often signaled by certain shapes, such as those in the following example (example 19-3). The essence of hemiola is that two short measures are telescoped into one longer measure with a corresponding shift of emphasis (see hemiola references in chapters 12 and 15). You may need to mark this strongly by adjusting the right-hand patterns.

Example 19-3.

General Points

Phrasing of the left hand should mirror the phrasing of the rest of the ensemble. If the bass is taking part in dialogue or imitation of the general thematic material, it is valuable to play such sections *with the left hand only* the first few times you rehearse. This will alert you to the melodic shape and phrasing of the bass.

Apply the general principles of articulation to your left-hand part. Allegros should be played with grace and animation; mark the beginning of each measure well, but lighten the unimportant beats of the measure. Movements in 4/4 with a preponderance of eighth notes in the bass respond well to a style that overlaps, or elongates slightly the first note in each group of four, but tapers the others away. Avoid slurring from weak beats to strong beats unless a particular effect is desired.

- Vary the delivery of your chords according to context. Incisive *secco* chords help good ensemble in allegro passages, while the softening effect of chords spread at different rates can enhance gentler passages. Use the techniques discussed in chapter 8 to provide warmth or brilliance as required.
- Learn to assess the needs of the ensemble. Sometimes you need to supply harmony notes that are not already present in the other parts, particularly when playing continuo to a single melodic line (voice or instrument). There are also some notorious little passages in *Messiah* in which the orchestra is suddenly silent and the continuo is left alone to support the singer. But at other times, for instance, in accompanying a choral work or concerto, the harmony is already complete: so the continuo is reinforcing, rather than filling in the harmony. You then might need only to play strong, full chords at crucial points in the measure: or you might double important strands of the choir's music. In choral works, some of these functions may be taken by the organ.
- Cover all significant changes of harmony (which are usually more frequent as cadences approach), but never feel obliged to play every single chord. A ceaseless succession of four-part chords is particularly inflexible and wearing. Do some weeding, and give shape and animation by the way you phrase and weight the remaining chords. This is particularly applicable to allegros.
- In instrumental ensemble music, if the bass part has very rapid figuration or arpeggios, it is best not to double all these notes in the left hand of the harpsichord part. This will detract from the effect and possibly sound untidy. Just play the outline—the notes on the beat, for example—to support the texture and maintain propulsion, leaving the figuration to the bass player. But come to an agreement with your bass player, who may in some cases prefer to leave the quick notes to *you*.
- As you gain experience, learn to pay increasing attention to the melodic line of the solo part(s), particularly where ornaments are involved. For instance, it is sad to hear a continuo chord with a major third at the top when at the same time the soloist has a beautiful, expressive appoggiatura resolving to the same third from the

dissonant note above: the continuo part kills the soloist's effect. Learn to recognize these harmonic contexts, and tuck the third tactfully away in a lower part, or—better still—omit it altogether and play a bare chord containing octave and fifth only.

• Take every chance to listen to skilled performers, particularly in chamber music, where detail is most easily observed. Even the way in which a final chord is decorated and spaced can be the subject of considerable artistry.

The early eighteenth-century writer Roger North summed up every aspect of continuo-playing splendidly:

There is occasion of so much management in the manner of play, sometimes striking only the accords, sometimes arpeggiando, sometimes touching the air [melody], and perpetually observing the emphatick places, to fill, forbear, or adorne with a just favour.[3] [I particularly like the word "forbear."]

A Special Note About Bach's Precepts and Principles

As mentioned above, Bach's own treatise on figured bass, printed as early as 1880 by Spitta, has recently appeared in a new edition. Originally a small manuscript work that Bach dictated to his scholars, it contains:

• sets of rules with four-part illustrations by Bach himself, largely adapted from a treatise by F. E. Niedt;
• additional examples, where Bach set the bass and figuring, but the realization was done by a student and bears no signs of correction (how interesting it would be if we had Bach's comments);
• "Principles for playing in four parts." Here the bass and figures were set and advice on playing offered, but no realization was given. The basses are mostly sequential and the harmonies slow moving; the figuring is skillfully graduated from simple to complex (figure 12).

Bach would not have claimed that his treatise did anything more than give an abstract outline of the subject: he preferred oral instruction and hands-on teaching, as many of his remarks show. Nevertheless, there are two important points to note in Bach's formal four-part realizations:

Figure 12. Exercise 6 from J. S. Bach's *Principles for Playing in Four Parts* (1738). Bach's instructions for filling out the figured bass read: "The seventh is resolved to the third [of the next chord]. To realize this passage in four parts, one can take the fifth or octave with the seventh." Note how the bass is reiterated: the player would add one half-note chord in the right hand to each group of eighth notes. This allows space for thought, but ensures that the player plays in time, however slowly—a sensible piece of pedagogy. Three keys—C major, G major, and A minor—are covered, and each phrase is rounded off by a conventional cadence. *Published, with modern transcription and commentary, by Oxford University Press.*

- **Doubling of notes**. Most chords are triads, that is, they contain three different notes. In four-part harmony, one of these notes needs to be doubled. Bach had an exceptionally keen ear for the best-sounding doubled note, and one reason he insisted on students working in four parts was to develop their skill in this respect. When playing in four parts, be careful not to double sensitive notes—dissonances, for example the seventh of a dominant-seventh chord, or the leading note of the key. Neither produces a balanced sonority, especially a doubled leading note.
- **Preparation of dissonance**. Salt and savor is added to harmony by the controlled use of the regular suspended dissonances—9 8, 7 6,

and 4 3. However many (or few) parts you are playing in, be alert to the way these dissonant notes are threaded through the musical fabric. It is not merely academic to ensure that suspended dissonant notes are prepared in the previous chord, and resolved down a step into the next chord: it really does sound better. (Note, though, that sometimes the resolution may be taken over by the solo part.)

Accompanying Recitative

Unless you are in the happy position of playing continuo for the revival of a baroque opera (Purcell's *Dido and Aeneas* is a frequent and welcome possibility), your involvement with recitative will probably be only in a church cantata or oratorio. Today, the preferred continuo instrument for sacred music is the chamber organ, but in practice many modern choral societies use the harpsichord, for various reasons.

You will be working with not only a singer but also a cellist or gamba player. The cellist should be placed near you, so that you can see the bow easily, or the cellist can see your hands. If the singer stands in profile, you will find that good ensemble is easy. Before starting, check that everyone is ready: then play a confident chord, spreading it slightly. Unless the conductor does it for you, one of the continuo players, cello or harpsichord, must lead—let it be the more experienced person. It is helpful if the top note of your chord provides the singer's first note.

Cadences are your next priority. They act as the punctuation marks of recitative. Two main types recur constantly, and it is worth becoming really familiar with these (example 19-4, 4a). Practice them until your hands will fall automatically on them *in any key*. To assist in this, it is advisable, especially for beginners, to space the chords exactly as follows. (Because the tonic note is at the top, this arrangement gives a clear indication of tonality.)

Note that conventions are attached to the timing of cadences. In certain contexts, the two cadence chords are played simultaneously with

Example 19-4.   **Example 19-4a.**

217

the vocal cadence, instead of afterward. The cadence is then sometimes referred to as **occluded** or **truncated**. Your singer, or conductor, or sometimes the composer will tell you what is required.

Between the first chord and the cadence other chords will occur. These chords will often be realized as half notes or whole notes, and the bass (cello) part may be written in long, perhaps tied, notes: but this does not mean that all must be sustained. It is merely a convenient and tidy way of writing down recitative. There is a lot of documentary evidence from eighteenth-century Germany that recitative chords, however notated, were often played fairly short, even on the organ, so as not to obscure the singer's text.[4] Be prepared to play quite brief chords accompanied by no more than a gentle cello stroke. You can restrike the right-hand chord at a strategic point if you feel it is necessary. (Sometimes a composer will indicate a change of chord in the right hand even when the bass is silent.)

When playing recitative from a vocal score, be careful—some older editions double the left hand in octaves, without indicating whether the cellist is playing the top or bottom left-hand note. It is not always an agreeable sound if your left hand is in octaves with the cello, so check the parts together.

Your own modest bit of creative input, as far as recitative is concerned, involves the texture of the chords you play, and the rate at which they are arpeggiated. Chords may be thick or thin; they may be played completely unspread, or spread in several ways—upward, downward, or both; fast or slow—and played with or without the added crushed notes, which give extra bite and sonority (see above).

In performing recitative, it is vital to convey the meaning of the words by controlling their pace. You will of course have rehearsed with your singer(s) previously and decided together when chords should follow precipitately, where they should be thoughtfully delayed, and generally how they should be spaced. You and your cellist must accompany the singer sensitively and support what he or she is trying to do.

Pacing the recitative is particularly important in a work such as a Bach Passion. (There is much uncertainty as to whether Bach used organ or harpsichord to accompany the recitative,[5] but, as I have indicated, modern choral societies often use the harpsichord, so I include these works here.) To go through the Evangelists's part properly with him involves a good day's work. Naturally you will not be undertaking big engagements of this kind without both experience and guidance; but you can help prepare by studying recordings of good continuo players. Aim at something that does not sound contrived, or draw much attention to itself—a good player underpins the singer's interpretation, but does not add a blatant commentary to it.

Historical Continuo Style

This chapter has so far concentrated on the problems beginners most need to address; but as you progress, you can investigate the style of different composers and periods. One certainly does not accompany, say, a violin sonata by Marini in the same style as a recorder sonata by Telemann, or a Monteverdi madrigal like a cantata by Montéclair. A valuable book for the purpose is Peter Williams's two-volume *Figured Bass Accompaniment* (1970). This contains copious quotations from many sources, practice material, and excellent commentary.

The historic sources that mention continuo playing are, however, not always as helpful as the beginner might wish. As I mentioned above, it is hard to write down the notes that a good continuo player plays without it looking slightly strange in places, and few old sources attempt to do so. The exceptions to this are interesting: look, for example, at the realization of a Scarlatti cantata in Donington (1982, p. 160), or of the Pasquali recitative in the first volume of Williams's work (1970, p. 56). The examples in Geminiani's *The Art of Accompaniament*, written about 1754 for the English market and available in S. P. E. S. facsimile, show an unusually full style of realization, often in six parts. But most sources take refuge in the unvarying, orthodox layout of three parts in the right hand and one in the left. A famous specimen of this technique is Gerber's realization of an Albinoni sonata,[6] which was done under Bach's supervision and might therefore be thought to have his *imprimatur*. We need, however, to remind ourselves of the purpose of such workings. In the eighteenth century, figured-bass passages were widely used as exercises for teaching written harmony and composition. C. P. E. Bach says of his father's methods of instruction:

His pupils had to begin their studies [in composition] by learning pure four-part thorough-bass. . . . The realization of a thorough-bass and the introduction to chorales are without doubt the best method of studying composition.[7]

Geminiani says, of his *The Art of Accompaniament*, "This Work will also be useful in leading the Learner into the Method of Composing, for the Rules of Composition do not differ from those of Accompagniament."[8]

Extant examples, therefore, should not always be assumed to be continuo realizations; they are equally likely to be harmony exercises written in formal textures. Certainly they do not agree with contemporary accounts of Bach's own extraordinarily full and contrapuntally inventive continuo parts.

As mentioned earlier, C. P. E. Bach's *Essay on the True Art of Keyboard Playing* contains in its second part (1762) a thorough and valuable discussion of continuo practice. C. P. E. Bach is writing about galant music rather than baroque, which was already in his day considered old-fashioned: as always, one must remember only to apply historic advice to the relevant style of composition. Nevertheless, some of his ideas are universally applicable, and he shall have the last word about historic continuo texture: "Sometimes chords must be thin, sometimes full, and, with reference to the number of parts, there are pieces that require all kinds of accompaniment."[9]

The Way Forward

As well as studying source material, you should experiment, and above all you should listen. Listening closely to experienced continuo players is one of the most stimulating pastimes imaginable. Also, a general familiarity with other aspects of music in the appropriate period will always bring benefits, by enabling you to distinguish important characteristics—dance rhythms; oratorical effects; and that elusive but vital feeling for the style of a country, a decade, or a composer.

In particular, develop your sensitivity to the speed of harmonic change, and to chord density and keyboard layout. For example, accompanying a gamba suite by Marais calls for close attention to the range of the solo part, so that your continuo chords are laid out to complement the gamba. When working off a facsimile copy that only gives the continuo line, you will need to spend a little time becoming familiar with the solo part(s). Again, a good way of doing this is to play the *bass only,* very attentively, when you first rehearse with the other player(s).

With time and talent you may eventually be able to approach the most demanding works of the continuo player's world—virtuosic violin sonatas of the early seventeenth century. These sonatas date from a time of phenomenal growth in violin idioms, and they display mercurial changes of mood and texture: the music surges impetuously forward, sports with contrapuntal motifs, or sighs into sumptuous cadences. It is in these sonatas, perhaps, that dramatic improvisation in continuo playing can most fully take wing.

Notes

1. Geminiani 1749/1969, 4 and following examples. Quoted in Cyr 1992, 78.

2. Couperin 1716/1974, 50.

3. Wilson 1959, 249.

4. This is discussed at length in Dreyfus 1987. Italian players were apt to indulge in perpetual, rattling arpeggios, which sustained the tone of the chord: but this was widely criticized as distracting.

5. These arguments are studied in Dreyfus 1987.

6. Printed in full in Spitta 1873/1951.

7. David and Mendel (eds.) *The Bach Reader*, 1966, 279.

8. Geminiani ca. 1754, 1.

9. C. P. E. Bach 1762, 175.

20

Simple Facts About Pitch, Tuning, and Temperament

Many people confuse these three words, so a little preliminary explanation may be useful.

Pitch, in the context of this chapter, means the acoustical standard adopted for any instrument (a' = 440, a' = 415, and so on). The figures refer to the number of vibrations per second: in the case of the harpsichord, the number of times per second that the string makes a complete vibration. There have been many standards of pitch in the past, many of them lower than our present-day norm of a' = 440: French diapason pitch (a' = 392), commonly used on seventeenth-century French harpsichords, produced an outstandingly grave and sonorous effect. The general consensus of harpsichord makers today is to set instruments at a' = 415, the pitch used by most period orchestras. The gauges of wire used for stringing are chosen accordingly.

Tuning should strictly mean no more than the physical act of setting the instrument in tune, but it is sometimes used archaically to refer to pitch: you may hear an organ described as "in the old tuning," meaning merely that the instrument is at a pitch other than the present standard. The word is also loosely used in the same sense as temperament, to mean a *system* of ordering intervals.

Temperament is the most complex and fascinating of the three topics. It deals with the minutiae of the mathematical relationships of intervals within the octave. In theory, the relationships can be adjusted almost indefinitely, even in a normal twelve-semitone octave; in practice, however, there are about twenty systems that have found favor during the development of European music. The systems bear different names—either that of their inventor (e.g., Werckmeister) or that of their distinguishing mark (e.g., equal temperament, the most recent development). The rest of this chapter is devoted to a consideration of such systems and of why we need them. Please do not stop reading because you notice a few mathematical ratios on the page: it is a bonus if you can cope with them, but I hope to explain the subject simply so that a nonmathematical person can understand.

The first operation that the tuner of a keyboard instrument must perform is to **set the octave**, or **set the bearings**. This means that all the notes in one octave must be properly spaced, so that harmonious chords are possible. This setting of the octave is the highly skilled part of the operation: it takes both knowledge and long practice. But it is a relatively simple process to copy the set octave all over the keyboard—all the As are tuned in pure octaves with the set A, all the B-flats with the set B-flat, and so on.

Musicians generally understand that pure musical intervals have simple frequency ratios. If a' = 440, then the A above that has a frequency of 880, and the one below it 220. So the frequency *ratio* of the octave is 2:1; going down an octave, the frequency halves (although the harpsichord string is longer), while going up an octave the frequency doubles (although the string is shorter). This is a fundamental law of physics, and—together with the phenomenon known as the harmonic series—can be studied further in text books.[1] Other natural intervals from the harmonic series also have simple frequency ratios: for instance, the pure fifth has a ratio of 3:2, the pure fourth 4:3, the pure major third 5:4. When an interval is pure, it has a completely clean sound, with no "beats." **Beats** in the context of tuning are disturbances or fluctuations in the volume of the sound: if the frequency ratio between the vibrations of the two strings sounding the interval is not quite true (i.e., simple) the sound waves interfere with one another. Slow beats (one or two a second) are only mildly distracting, but as the beat rate rises the interval becomes more dingy sounding, and if the two strings are mistuned a long way from the pure ratio, the result is acutely unpleasant.

One would think that everything within the set octave could be tuned in pure intervals, but oddly enough this is impossible—a Great Flaw exists in the musical universe. To understand its nature and consequences, consider the following example. An octave is made up of three major thirds—for example, C–E, E–G-sharp, and G-sharp–B-sharp. The frequency ratio for pure major thirds is 5:4. To add ratios, one multiplies them together: 5:4 × 5:4 × 5:4 = 125:64. But this resulting 125:64 is less than an octave, which is 2:1 or (for purposes of comparison) 128:64. Three pure major thirds will not quite stretch to an octave—the B-sharp is lower than C. Clearly, there will be problems if we try to pursue this line, since on a usable keyboard there is only one key for B-sharp and C: and obviously octaves must be perfectly in tune.

Now consider fifths. There are twelve possible fifths within the octave. (To visualize this, look at a full seven-octave piano, and from the C above the lowest A, go up by intervals of a perfect fifth, making sure you use letter names that ascend five each time; G, D, A, E, B, F-sharp, C-sharp, G-sharp, D-sharp, A-sharp, E-sharp, B-sharp.) Twelve successive fifths and, although we have just gone off the piano keyboard, we are back at C (i.e., B-sharp). Or are we? The mathematics are a bit harder this time, involving twelve multiplications; but they show that twelve pure fifths with frequency ratios of 3:2 exceed seven octaves—they have overshot the mark, and B-sharp is higher than C. Obviously, this will not do either.

These examples show that one cannot tune in pure intervals throughout and still manage with only twelve notes in each octave. String players, wind players and singers can to some extent adjust their intervals as they proceed, but for a keyboard with only twelve keys some system of compromise is necessary: the intervals must be modified, or tempered, according to some scheme. You can imagine the processes involved by picturing a measured length of sand into which you have to insert twelve pegs. Not only do these "semitone" pegs have to be a reasonably equal distance apart, but each peg must be an acceptable distance from the pegs with which it forms the major third and fifth. As you move each peg, you alter every other relationship at the same time. In real life, the adjustments involved in devising a temperament are done part empirically, part mathematically; the resulting relationships are often displayed on a circular diagram of fifths for ease of reference (see chapter 21). Another handy reference device is a pocket dial produced by Clayson and Garrett. This tabulates the resulting sizes of the major thirds and fifths in twelve common temperaments.[2]

Mean-Tone Temperament

Mean-tone is the earliest system of temperament of interest to harpsichordists. It starts by determining the size of the major thirds: the name mean-tone, incidentally, is given because in this system a tone is exactly half a pure major third. Mean-tone has eight pure thirds—the ones used in the simplest keys, i.e., C–E, G–B, F–A, D–F-sharp and so on. Pure major thirds (frequency ratio 5:4) are noticeably smaller than those in equal temperament (which is the system used on pianos and the one most people have grown up with); but these distinctive, unforced pure thirds give a serene, luminous quality to the major triad. The other four thirds within the octave series, however, have to be disastrously large in compensation: F-sharp–B-flat, G-sharp–C, B–E-flat and C-sharp–F sound quite unacceptable. (Notice that they are not really thirds: they are diminished fourths. When used as the latter, either melodically or harmonically, they have a remarkably tense and haunting effect.)

The size of the thirds obviously affects the size of the fifths, as the intervals are shunted about within the octave. No mean-tone fifths are pure. This does not matter much—the ear is quite tolerant of the eleven rather small fifths. But the remaining interval within the mean-tone octave, G-sharp–E-flat, comes out so much larger than a pure fifth that it is quite unusable: it was nicknamed "the wolf" because of its discordant howling, and for many years it was a considerable musical obstacle.

You will have noticed that the black keys are tuned to B-flat, E-flat, F-sharp, C-sharp, and G-sharp, but these notes will *not* work as their enharmonic equivalents—A-sharp, D-sharp and so on.[3] This means that keys with more than two flats or three sharps are unusable, and even E minor and B minor are not entirely harmonious, because the dominant chords of these keys (which contain D-sharp and A-sharp respectively) sound false. But the simple keys contain so many very satisfactory sounding chords that the compensations are great.

It is helpful to become accustomed to mean-tone temperament, as you will often hear it in recordings of seventeenth-century music. Its highly distinctive flavor is an integral part of the music, and its unique relationships were part of the composer's intentions. In practical terms, the main feature you may notice is that the semitones are not of equal size: the chromatic semitones (e.g., F–F-sharp) are smaller than the diatonic ones (e.g., F-sharp–G). This means that the leading notes of most of the simple keys are noticeably flat to modern ears. Another consequence is that chromatic melodies have a fascinating and expressive irregularity. The great seventeenth-century theorist Mersenne was one of many writers who observed how the inequality of the semitones lent beauty and variety to music. Once you are used to the richness and yet the asperity of mean-tone sound, and understand the reasons underlying it, this is an impressive temperament.

Modified and Well-Tempered Systems

The mean-tone system was later modified by eighteenth-century theorists such as Gottfried Silbermann. The restricting wolf fifth was retained, but made smaller and less objectionable, and the other fifths were slightly enlarged, so that they were now flatter than pure by only a fifth or sixth of a comma, instead of a quarter of a comma as in the original system. (The comma of Pythagoras is the amount by which twelve pure fifths overshot seven octaves, as illustrated earlier in the chapter.) This process evened out the semitone steps somewhat, and enlarged the thirds slightly; but keys such as F minor or A-flat major were still barely usable.

However, the restless urge of the late seventeenth century could not remain content with systems that were restricted to certain keys, and experiments began in producing systems that, although less than perfect in some keys, were at least usable in all: that is, they were *well-tempered*. This was done by abolishing the fixed abnormality of the G-sharp–E-flat fifth. Once this bottle-neck was removed, the imperfection of the fifths could be distributed freely and variably around the circle. For this reason, these temperaments are also referred to as *unrestricted* or *circulating*. Werckmeister and Kirnberger devised many such temperaments, and Bach's *The Well-tempered Clavier* may have been written for a system of this kind (although this is much debated). Great ingenuity was displayed by musicians in deciding how to allocate the imperfection of the fifths. Occasionally a few widened fifths were used as well as the narrowed ones, particularly by the French. Of the varying sizes of third that resulted, none was so unbearably large as the four bad thirds in mean-tone temperament.

One pronounced result of any unequal temperament is that each of the twenty-four keys has very slight differences in the quality of its intervals and the character of its chords. The differences are small, and no one could ever identify every key, in any temperament, by the sound alone; but there is nevertheless in all unequal temperaments a perceptible change of character from the simple keys to the remoter sharp or flat keys, which have greater intensity. (Perhaps a memory of this difference lingers on in the characteristics that various musicians have ascribed to certain keys—Beethoven's "black key" of B minor, for example.) Note that this distinctive character would remain whatever *pitch* was in use—the *relationships* within the key matter, not its absolute pitch.

Well-tempered systems were in use for organs until well into the nineteenth century and sometimes even later. It is an expensive and laborious job to change an organ temperament, as it involves cutting and altering pipes. But developments in nineteenth-century music soon relegated the organ and the temperaments that it used to a relative backwater. Mainstream romanticism, with its love of diminished-seventh chords, its freedom of modulation, and its vast development of instrument technology, consorted naturally with the development of our modern system of **equal temperament**—the system in which all fifths are narrower than pure by the same amount, all semitone steps are equal, all thirds are wider than pure by the same amount, and no interval except the octave is pure.

One might think that this was an obvious answer to the Great Flaw, but a price has to be paid for the simplicity of the solution. There is infinite freedom of modulation; but key subtlety, purity of triads, and the expressive tensions and relaxations created in both melody and harmony by the slightly different-sized semitones, have all disappeared. And although it suits the piano, equal temperament (besides being very difficult to tune accurately) does not produce a good sonority on the harpsichord. The rich harmonics of harpsichord sound derive much of their strength from the sympathetic resonance of nearby strings with which they share simple frequency-relationships; if there are no pure intervals, this reinforcement cannot take place.

A harpsichord is usually tuned in one of the well-tempered systems today, unless it is required to play music written before about 1650. The temperament of Vallotti (1741) is popular and quite easy to tune: instructions are given in the next chapter. Vallotti used six pure and six tempered fifths, and tucked away the least harmonious thirds (F-sharp–B-flat, G-sharp–C, and C-sharp–F) in the remoter keys. Eighteenth-century French music is enhanced by the use of temperaments such as that of Rousseau/d'Alembert, or Rameau's *tempérament ordinaire*, both of which have three fifths slightly larger than pure tucked around the back of the circle (G-sharp–E-flat–B-flat–F). All these systems may be studied in detail in Klop's *Harpsichord Tuning* and other publications.[4]

Recordings of music involving harpsichord usually mention the temperament used, and this is a good way both to observe the characteristics of the different systems and to see what music they best suit. Kenneth Gilbert, for example, uses Rousseau's temperament from the *Dictionnaire de musique* (1768) for recordings of Couperin and Rameau, but Werckmeister III for the Bach Suites. The Parley of Instruments uses Vallotti for a wide range of ensemble music. The Vallotti temperament also suits music for harpsichord and viola da gamba well, its intervals agreeing readily with the stringing and fretting of the gamba.

In the recording studio, it is easy to use a different temperament for each piece of music: Trio Sonnerie's recording of Rameau's *Pièces en Concert*, for example, uses three different temperaments—Young (for C minor), Bendeler (for G major), and Werckmeister III (for A major, B-flat major, and D minor)—in order to favor the keys of the different pieces. This is obviously a perfectionist approach, which cannot be applied to live performance. Skilled tuners may however compromise when setting up an instrument for a recital, by using a certain basic temperament but modifying one or two of its notes very slightly to favor a key that is prominent in the recital.

Such subtleties are for professionals, and if all this seems abstruse and daunting, there is no need to worry about how it is achieved. The results, however, are important, for temperament forms part of the music in a profound sense. We have gradually come to perceive that the harmonic and melodic effects intended by a composer derive from the temperament he heard in use around him. The care that is now taken to perform keyboard music in an appropriate temperament is a highly interesting aspect of historical performance practice.

If a temperament sounds strange to your ear, do not resist it, but try to analyze what constitutes the strangeness, and what musical point it is underlining. The uneven chromatic steps or the strained diminished fourths in mean-tone tuning, or the tense and bitter C-sharp major chords in *tempérament ordinaire*, are conveying a unique point. Pay particular attention to the size and quality of the thirds—contrary to one's natural assumption, it is the tuning of the major thirds, not the fifths, that strikes the ear most forcibly. When Bach was trying to show, in *The Well-tempered Clavier*, how a system can sound satisfactory in all the twenty-four keys, he took great care over the placing and textures of the more extreme thirds, either putting them in a low register where they beat less rapidly, or disguising them with a cadential trill. This care is typical of his painstaking intellect. Many other composers, however, seemed to enjoy and exploit the slight asperity of chords with large thirds. Your aural perception will gradually become enriched by this fascinating diversity, and a new dimension of music will begin to unfold.

Notes

1. In simple terms, the harmonic series consists of the notes obtained when a string of fixed length is caused to vibrate in two sections, then three, then four,

and so on. The same series is obtained from progressively subdividing the vibrations of an air column, e.g., in a bugle.

2. *Clayson and Garrett Tuning Compass*. A pocket indicator with booklet, 1980. Available from Early Keyboard Instruments, Lyminge, Folkestone, Kent, U.K.

3. On seventeenth-century instruments, the G-sharp key is often divided into back and front halves, one half plucking a G-sharp string, the other half plucking a string tuned to A-flat. This mitigates some of the worst evils of mean-tone temperament. D-sharp and E-flat may be similarly divided.

4. Klop 1974; Tittle 1987; Barbour 1951–53; Padgham 1986.

21

Care, Maintenance, and Tuning of the Harpsichord

If you have built your own instrument from a kit, you will have absorbed many of the basics of maintenance and repair, or will be able to find them in your manual. If you have bought your instrument, you will not have such useful experience at first, but a good supplier should show you how to do certain necessary operations, such as voicing a new plectrum, and you will gradually build up your knowledge of the instrument. If a problem occurs while you are playing someone else's instrument, you should proceed with great caution. When in the slightest doubt, leave the problem alone and report it to the owner.

General Care

The harpsichord prefers a modest, equable temperature (certainly not more than 70°F [21°C]) and reasonable humidity.[1] Keep the instrument away from radiators, fires, direct sunlight, and drafty places.

Being made of wood, the instrument responds strongly to changes of humidity. The interaction is complex. Put simply: in humid conditions, the wood absorbs moisture and expands, which means that the strings are required to stretch more. The greater tension will raise the pitch slightly, although this will not be uniform over the whole instrument. Conversely, in dry conditions the wood shrinks and tension slackens.

Extremes of dryness are very bad for the instrument, cracks in the soundboard being a particular danger. You cannot do much about avoiding humid conditions in damp weather; but you can, by using humidifiers, protect your instrument from the worst drying effects of central heating. Even having some copiously watered plants in the room will help.

It is worth while buying a hygrometer and taking trouble to discover what conditions suit your instrument. Always remember that when a harpsichord is moved to a different environment there will be some degree of stress.

An open harpsichord lid looks decorative, but there are snags about leaving it open for long periods. With the lid up, the soundboard is exposed to the atmosphere, and is more vulnerable to drying and instability of tuning. If the soundboard is painted, it may tend to discolor with prolonged exposure to light. Also, dust will gather on it in time: this will need to be brushed out carefully, using an artist's brush, and vacuumed away. So on balance the lid is best kept shut when the instrument is not in use. Obviously, in an institution, keeping the lid closed avoids damage and disturbance, although you then need to take care that things are not placed (or even stacked) on top of it. If the instrument has its own cover, use it.

If you use an eraser of any kind while practicing, take care not to let the debris drop down from the music rest into the interior. Put the music on your knee while you rub. Be careful with pencils too; on some types of harpsichord, they can roll under the keys or even under the name-board and be very hard to retrieve. This can also cause damage to the action.

Simple Trouble Shooting

To act effectively, you need to understand the principle of registers, and know a little about how jacks behave. You may need to reread chapter 2.

If a note fails to sound, there are several possible causes.

- The string may be broken.
- The plectrum may be broken.
- The plectrum may be missing the string.
- The jack may be damaged.
- The jack may be sticking in the register, and failing to return.
- The plectrum may be hanging—that is, not slipping back beneath the string after playing.
- A key may be sticking.

If the string is broken—an infrequent mishap in normal circumstances—you will see misplaced wire. Remove both ends with care (harpsichord wire is dangerously sharp-ended and whippy), roll it up and dispose of it safely. If you know how to restring, check the gauge of wire appropriate to that note. The new string will need a few days to stretch out fully, and you will have to keep easing it gently up to pitch.

If no strings are broken, take off the jack rail, depress the key in question, and identify which jack, in which register, is the faulty one. Lift it out and examine it. (Notice that it will bear a number, indicating to which place, in which register, it belongs. Jacks are not freely interchangeable, and if you remove more than one, it is vital to replace them correctly.)

If the plectrum is broken—a commoner occurrence—a new one must be fitted and voiced. It will be necessary first to remove the stub of the broken plectrum. Sometimes this can easily be done with pliers, by pushing it back the way it was put in. If it has sheered off flush with the jack, you may need to push it out with a small screwdriver, resting the jack across a voicing-block or other piece of wood.

It is hard to describe exactly how to voice a plectrum to someone who has never done it, but if you are in sole charge of a school harpsichord and have an emergency on your hands, the following summary may help.

You need a very sharp knife with a smallish blade (a scalpel or modeling knife), a block of hard wood, and care and patience. Find a new uncut plectrum and insert it through the hole in the jack tongue, so that it points out on the same side as the damper. Then drop the jack into its slot and cut the plectrum approximately to length, so that it projects about 1 mm beyond the string it should pluck. Now, take the jack out again and start to shape the plectrum so that it tapers *in* toward the tip on both sides as you look down on it, and also tapers *up* toward its tip from beneath. Do not cut the top surface at all (look at other plectra as a guide). It will be easier to work if you remove the damper, using tweezers or pliers. You are aiming to create a plectrum that will flex uniformly and willingly along its entire length, so be sure to thin the plectrum right back to where it enters the jack. Use a light whittling action, and never cut too much at once, or you may spoil the job and have to start all over again. Work tidily, leaving no rough bits or snags, which might cause problems.

As you progress, drop the jack in occasionally, play the note and see how it sounds. A fierce, explosive "boing" means that more whittling is needed. Compare the neighboring notes for relative strength and attack.

Final shaping involves removing mere wisps of material. When you are satisfied, replace the damper felt (making sure the damper is not too low), and replace the jack and jack rail.

If the plectrum is missing the string, make sure that the register is fully on. If it is, but the note still misses or is weak, it may be possible to lengthen the plectrum slightly by easing it carefully through the tongue a little, using a small screwdriver or pair of fine pliers. Support the tongue against a voicing-block while you push. If this does not work, you will probably have to cut a new plectrum.

A damaged jack is most likely to have trouble with the spring or the tongue—the little piece of hinged wood in which the plectrum is set. Make sure that the pivot pin is intact, and the tongue is able to swing freely. Check that the spring at the back is operating properly, so that it can return the tongue to its place. Jack design varies so much that it is only possible to give a few hints, but a one-piece plastic tongue-and-hinge can often be activated by a little gentle flexing, whereas an ineffectual bristle spring may have to be replaced.

If the jack is failing to return after playing, you will need to free it in the register. Rub it up and down in the register, maintaining gentle friction with the sides; failing that, apply a little talc or graphite, or rub it gently with fine sandpaper.

If the plectrum is hanging above the string, there can be several causes. The tongue may be too stiff, or the spring faulty (see above). The damper may be set too low, preventing the jack from falling to its full extent. The plectrum itself may be marginally too long or inflexible, or have a whisker of plastic that needs trimming: get the scalpel out. Hanging can also result from a playing problem; on a badly regulated instrument, merely raising the finger from the key too lazily can cause the plectrum to hang. Cultivate a more positive release.

A key that sticks may be binding with its neighbors, and you will probably have to take the keyboard(s) out and do some sandpapering. To remove the keyboards, unscrew the name-batten, which runs across the upper manual, stand all the jacks up in their slots so that they do not fall through, and then find the release catch of the keyboard unit so that you can pull it out. Again, this is a simple job once you have done it several times, but not on first acquaintance.

Good regulation and ease of playing of an instrument depends on a complex and very precise balance between several factors: the length of the plectrum and the tension of the string; the height of the jack, and hence the distance of the plectrum below the string; the depth and freedom of the key-travel; the set of the damper, and its freedom from whiskers or other accretions; the **stagger**, or tiny interval between the pluck of the different registers; and so on. Getting all these right, and *consistent*, is the work of an expert, but you may be able to correct obvious minor upsets.

If the harpsichord is your own, you should aim to become friends with what is under the lid. You may not be technologically minded yourself, but perhaps a friend will help. Do beware, though, of enthusiastic meddlers.

Transposing Instruments

Some harpsichords are built with an integral transposing facility, to enable you to play at either a' = 415 or a' = 440. Certain builders also offer the facility to transpose to a' = 392 (French diapason pitch). The general principle is, that to play at a' = 415, you use the keyboard in its basic position, but to play at a' = 440, you move the entire keyboard one note to the right (thereby wasting one string in the bass and losing the top note of the treble, unless the instrument is equipped with extra strings). For a' = 392, you move the keyboard one note to the left.

To move the keyboard, find the release catch. Now adjust the end blocks of wood that govern the position of the keyboard—for example, to transpose up, take the movable block away from the treble end, push the keyboard to the right as far as it will go, and insert the block at the bass end. Finally secure the catch again. In a few types of instrument it may be necessary to stand the jacks up before moving the keyboard. Note that when you have transposed, you will need to retune the instrument, if it is in anything other than equal temperament. A moment's thought will reveal why this is so.

Practical Aspects of Tuning

You should gradually be learning to tune your own instrument. The harpsichord is vulnerable to climatic changes and other man-made hazards (of which central heating and stage lighting are the worst), and needs fairly frequent attention. It is simply not possible always to rely on the services of a professional tuner. Besides, as should be evident from the previous chapter, the whole fascinating procedure of tempering the intervals of your instrument's scale is a really creative preliminary to playing, and a vital part of making the music.

It is of course possible to buy electronic tuning aids. These are available in two basic forms. The first type generates a sound for each note, which you then match by tuning. The second, more common, type is a meter. One uses this according to the instructions supplied; but most meters on the market have a dial calibrated in units called **cents** (a cent being a small logarithmic unit equal to one hundredth of an equal-tempered semitone). The dial shows when you have reached the required frequency, or how far flat or sharp you are. There is no doubt that meters are the simplest and most foolproof: tone generators take skill to operate well, although they teach you how to listen for beats. Both types are generally set to equal temperament, but several temperament options can usually be obtained for a little extra expense. The data in cents for many different temperaments can be found in Padgham (1986) or Barbour (1951–53).

If you are in charge of a school harpsichord, or live a hectic life, an electronic tuner is probably your best ally. There is, however, no real substitute for learning to tune by ear, which can give great pleasure and vouchsafe much insight. It is not difficult, provided you understand what you are trying to do. The next few pages may look complicated, but you may not need to absorb all the information that they contain—in practice, a selection will probably suffice. Nevertheless, read it all in the first instance.

Preliminaries

One first needs a few practical hints about the physical action of handling a tuning pin or hammer, and applying it to a string.

- Isolate the register you intend to tune by silencing the others.
- Locate the tuning a'. On some harpsichords, it is easy to see which tuning pin relates to which string, since the pins are offset in a pattern mirroring the sharps and naturals of the keyboard. If this is not so, select the front eight-foot, touch your tuning a', and notice which jack moves. You can then locate the tuning-pin, once you have noted which way the jack plucks.
    On most harpsichords, the row of tuning pins for the front eight-foot lies *behind* the row for the back eight-foot. The four-foot tuning pins, if any, are located further back still, near the jack rail.
- Hold the tuning hammer in whichever hand is more comfortable for each part of the keyboard, and rest your wrist on the top of the name-board: this will prevent you pulling the tuning pins toward you. Place the slot gently over the head of the tuning pin—without forcing it down—and turn *very slowly, keeping the hammer*

235

absolutely vertical: clockwise to sharpen; counterclockwise, to flatten. On a well-regulated instrument, the pins will turn smoothly without jerks, although they should not seem loose. (If they do slip, a precise tap on the head of the pin with the tuning hammer is quite in order.)

•   Fine tuning involves easing the pin through a very small arc; in fact, tiny adjustments of pitch call for a mere squeeze on the tuning hammer. Experiment to find a way of holding the hammer to make this fine degree of control possible. Personally, I find that the best grip involves holding the T-bar of the hammer between second and third fingers, steadying the fourth and fifth fingers against the upright, and pressing the thumb gently against the end of the T-bar. When I discovered, in the National Portrait Gallery in London, a picture of the harpsichord builder Shudi tuning one of his harpsichords (figure 13), it was interesting to find that he seemed to be using the same grip.

•   Whatever pair of strings you are tuning together, always adopt the sequence: play, listen, tune; play, listen, tune . . . Give yourself time to hear the interval die away, and to see if beats are present.

•   It is best to set each note to the required pitch *from below,* so slacken the tension ever so slightly (not letting the pin unwind) and then ease it very gently up to pitch.

•   When you have finished, take the tuning hammer very gently off the pin, so as not to disturb the result.

Before you think of attempting actual tuning, other preliminaries need to be understood, and a few processes practiced, as follows:

All tuning systems involve setting some intervals pure (that is, without beats) and other intervals to beat by certain amounts. **Beats** are disturbances in the plainness and cleanness of sound that occur when two notes are not perfectly related. Most musicians need practice in hearing beats: indeed, a good musical ear can be a positive hindrance, because it tends to make one focus on the aesthetic aspect of the interval, rather than on the beats.

To start with, practice listening for beats by taking the same note—it should be in the tenor range—on two eight-foot registers, and very gradually mistuning one with the other. You will hear slow, wavy unevenness, which will get faster and eventually merge into an unpleasant sound the further you mistune. Then return the tuning gradually to where you started, and listen as the beats get slower and then disappear. A true unison has a dead, dry sound which you should learn

Figure 13. *Portrait of the Shudi Family* by Marcus Tuscher (ca. 1742). Burkat Shudi, the noted London-Swiss harpsichord builder, is here shown tuning one of his instruments: probably a unique depiction of the process. His son's pointing finger makes sure that the uninitiated viewer does not miss this inconspicuous but important action. Note Shudi's grip of the tuning hammer. *Reproduced by permission of The National Portrait Gallery, London.*

to recognize. It is important not to let subjective judgments intrude: you are not listening for the kind of unison produced by a string orchestra, which has a warm, comforting ambience because its unison is not exact.

When you can tune good clean unisons between your eight-foot strings, try tuning pure fourths and fifths on the front eight-foot register. Do this in the tenor region where, because of the lower frequencies involved, beats are also slower and easier to hear. Again, the beats will be faster the more mistuned your interval is, and will then get slower and disappear as you return to a pure interval.

Whatever temperament you use, you need to be able to tune both pure and modified fourths and fifths. (Note that fifths, if not perfect, are usually *narrowed,* whereas fourths are usually *widened:* make sure you are adjusting your interval in the right direction.) The pure intervals will have no beats; the modified ones will have a stated number—see below. It is helpful to know where the beats for these intervals actually *sound,* so that you can listen for them at the right pitch.

237

- Between any two notes a fifth apart, the beats will be at a pitch an octave above the *higher* note, where the third harmonic of the lower note coincides with the second harmonic of the upper (example 21-1).
- Between any two notes a fourth apart, the beats will be at a pitch two octaves above the *lower* note, where the fourth harmonic of the lower note coincides with the third harmonic of the upper (example 21-2).

Example 21-1.   **Example 21-2.**

(Explanations of these matters can be studied in any good physics reference book.) Playing this higher note where the beats occur will direct your ears to the right pitch and help you to focus on what you are hearing.

After mastering the tuning of unisons, fourths and fifths, you can begin to tackle octaves. This is not quite as simple as it might seem, and you should give yourself enough time to listen to each octave—probably four or five seconds. Reject any interval with the slightest rolling or burring in the sound: there must be no beats at all. It can be difficult at first to muster the patience and the physical coordination to search for the tiny point at which this is true. Believe that it does exist. You will gradually become familiar with the sound which marks the exact spot— it has a diamond-like clarity.

It is also a help to check your octaves by sounding (successively) the fifth and the fourth of which they are composed. Remember that a pure fourth plus a pure fifth equals a pure octave; and if your chosen temperament instructs you to temper either interval, the complementary interval will beat at the same rate, and sound similarly softened.

Starting to Tune by Ear

As described in the previous chapter, temperament is an inescapable necessity, not a luxury or an anachronism that can be evaded. Choose a temperament that suits the majority of the music you intend to play. Then look up its data: not the kind of data expressed in *cents*, which are intended for those using meters, but the kind expressed in little diagrams showing where the pure fifths occur and by how much the others are mistuned: usually expressed as a **fraction of a comma—** one-quarter, one-fifth, one-sixth. The following diagram shows the spacing of Vallotti's temperament, which was quoted by Tartini in his *Trattato di Musica,* (Padua, 1754): six perfect fifths, indicated by a small circle, and six fifths narrowed by one-sixth of a comma (figure 14). Vallotti's is a useful general temperament that is fairly easy to tune, so I use it here as my illustration.

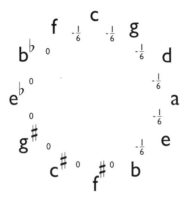

Figure 14. Tuning diagram showing Vallotti's temperament (1741). *Reproduced by courtesy of Gerrit Klop.*

The pure fifths present no problem, but how does one know how much to narrow the tempered fifths? There are various ways of judging a sixth of a comma. The Clayson and Garrett Tuning Compass mentioned in chapter 20 has a booklet containing various exercises aimed at achieving an understanding of the process. Klop's *Harpsichord Tuning* (1974) has tables showing the beat rates for all the imperfect (i.e., tempered) intervals; these are given in beats *per minute,* which are measured using a metronome.

Some people find this rate per minute difficult, however, and prefer to work with beat rates *per second.* These are easy to judge using a wrist watch, since in the tenor register, where you set your first octave, the beat rates you need are not more than about three per second. Beats per second will not give quite such a precise result, but the following method of tuning Vallotti's temperament, based on a method devised by Peter Bavington, will produce a very acceptable result:

• Set your a' on the front eight-foot (which is usually the easiest to hear beats on) using a tuning fork. Be clear as to whether your fork is a′ = 415 or a′ = 440. Sound the fork, then hold the shaft in your mouth while it sounds, to leave both your hands free for tuning.

• Next, transpose the a′ down an octave into the tenor register: check this lower a against the fork, too.

• Then set the octave which runs between c and b in the tenor region, thus:

Tune the f, a third below a, to beat three times per second.

Tune successively, the b-flat a pure fourth above; the e-flat a pure fifth below; the g-sharp a pure fourth above; the c-sharp a pure fifth below; the f-sharp a pure fourth above; the b a pure fourth above.

Considering the e below that b: tune it so that it beats equally— about once a second, really only perceptible as a slow soft wave— with both the b and the tenor a you started from. If this does not work at first, go back and check, adjusting as necessary. Do not, of course, alter the a.

Then, taking the tenor f, tune the c below that so that it beats a little more than once a second. Next, test this c with the e above it; there should be rather less than three beats per second.

Returning to the c, tune the g above it to beat about once a second.

Lastly, considering the only note you have not already tuned, d, tune this so that it beats equally with the previous g and the tenor a above. Again, make any necessary adjustments by working back-ward (so that you do not alter the a).

• Now try out all the following fourths and fifths between the white notes of this primary octave: c–f, c–g, d–g, d–a, e–a, e–b. They should all sound about equally impure and have about one beat per second; just enough for the interval to sound gently wavy or fuzzy, without being at all unpleasant. Any interval that beats really noticeably is too small (if a fifth) or too large (if a fourth).

• Finally, check the major third d–f-sharp, which should beat three times per second, and the major sixth c–a, which should beat about four times.

Once your octave is set thus, you use it as a model for the rest of that register, each note being copied carefully in pure octaves. After you have copied about eight notes of the model, try out a few major and minor chords, using notes you have already tuned, to see if any are notably false. Certain chords, notably F-sharp major, B major, and A-flat major, will have conspicuously large, somewhat dissonant thirds— this is correct, because it is a property of Vallotti's temperament. If nothing else sounds amiss, you can proceed to copy the model all over the rest of the front eight-foot.

The tuning of the front eight-foot can then be copied on to the other eight-foot register on the instrument unison by unison, starting in the bass. As you do this, start to check the octaves on *this* register, as soon as there is room to do so: it will act as a double check on your tuning of the first eight-foot. The four-foot, if any, is best tuned in octaves with the front eight-foot.

I stress that this is only a first guide. Greater insights into tuning will come through using Klop's booklet or the Clayson and Garrett tuning compass. Klop has good instructions on mean-tone tuning, which is a particularly rich system. To play music written before about 1650 in mean-tone tuning is a revelation. Indeed, after gaining a little experience, you will probably be gripped by enthusiasm and want to try out various other temperaments, in order to hear how different pieces of music actually sounded to their creators. Few processes could be more rewarding.

Other Information

To check the tuning quickly when you come to an instrument, you can simply try major and minor chords in the middle area of the keyboard, and if these seem satisfactory, it is a fairly simple process to tidy up the extremities of the keyboard by tuning notes in octaves with notes in the area you have checked. As it is the small strings which go out of tune most readily, these may be the only ones needing attention. If any chords in the middle area are poor, however, it has to be said that this quick tidying-up process is rarely satisfactory; one alteration leads to another, and often tuning the whole register is just as quick in the long run.

- If the instrument has not been tuned for some time and has moved some way from its normal pitch, it may need an extra tuning to restabilize it after it has been brought back to pitch.
- If you want to set Vallotti's temperament using a *meter*, and it does not have this option, you can use the equal temperament setting and convert it to Vallotti by adding or subtracting the following numbers of cents:

B♭: + 6. E♭: + 4. G♯: + 2.

C♯: 0. F♯: − 2. B: − 4.

E: − 2. A: 0. D: + 2.

G: + 4. C: + 6. F: + 8.

241

- If you are having to tune in noisy conditions, it can be helpful to leave the main lid closed and put your head under the front flap. This may appear slightly eccentric, but you will hear more clearly and be less distracted by other sound.

In Conclusion

All harpsichords have their own patterns of behavior, but many tend to go sharp in the bass and flat in the treble in cold dry weather (as if the instrument was huddling close to get warm). Conversely, they may go sharp in the treble and flat in the bass (as if stretching out) in warm or humid weather. Thunderstorms and sharp barometric changes can be particularly hard on tuning. But do not imagine that tuning is an endless chore—a good professionally built instrument in a sympathetic environment can stand in tune for many weeks.

If you take your instrument out to a concert venue, allow it to acclimatize to the new conditions for at least an hour before tuning, if possible. Onlookers may at times be patronizing about the apparent tuning instability of the harpsichord, but they are usually silenced if you ask them how often a string quartet tunes during a concert.

Most people who take instruments about with them soon work out their own methods, but a surprisingly small vehicle will suffice provided that its internal arrangement is flexible. Vehicles with right-hand drive have a natural advantage—if the front passenger seat can be folded down so that the tail of the harpsichord reaches the dashboard, the bentside of the instrument will fit neatly around the driver. The instrument needs a well-fitting padded cover to protect it; the stand can be dismantled and is easily stowed. A small trolley can be useful, but if stairs are involved a couple of stalwart helpers are preferable.

To travel with one's instrument is to make friends; people are almost invariably interested and helpful. Also, over a period of time, you will develop a close friendship with the harpsichord itself. It is my hope that this book will enable you to draw the best from the instrument, and to play it with ever-increasing enjoyment and understanding.

Notes

1. Various factors condition what is regarded as satisfactory. Relative humidity is by definition linked to temperature, since warm air can absorb more moisture than cold. In places with a continental climate the relative humidity may fluctuate very widely—between 20% or less (in cold, snowy weather with the central heating well turned up) to 80% or more in trying summer conditions. The

Hubbard workshop seems to prefer a relative humidity of about 40%, given a temperature of 70°F [21°C]. In the United Kingdom, where the relative humidity is in any case more constant, that would be regarded as rather low, builders being happier with about 60%.

A harpsichord's well-being can depend upon the conditions prevailing at the time when the soundboard is glued into the case. Obviously a thin sheet of spruce, glued all around its edges to a framework of greater solidity, will be at risk of cracking if it is humid when installed but later dries out. Builders therefore aim to dry out the soundboard beforehand, and to fit it in dry weather. One cannot, however, always win: a soundboard installed in dry conditions may bulge upward when it absorbs moisture, and I have known harpsichords with a bulge that could foul the four-foot strings.

APPENDIX A

Twentieth-Century Harpsichord Music

The revival of the instrument has naturally led to a certain amount of modern composition for harpsichord. Some of this has at least a hint of pastiche in its make-up, in that it invokes historic genres, idioms, or textures to a greater or lesser degree, even when the harmonic idiom is fairly modern. Increasingly, though, there is a preoccupation with the actual acoustic properties of the instrument, which lend themselves readily to avant-garde treatment. Harpsichord sound is fairly evenly dispersed through the frequency spectrum: that is to say, the sound is not particularly strong in the fundamental frequencies, but possesses a wealth of overtones. This characteristic enables it to be combined effectively with electronically generated sound of many kinds, as well as with conventional instruments. The instrument's percussive potential has likewise not been overlooked.

In the United States, the Southeastern Historical Keyboard Society (see appendix B) offers Aliénor Harpsichord Composition Awards to stimulate interest in new music for the instrument. Japanese composers are also showing a lively interest in the harpsichord. Three publications ought to be mentioned.

Frances Bedford, *Harpsichord and Clavichord Music of the Twentieth Century* (Berkeley, Fallen Leaf Press, 1993) is a very comprehensive catalog of contemporary harpsichord music.

Larry Palmer, *Harpsichord in America: A Twentieth-Century Revival* (Bloomington, Indiana University Press, 1989) is more anecdotal, but gives a lively and readable picture of the contemporary music scene in America as it involves the harpsichord.

Martin Elste, *Modern Harpsichord Music: A Discography* (London, Greenwood Press, 1995) gives details of recordings of twentieth-century music for harpsichord.

The following selection of music includes pieces (marked *) that might be played by the amateur:

Ahlgrimssen: *Strond*

Andriessen, Louis: *Overture to Orpheus** (a simple but lengthy piece needing two manuals)

Bialas, Günther, Hugo Distler, and others: pieces* in *New Music for Harpsichord* (Bärenreiter)

Bryars, Gavin: After Handel's Vesper

de Falla, Manuel: Chamber Concerto for harpsichord (piano)

Dodgson, Stephen: Various neobaroque pieces*

Emmerson, Simon: *Points of Departure* for harpsichord and live electronics

Górecki, Henryk: *Concerto*

Jacob, Gordon: *Suite for Virginal**

Leigh, Walter: *Concertino*

Ligeti, György: *Continuum; Hungarian Rock; Passacaille Ungarese**

Poulenc, Francis: *Concerto*

Nyman, Michael: *The Convertibility of Lute Strings*

Vaughan, Mike: *Crosscurrents* for harpsichord and tape

APPENDIX B

Useful Information

Organizations

UNITED KINGDOM

National Early Music Association, 8 Covent Garden, Cambridge CB1 2HR. An organization concerned with many aspects of early music. It publishes a quarterly newsletter, a twice-yearly journal *Leading Notes*, and the invaluable *Early Music Yearbook*. This contains a register that lists players, teachers, and ensembles, and a Buyer's Guide to instrument makers worldwide (makers are listed under categories: British Isles, Continental Europe, North America, and Rest of World). It also lists early music organizations and publishers worldwide.

Under the Association's auspices, thirteen regional Early Music forums operate in Great Britain. These offer newsletters, workshops, contact registers, and other facilities. The Welsh College of Music and Drama (Castle Grounds, Cardiff CF1 3ER) has taken a welcome initiative in setting up Early Music Wales.

The Early Music Centre, Sutton House, 2–4 Homerton High Street, London E9 6JQ. Administrative center for the Early Music Network, which promotes concerts by outstanding performers. It also runs a competition for international young artists.

UNITED STATES

Early Music America, 11421 1/2 Bellflower Road, Cleveland, Ohio 44106. Publishes bulletins, a twice-yearly journal *Historical Performance,* and a booklet listing makers of historical instruments classified by category.

A large amount of activity is based on universities. A few extra addresses follow:

Southeastern Historical Keyboard Society, P.O. Box 32022, Charlotte, North Carolina 28232. An important meeting ground for enthusiasts. Newsletters twice yearly, and *The Early Keyboard Journal*, published jointly with the Midwest Historical Keyboard Society.

Midwest Historical Keyboard Society, Nanette G. Lunde, Department of Music, University of Wisconsin, Eau Claire, Wisconsin 54702-4004.

Cambridge Society for Early Music, P.O. Box 336, Cambridge, Massachusetts 02238. America's oldest society for the presentation of music up to the early nineteenth century.

MusicSources, 1000 The Alameda, Berkeley, California 94707. A center for historically informed performance in Berkeley.

Westfield Center for Early Keyboard Studies, 1 Cottage Street, Easthampton, Massachusetts 01027.

Periodicals

UNITED KINGDOM

The Harpsichord and Fortepiano (twice yearly), Peacock Press, Scout Bottom Farm, Mytholmroyd, Hebden Bridge, West Yorkshire HX7 5JS. Articles of interest to players, listeners, and builders.

Early Music (quarterly), Oxford University Press, Ely House, 37 Dover Street, London W1X 4AH. Excellent specialist articles and reviews. Available also in the United States.

Early Music Today (bimonthly), Rheingold Publishing Ltd., 241 Shaftesbury Avenue, London WC2H 8EH. Popular in style but well informed; a good introduction to the early music scene.

Early Music Review (monthly except December and August), King's Music, Redcroft, Banks End, Wyton, Huntingdon, Cambs PE17 2AA. Succinct and knowledgeable reviews of published music and recordings, and articles on related topics. Excellent for keeping up with the early music scene.

UNITED STATES

Continuo: The Magazine of Old Music (bimonthly), P.O. Box 327, Hammondsport, New York 14840.

The Early Keyboard Journal (annual), P.O. Box 32022, Charlotte, North Carolina 28232-2022.

Performance Practice Review (twice yearly), 1422 Kroll Park Lane, Fallbrook, California 92028.

Harpsichord Retailers

RECONDITIONED INSTRUMENTS

United Kingdom

The Early Music Shop, 38 Manningham Lane, Bradford, West Yorkshire BD1 3EA. Kits, reconditioned instruments.

The Early Keyboard Agency, Martin Robertson, Heyford Galleries, High Street, Upper Heyford, Bicester, Oxon. OX6 3LE. Specializes in good quality reconditioned instruments.

United States

Harpsichord Clearing House, Glen Giutteri, 9 Chestnut Street, Rehobeth, Massachusetts 02769.

MusicSources, 1000 The Alameda, Berkeley, California 94707. This concert and teaching center carries a large number of harpsichords, in varying states of repair, that are seeking new owners.

NEW INSTRUMENTS

It would be invidious, and it is not realistic, to name individual makers of new instruments, of whom there are now a great number. In Boston alone, there are said to be more harpsichord makers than there were in Antwerp in its seventeenth-century heyday.

Some firms are large and well established; some are small new ventures that may nevertheless produce excellent work. Any early music periodical can be relied on to produce several advertisements, and the builder's list in the *NEMA Yearbook* is comprehensive and worldwide. The periodical *Early Music* contains many advertisements for builders in both the United Kingdom and the United States. *Early Music America* publishes a booklet of builders (see above for details of all these publications). Some builders also sell reconditioned instruments.

Two firms are particularly well known worldwide as suppliers of kits and parts:

KITS

Zuckermann Harpsichords Inc. (Ricard Auber), Box 151, 65 Cutler Street, Stonington, CT 06378.

Hubbard Harpsichords, Inc. 31 Union Avenue, Sudbury, Massachusetts 01776.

These kits can also be obtained in the United Kingdom through the Early Music Shop (see above).

Books and Music:
A Small Selection of Specialist Dealers

UNITED KINGDOM

Brian Jordan, 10 Green Street, Cambridge CB2 3JU (tel. 01223 322368).

The Early Music Shop, 38 Manningham Road, Bradford, West Yorkshire BD1 3EA (tel. 01274 393753).

Banks' Music, 18 Lendal, York YO1 2AU (tel. 01904 658836).

Jacks, Pipes and Hammers, Bridge View, Garrigill, Alston, Cumbria CA9 3DU (tel. 01434 381583). The latter dealer operates a particularly prompt and knowledgeable personal service.

UNITED STATES

Early Music Shop of New England, 59 Boylston Street, Brookline, Massachusetts 02146.

Boulder Early Music Shop, 2020 Fourteenth Street, Boulder, Colorado 80302.

E. C. Schirmer, 138 Ipswich Street, Boston, Massachusetts 02215-3534.

The Musical Offering, 2430 Bancroft Way, Berkeley California 94704.

Publishers of Facsimile Music

Performers' Facsimiles, Broude Brothers, 141 White Oaks Road, Williamstown, Massachusetts 01267, U.S.A.

Editions J. M. Fuzeau, Boite Postale No. 6, 79440 Courlay, France.

Editions Minkoff, Rue Eynard 8, Casse Postale 377, 1211 Geneva 12, Switzerland.

Minkoff UK, 36 Sundridge Road, Bradford, West Yorkshire, BD1 2AE, United Kingdom.

Minkoff and Fuzeau facsimiles are both available in the United States from:

OMI (Old Manuscripts and Incunabula), P.O. Box 6019 FDR Station, New York, New York 10150.

Festivals and Exhibitions

UNITED KINGDOM

The York Festival of Early Music is preeminent. It takes place about the second week of July and lasts ten days or more. Concerts featuring top-ranking artists take place in many historic locations in York. There is an exhibition of instruments. Contact Delma Tomlin, York Early Music Festival, 65 Rawcliffe Lane, York YO3 6SJ.

In London, the Lufthansa Festival of Baroque Music is held in St. James's Church Piccadilly. Smaller but worthwhile festivals also take place in Beverley, Yorks (early May), and Leicester (late May): this list is expanding rapidly. Aldeburgh in Suffolk has just added an Early Music Festival (April) to its famous international program. One can also find excellent little summer events, such as the Suffolk Villages Festival directed by Peter Holman, where well-known professionals perform in a relaxed setting.

Festivals are often arranged around themes: the amount of actual harpsichord music contained may vary, but there's nearly always a harpsichord around!

The London International Exhibition of Early Music takes place annually in the early autumn, and gives a splendid opportunity to sample the wares of harpsichord builders, publishers, etc., and to hear informal concerts.

In Europe, mention should be made of the prestigious and long-established Flanders Festival in Bruges, Belgium, which combines concerts by outstanding artists and a trade fair of instruments and music, and the Utrecht Early Music Festival.

UNITED STATES

The prestigious Boston and Berkeley Early Music Festivals operate in alternate years: Boston in odd-numbered years, Berkeley in even. The Boston Festival takes place in the second week of June and offers a comprehensive program of events and an exhibition of instruments. Contact address for the Berkeley Festival is 1 Zellerbach Hall, Berkeley, California 94728.

Museums and Collections Containing Harpsichords

UNITED KINGDOM

Fenton House, Hampstead Green, London NW3 6RT.
Royal College of Music, Prince Consort Road, London SW7 2BS.
Finchcocks Living Museum of Music, Goudhurst, Kent TN17 1HH.
Russell Collection (Edinburgh University), Saint Cecilia's Hall, Niddry Street, Cowgate, Edinburgh EH1 1JF.
Victoria and Albert Museum, Cromwell Road, South Kensington, London SW7 2RL.
Horniman Museum, London Road, London SE23 3PQ.
The Bate Collection, Faculty of Music, Saint Aldate's, Oxford OX1.
Many of these collections hold recitals from time to time.

UNITED STATES

Preeminent examples include:
The Musical Instruments Gallery, Boston Museum of Fine Arts, 465 Huntingdon Avenue, Boston, Massachusetts 02115.
The Skinner Collection (Yale University), 15 Hillhouse Avenue, P.O. Box 208278, New Haven, Connecticut 06520-8278.
Smithsonian Institute, Washington, DC.

Education

Many colleges of music in Britain offer instruction in harpsichord (see the *Early Music Yearbook*). British universities do not always include instrumental tuition in their degree courses, but have nevertheless produced many well-known players. American colleges of music and universities, with their enviable resources, have attracted many notable teachers. Many students from all over the world, however, contrive eventually to make their way to Utrecht, the Mecca of early music.

SUMMER SCHOOLS

United Kingdom
Benslow Music Trust, Little Benslow Hills, off Benslow Lane, Hitchin, Herts SG4 9RB. This organization runs a very wide variety of short courses for amateur musicians. These are internationally respected and often include various aspects of early music, particularly ensemble playing.

Many local forums of the National Early Music Association (above) run summer schools. These are often concerned mostly with consort music, but you may find harpsichord courses occasionally.

Other trusts and educational bodies run summer schools: that at Dartington in Devon is long-established and prestigious, that associated with Early Music Wales (above) is new and promising. For details, see *Early Music Today* or the *Early Music Yearbook*.

United States

From the vast number on offer, I select three:

The San Francisco Early Music Society, P.O. Box 10151, Berkeley, California 94709. This society runs a particularly comprehensive series of summer schools.

Baroque Music and Dance Workshop run by the Music Department of Stanford University, Stanford, California 94305-3076.

Oberlin Baroque Performance Institute, 77 West College Street, Oberlin, Ohio 44074. Summer schools with various specializations.

The Internet

If you have access to the Internet, much recent information about organizations, events, harpsichords, suppliers, etc., can be found in various ways; you could start by subscribing to the *Harpsichord and Related Topics* discussion list by sending an e-mail to:

LISTSERV@ALBNYVM1.BITNET. The message should consist of: SUBSCRIBE HPSCHD-L John Smith (put your own name here).

If you also have access (a browser) to the World Wide Web (WWW), an excellent starting point is the Early Music FAQ (Frequently Asked Question) page at:

http://www.best.com/~mccomb/music/early/faq/rmefaq.htm This in turn will point you to the Early Music America home page, which is a good source of further onward links:

http://www.cwru.edu/orgs/ema/

Another useful collection of links is maintained by The Renaissance and Baroque Society of Pittsburgh at:

http://ivory.lm.com/~kholt/R-and-B/EMLinks/

There are obviously gaps: you can only contact organizations that have a presence on the Internet, but there are very many others. The Internet, however, is developing at an amazing rate, and by the time you read this it will contain a great deal more than at the time of writing. Although all the above addresses are in the United States, they are truly international and will point you to information worldwide.

Bibliography

Anthony, James R. 1974. *French Baroque Music from Beaujoyeulx to Rameau*. Rev. ed. Portland, OR: Amadeus Press, 1997.

Bach, Carl Philipp Emanuel. 1753–62. *Versuch über die wahre Art, das Clavier zu spielen*. Trans. and ed. W. J. Mitchell, *Essay on the True Art of Playing Keyboard Instruments*. New York: Norton, 1949.

Bach, Johann Sebastian. 1738. *Vorschriften und Grundsätze*. Trans. Pamela Poulin, *Precepts and Principles for Playing the Thorough-bass or Accompanying in Four Parts*. Oxford: Clarendon Press, 1994.

Barbour, J. Murray. 1951–53. *Tuning and Temperament: A Historical Survey*. East Lansing, MI.

Bent, Ian, ed. 1981. *Source Materials and the Interpretation of Music*. London: Stainer and Bell.

Boalch, Donald H. 1956. *Makers of the Harpsichord and Clavichord, 1440–1840*. 3rd ed. Edited by C. Mould. Oxford: Clarendon Press, 1996.

Boxall, Maria. 1977. *Harpsichord Method*. London: Schott.

Boyd, Malcolm. 1986. *Domenico Scarlatti, Master of Music*. London: Weidenfeld and Nicholson.

Brown, Howard M. 1976. *Embellishing Sixteenth-Century Music*. London: Oxford University Press.

Brown, Howard M., and Stanley Sadie, eds. 1989. *Performance Practice*. 2 vols. London: Macmillan; New York: Norton, 1990.

Buelow, George J. 1980. Rhetoric and Music. In *The New Grove Dictionary of Music and Musicians*, vol. 15. Ed. Stanley Sadie. London: Macmillan. 793–803.

Burney, Charles. 1775. *The Present State of Music in Germany, the Nether-lands, and the United Provinces.* London.

Butt, John, and Peter le Huray. 1985. In Search of Bach the Organist. In *Bach, Handel, Scarlatti: Tercentenary Essays.* Ed. Peter Williams. Cambridge: Cambridge University Press.

Clark, Jane. 1980. Les Folies Françoises. *Early Music* (April): 163–169.

Couperin, François. 1716. *L'art de toucher le clavecin.* Paris. Trans. Margery Halford, *The Art of Playing the Harpsichord.* New York: Alfred Publishers, 1974. This edition is preferable to others available.

Cyr, Mary. 1992. *Performing Baroque Music.* Portland, OR: Amadeus Press. A cassette of musical examples is available.

Dart, Robert Thurston. 1954. *The Interpretation of Music.* London: Hutchinson. Expanded and updated as *Performance Practice. See* Brown 1989.

David, Hans, and Arthur Mendel, eds. 1966. *The Bach Reader.* Rev. ed. New York.

Donington, Robert. 1974. *The Interpretation of Early Music.* Rev. ed. London: Faber Music.

———. 1982. *Baroque Music: Style and Performance.* London: Faber Music.

Dreyfus, Laurence. 1987. *Bach's Continuo Group: Players and Practices in his Vocal Works.* Cambridge: Harvard University Press.

Elste, Martin. 1995. *Modern Harpsichord Music: a Discography.* London: Greenwood Press.

Faulkner, Quentin. 1984. *J. S. Bach's Keyboard Technique: A Historical Introduction.* St. Louis: Concordia.

Ferguson, Howard. 1975. *Keyboard Interpretation.* Oxford University Press.

Fuller, David. 1986. Notes inégales. In *The New Harvard Dictionary of Music.* Ed. Don M. Randel. Cambridge: Harvard University Press.

Gasparini, Francesco. 1708. *L'armonico pratico al cimbalo.* Trans. F. S. Stillings and ed. D.L. Burrows, *The Practical Harmonist at the Keyboard.* New Haven: Yale School of Music, 1980.

Geminiani, Francesco. 1749. *A Treatise of Good Taste in the Art of Musick.* Rpt. New York: Da Capo, 1969.

———. ca. 1754. *The Art of Accompaniament.* London. Facsimile edition, Florence: S. P. E. S., 1990.

Gilbert, Kenneth, ed. 1969. *F. Couperin: Pièces de clavecin.* Paris: Heugel.

Gustafson, Bruce, and David Fuller. 1990. *Catalogue of French Harpsichord Music.* Oxford University Press.

Harley, John. 1992–94. *British Harpsichord Music.* Vol. 1, *Sources;* vol. 2, *History.* Aldershot: Scolar Press.

Hubbard, Frank. 1965–67. *Three Centuries of Harpsichord Making.* Cambridge, MA: Harvard University Press.

Humphreys, David. 1983. *The Esoteric Structure of Bach's Clavierübung III.* Cardiff: University College Press.

le Huray, Peter, ed. 1981. *The Fingering of Virginal Music.* London: Stainer and Bell.

———. 1990. *Authenticity in Performance: Eighteenth-Century Case Studies.* Cambridge: Cambridge University Press.

———. 1992. Dom Bédos, Engramelle, and Performance Practice. In *Aspects of Keyboard Music.* Ed. R. Judd. (Essays in honour of Susi Jeans.) Oxford: Positif Press.

Kenyon, Nicholas, ed. 1988. *Authenticity and Early Music, a Symposium.* Oxford University Press.

Kircher, Athanasius. 1650. *Musurgia Universalis.* Rome.

Kirkpatrick, Ralph. 1953. *Domenico Scarlatti.* Princeton, NJ: Princeton University Press.

Kirnberger, Johann. Ca. 1777. Preface to *Recueil d'airs de danse caractéristiques.* Ed. Ulrich Mahlert. Berlin: Breitkopf, 1995.

Klop, Gerrit C. 1974. *Harpsichord Tuning: Course Guide.* Netherlands: Garderen.

Ledbetter, David. 1988. *Harpsichord and Lute.* London: Macmillan.

Loulié, Étienne. 1696. *Eléments ou Principes de Musique.* Paris.

Mellers, Wilfrid. 1950. *François Couperin and the French Classical Tradition.* Rpt. London: Faber and Faber, 1987.

Neumann, Frederick. 1982. *Essays in Performance Practice.* Ann Arbor: UMI Research Press.

———. 1993. *Performance Practice of the Seventeenth and Eighteenth Centuries.* New York: Schirmer.

O'Brien, Grant. 1990. *Ruckers: Harpsichord and Virginal Building Tradition.* Cambridge: Cambridge University Press.

Padgham, Charles. 1986. *The Well-Tempered Organ.* Oxford: Positif Press.

Palmer, Larry. 1989. *Harpsichord in America: A Twentieth-Century Revival.* Bloomington: Indiana University Press.

Rishton, Timothy J. 1992. The Eighteenth-Century British Keyboard Concerto after Handel. In *Aspects of Keyboard Music.* Ed. R. Judd. (Essays in honour of Susi Jeans) Oxford: Positif Press.

Rodgers, Julane. 1971. *Early Keyboard Fingering, ca. 1560–1620.* Ph.D. Dissertation, University of Oregon. Ann Arbor, MI: Xerox University Microfilms, 1976. Facsimile.

Rosenhart, Kees. 1977. *The Amsterdam Harpsichord Tutor.* 2 vols. Amsterdam: Muziekuitgeverij Groen.

Russell, Raymond. 1959. *The Harpsichord and Clavichord.* Rev. ed. London: Faber, 1965.

Saint-Lambert, Michel de. 1702. *Les Principes du Clavecin.* Paris. Trans. Rebecca Harris-Warrick, *Principles of the Harpsichord.* Cambridge: Cambridge University Press, 1984.

Santa Maria, Tomás de. 1565. *Arte de tañer fantasia.* Valladolid. Quoted in translation in *Early Keyboard Fingering, ca. 1560–1620. See* Rodgers 1971.

Sloane, Sally Jo. 1995. *Music for Two or More Players at Clavichord, Harpsichord, Organ: An Annotated Bibliography.* London, Greenwood Press.

Spitta, Philipp. 1873–80. *Johann Sebastian Bach.* Leipzig. Trans. rpt. 3 vols. in 2. New York: Dover Publications, 1951.

Strunk, Oliver. 1950. *Source Readings in Music History.* Rpt. in 3 vols. London: Faber and Faber, 1981. Volume 2, *The Renaissance,* and volume 3, *The Baroque Era,* are especially relevant.

Tilney, Colin. 1995. *The Art of the Unmeasured Prelude for Harpsichord.* London: Schott.

Tittle, Martin. 1987. *A Performer's Guide through Historical Keyboard Tunings.* Ann Arbor, MI: Anderson Press.

Williams, Peter. 1984. *Bach's Organ Music.* Volume 3: *A Background.* Cambridge: Cambridge University Press.

———, ed. 1985. *Bach, Handel, Scarlatti: Tercentenary Essays.* Cambridge: Cambridge University Press.

Wilson, John, ed. 1959. *Roger North on Music.* London: Novello.

Index

Page numbers in **bold** indicate key (definition) references. Page numbers in *italic* refer to illustrations and musical examples. Names followed by dates in parentheses are those of composers, unless otherwise stated.